B-24
COMBAT MISSIONS

B-24

COMBAT MISSIONS

FIRST-HAND ACCOUNTS OF LIBERATOR OPERATIONS OVER NAZI EUROPE

MARTIN W. BOWMAN

FOREWORD BY EARL WASSOM

METRO BOOKS

NEW YORK

This 2010 edition published by Metro Books, by arrangement
with Elephant Book Company Limited, 35, Fournier Street,
London E1 6QE, United Kingdom.

Editorial Director: **Will Steeds**
Project Editors: **Laura Ward, Chris Stone**
Designer: **Philip Clucas** MCSD
Photographers: **Pat Bunce** (B-24 interior and exterior photography);
   Mark Winwood (memorabilia photography)
Production: **Robert Paulley**
Color reproduction: **Modern Age Repro House Ltd**, Hong Kong

Jacket and front cover illustration: *Under Attack: Tall, Torrid & Texas*
by Roy Grinnell, Artist of the Aces (website: www.roygrinnell.com)

Metro Books
122 Fifth Avenue,
New York, NY 10011

ISBN: 978-1-4351-1220-9

Printed and bound in China

10 9 8 7 6 5 4 3 2

Author dedication
This book is dedicated to Forrest S. Clark and to the memory
of those other fine "Flying Eightballers"—John W. McClane, Bill
Cameron, Bill Robertie, and Don Chase.

Elephant Book Company and the author particularly wish to thank the
following for their help in preparing this book: Pat Bunce and everyone at
the Collings Foundation; Pat Everson of the 448th Bomb Group Collection
and the veterans of the 448th Bomb Group, and also the people involved at
Station 146 USAAF WWII Control Tower, Seething, near Norwich, Norfolk;
Jonathon Moran at Liberatorcrew.com; Paul Thrower, Curator, 93rd Bomb
Group Museum, Hardwick, Norfolk, England; the Tower family, for kindly
allowing us to use the "V-mail" illustrations by T/Sgt. Harry L. Tower Jr.;
and Earl Wassom, EdD, Director, 8th Air Force Historical Society.

Contents

Foreword and Introduction 10-11

Part 1:
History and Development 12
Preparing for a mission 20

Part 2: The Crew
The Pilot and Copilot 28
The Navigator and Nose Gunner 42
The Radio Operator 56
The Bombardier 70
The Engineer/Top Turret Gunner 84
The Waist Gunners 98
The Ball Turret Gunner 112
The Tail Gunner 126

Part 3:
Rest and Recreation 140

Glossary 154
Further Reading 155
Picture credits and acknowledgments 156

Foreword

I first met Martin Bowman in a book store in Norwich, England, in November 1995. The occasion was a very special one, for it was the 50th anniversary celebration of Victory in Europe (VE Day). Hundreds of American veterans, air and ground crewmembers, and the families of the Second Air Division Association, Eighth Air Force, were in the city for these commemorative celebrations. Soon after this occasion, I realized that "our war," and the particular military group I served in, would be forgotten if our legacy was not maintained by the younger generation. Martin Bowman is one of this new generation, and his interest and dedication to maintaining the spirit and accuracy of World War II US Eighth and Fifteenth Air Force history, and in keeping alive the memories of the men who fought in these combat missions, has been an inspiration to me, and to many others like me.

Through photos, graphics, memorabilia, and—above all—personal accounts, Martin Bowman's *B-24 Combat Missions* portrays the acts of brave young Americans of the air forces. These men put their lives "on-the-line" for the cause of freedom, for their country, and for the world. The story line for this work includes fascinating first-hand accounts from, and anecdotes about, the ten men—the four officers and the six enlisted men—who formed the crew of a B 24 Liberator bomber. Each airman's responsibility as a crewmember is carefully detailed. Information about his training and careful descriptions of his particular duties in the aircraft are included. The author has contacted and interviewed hundreds of veterans, and these personal stories make the book come alive with never-before published accounts. As a B-24 Aircraft Commander, as we were called, I have read and can verify that the author has carefully and movingly portrayed the lives and experiences of the flight crew. He has also included in this volume accounts, in great detail, of the so-called unsung heroes of the Eighth and Fifteenth Air Forces. The author points out: ". . . less than a third of its men fly the airplanes; everyone on the field, whatever his job, shares the victories and losses of heavy bombardment." The unsung heroes, as Martin correctly states, are the "groundpounders or paddle feet," as they were affectionately called. And, importantly, it was not all work and no play for these men. The final section of the book portrays rest and recreation ["R and R"] activities, such as the liberty run to town, which might include a movie, or the dance hall at the "Sampson and Hercules," or the Norwich Hippodrome. Near my base were pubs such as the Parson Woodford Public House for nightly entertainment, or the Saturday night dances on base. A long-sought-after leave to London was always refreshing.

Martin Bowman has reconstructed the life and times of the men in the "Mighty Eighth" and Fifteenth Air Forces during one of the most critical times in American history. He has done so with skill and with historic accuracy.

Earl Wassom, EdD
Past President, Second Air Division Association
Director, 8th Air Force Historical Society
1st Lieutenant, 8th Air Force, 785th Bomb Squadron, 466th Bomb Group (1944–45);
35 combat missions flown between September 1, 1944 and March 18, 1945

Introduction

Wendell Wilkie, after he had circled the United Nations in a four-engined bomber, dedicated his book to the crew of the Liberator that had showed him how air power had made all nations shrink into "One World." The "Libs" [Liberators] of the Eighth, more than any other bomber, helped to shrink Hitler's conquests, too. In helping to free Europe, the part played by the Liberators of the 8th, 9th, 12th, and 15th Air Forces cannot be overestimated.

Largely overshadowed by the B-17 Flying Fortress, the B-24 Liberator was never to gain the recognition it deserved from press and public alike. It was one of the most maligned aircraft of the war, lampooned by cartoonists and aircrews alike. Flying Fortress crews referred to the B-24 as "the crate that ours came in," and the "Banana Boat," because the B-24 "has been designed as a flying boat but they couldn't plug the leaks and turned it into a bomber instead!"

The Davis high-aspect ratio wing proved ideal for long, over-water patrols at medium altitudes. Because this wing provided far less lift than the B-17 wing, it was never really successful in the European Theater of Operations (ETO), where the Liberator was required to fly high-altitude bombing missions with the Flying Fortress, an aircraft of totally different performance. The B-24 was bigger than the B-17, with a 110-ft (33.53m) wingspan versus 103ft 9in (31.62m) for the B-17. The B-24 could easily fly as fast with three motors as the B-17 with all four. The bomb bay on the B-24 was twice the size of the bomb bay on the Fortress—but would not carry twice the bomb load that the B-17 would carry—and the B-24 had a tricycle landing gear, which made taxiing, taking off, and landing easier. In addition to improved performance, there were several comfort and control features that were superior to the B-17's.

In September 1944, 6,043 B-24s (24 per cent more than the peak B-17 force) were in operation with the USAAF (United States Army Air Forces), equipping 45 groups worldwide. But enough B-17s became available to convert the entire 3rd Division to B-17s, and if the war in Europe had continued for any longer than it did, then the Liberator might, in England at least, have been replaced totally by the Flying Fortress. One report in the US Strategic Bombing Survey concluded that "the B-17 was a more efficient combat aircraft than the B-24 from a viewpoint of bombing accuracy, life of aircraft, tons dropped for each effective sortie, and losses."

The Liberator was produced in far greater numbers (18,188) than any other American aircraft during World War II, and it was probably the most versatile of all the four-engined bombers built during 1941–45. Libs served with no fewer than 15 air forces, its capacious fuselage making it ideal for a multitude of roles that included strategic bombing in all theaters of operation, maritime reconnaissance, VIP, supply and troop transport, photo-reconnaissance, radio countermeasures, and flying tanker—hauling fuel to France during the push toward Germany. Liberators fought the U-boat in the Atlantic and they made a vital contribution toward winning the war in the Pacific. Its most famous single exploit is possibly the raid on the Ploesti oilfields in August 1943, but the plane is perhaps best remembered for its daylight raids with the USAAF 8th and 15th Air Forces and in the Pacific, where its "masthead bombing" of Japanese shipping was a constant source of fear to the enemy.

Martin W. Bowman
Norwich, England, 2009

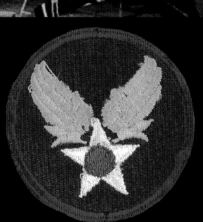

PART 1

History & Development

Preparing for a Mission

History and Development

"We knew that the first Lib would land in a few minutes. The Fortress boys scornfully call the big-bellied Libs 'pregnant cows.' The RAF officers were cracking jokes about the big-bellied ship: 'Doubt if she'll be able to set down here, old boy. They tell me she takes three counties to get down in. Great cargo ship—never do as a bomber.' Five minutes later, the Lib came in, easy as a Cub. The skeptics squirmed . . ."

—Captain John R. "Tex" McCrary and David E. Scherman, *First Of The Many*

I t is generally believed that the name "Liberator," which surpassed every other type of US military aircraft in World War II in terms of numbers produced, was chosen by the British, whose practice was to give nicknames rather than numerical designations to aircraft. The reality is that the aircraft acquired the name as a result of a contest held at the Consolidated Aircraft Corporation plant at San Diego, California. Dorothy Fleet, wife of the company's founder, the aviation pioneer Reuben H. Fleet, selected the name and submitted her entry anonymously.

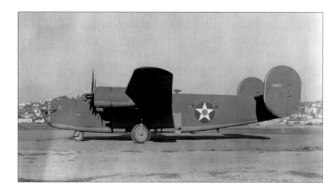

Left: Model 32 first flew on December 29, 1939. It was followed in 1940 by six YB-24s (pictured is 40-0697), which had been ordered by the Air Corps just prior to the contract for the prototype.

Consolidated had a lengthy history in long-range aircraft design, led by Isaac Machlin Laddon, who joined the company in 1927 as chief engineer. He was responsible in 1928 for the Admiral flying boat and, later, for the Catalina flying boat. In May 1938 the French government had issued a specification for a heavy bomber. Consolidated's early study, designated LB-30, was a landplane version of their new Model 29 flying boat (PB2Y). Then, early in 1939 the US Army Air Corps drew up a requirement for a heavy bomber capable of more than 300mph (483kmh) with a range of 3,000 miles (4,828km) and a ceiling of 35,000ft (10,668m). Consolidated responded with the XB-24 (Model 32), which had a high-aspect ratio wing designed by David R. Davis and twin-finned empennage (tail assembly arrangement) as used on the Model 31 flying boat (P4Y-1). Of conventional structure, among the Model 32's more unusual features was a tricycle undercarriage. The main gears had to be long to exceed the tall bomb bays and were retracted outward by electric motors. Roller-shutter doors protected an 8,000lb (3,629kg) bomb load, which was stowed vertically in the two halves of the bomb bay and separated by a catwalk connecting the flight deck and the tail section.

By January 20, 1939 preliminary specifications were ready and construction began. In February a wind tunnel model was tested on the strength of which the designers ventured to Wright Field to discuss their design with senior Air Corps officers. On March 30 a contract for a prototype was signed after Consolidated had made almost 30 changes to the preliminary specifications on the recommendation of the Air Corps. In September, France followed up its tentative order with a production contract for 139 aircraft under the original LB-30 designation. On December 29, 1939 the Liberator flew for the first time when William Wheatley took off from Lindbergh Field, next to the Consolidated plant in San Diego. In 1940 seven YB-24s, which had been ordered by the Air Corps shortly before the contract for the prototype, were delivered for service trials. The wing leading edge slots had been deleted and de-icing boots fitted to the wings and tail. In the tail 0.5in machine-guns replaced the 0.30in guns of previous models. Six YB-24s and 20 B-24As were

Far left: P-38 Lockheed Lightnings zoom low over Liberator Mk.VIs of 614 Squadron RAF, which are dispersed on the Foggia Plain in Italy in 1944.
Left: One of the two B-24As that conveyed members of the Harriman mission to Moscow, via England, in September 1941. The Stars & Stripes are prominently displayed to proclaim US neutrality.

preemptive attack on the US Naval base at Pearl Harbor in Hawaii. A specially modified B-24A, ready for an armed reconnaissance of Japanese installations in the Marshall and Caroline islands—and particularly the Truk and Jaluit islands—was destroyed on the ground at Hickam Field. (Two B-24As had been prepared, but only one had arrived by the time of the Japanese attack.) Immediately following the attack, the USAAF repossessed 15 Liberators, which retained their RAF serial numbers and the designation, LB-30; they were dispatched to the Pacific but none reached the Philippines before the Japanese occupied the islands. Four of these aircraft eventually reached the 7th Bombardment Group in Java and on January 16, 1942 three LB-30s and two B-17s from this group carried out the first Liberator action of the war by USAAF crews with a raid on Japanese shipping and airfields from Singosari, Malang.

Left and below: The Ford Plant at Willow Run, Michigan, where Ford produced 6,792 examples of the B-24L model and 1,893 more in component form; below, B-24Ds with "buzz numbers" on the nose, which were used for training, on the line at Wendover Field, Utah, early in 1944. Behind the hardstanding are the famous salt flats.

diverted to the RAF (Royal Air Force) and after the fall of France in June 1940 Britain took over the French contract for 139 LB-30s. As a result of combat in Europe, the XB-24 was fitted with self-sealing fuel tanks and armor plate. By the end of the war almost 2,500 Liberators had been delivered to the RAF, RCAF (Royal Canadian Air Force), and the RAAF (Royal Australian Air Force), of which 1,694 were supplied by Consolidated alone. Had more Liberators been available to RAF Coastal Command in sufficient quantities during the early part of the war, the U-boat menace might have been better contained.

On December 7, 1941 the Liberator was on the brink of entering US operational service in the Pacific when the Japanese launched their

Right: *Recruitment poster showing a B-24D warding off Japanese fighters in the Pacific Theater. Most potential bomber crews wanted to fly in the B-17 Flying Fort, so a poster like this would call on a sense of patriotism.*

Above: *B-24D of the 308th BG in the China-Burma-India (CBI) Theater, taking off at Kunming, China. In March 1943 the group transferred from the 10th Air Force to Gen. Claire L. Chennault's China Task Force, later 14th AF. The B-24s doubled as transports, carrying supplies.*

Left: *AAF poster with a story about the "Rambler" that roared into Rangoon. Liberators served in every theater of war and on every front in World War II—as bomber, transport, tanker, and naval attack aircraft.*

to full strength and remained on the Indian side of the Himalayas, while the 308th Bomb Group, which was also equipped with Liberators, was sent to the Chinese side of the mountain range. In March 1943 the 308th joined General Claire L. Chennault's China Task Force (later 14th Air Force). The Liberators had to double as transports, carrying their own supplies over the "Hump" before flying their first mission in May 1943. For his actions in the South China Sea on the night of October 25–26, 1944, Major Horace C. Carswell Jr. in the 308th Bomb Group was awarded the Medal of Honor.

In September 1942 the B-24 entered the fray in Europe when the Second Bombardment Wing was established in East Anglia (the easternmost counties of England). Two B-24 Groups (and four B-17 Groups) had to prove that daylight precision bombing could succeed in the skies over Europe. But the RAF remained unconvinced, and even some American instructors doubted their crews' ability to bomb in daylight and survive against German opposition. However, by March 1944 the Second Bombardment Division numbered 11 groups and during April five more B-24 groups arrived in England. Despite the obvious drawbacks of mixing two types of heavy bomber, they joined the Third Bombardment Division, hitherto equipped with the Fortress. General Doolittle had wanted to bring the 8th Air Force up to strength with Fortresses but, by the late spring of 1944, five B-24 plants in America were producing more than enough Liberators. The uneasy marriage between the Fortress and Liberator in the Third Bombardment Division ended when, during July to September, all five Third Bombardment Division Liberator groups were converted to Fortresses. On New Year's Day 1945 the Second Bombardment Division was redesignated the Second Air Division.

Of all the theaters of operations in which the B-24 served, only in the Mediterranean did it see such widespread and diversified service with both the RAF and the USAAF. In July 1942 the 98th Bomb Group arrived from the US and was based in Palestine. They and the 376th Bomb Group flew missions in support of the Eighth Army and in 1943, further afield to targets in Sicily and Southern Italy. In February 1943 the Mediterranean Air Command and North West African Air Forces, commanded by General Carl Spaatz and consisting of Eastern Air Command, 12th Air Force and other units were officially created. In

To the small 11th Air Force fell the task of defending the vast Alaskan wastes and the Aleutian Island chain. By 1942 there were three B-24 Squadrons in Alaska and in 1943 they pounded Japanese shipping and positions in the Aleutians from Adak, 250 miles (402km) from Kiska.

In February 1942 the 10th Air Force was activated for action in the CBI (China-Burma-India) Theater and by the end of the year the 7th Bomb Group was equipped with B-24s. On October 21, 1942 the group flew its first offensive mission north of the Yellow River when a flight bombed the Lin-hsi mines. By January 1943 the 7th Bomb Group was up

Above: Crew in the 404th "Pink Elephants" BS in the 28th Composite Group of the Alaskan Air Force study details before a raid on Japanese targets in the Aleutians.

November, General Louis Brereton was authorized to activate Ninth Bomber Command. On May 6, 1943 Operation Husky, the invasion of Sicily, began and the Liberators attacked Reggio di Calabria, the terminus of the San Giovanni-Messina ferry service to Sicily. That summer three 8th Air Force groups in East Anglia joined the 98th and 376th Bomb Groups for a raid on the Ploesti oilfields. Of the 177 Liberators that took part, 54 failed to return. The plants were repaired and operating at pre-mission capacity within a month.

After Ploesti the two 9th Air Force groups were transferred to the 12th Air Force. In October 1943 General Henry "Hap" Arnold proposed a plan to split the 12th Air Force in two to create a Strategic Air Force in the Mediterranean, leaving the remaining half of the 12th as a tactical organization. The possibility of a Strategic Air Force based in southern Italy would effectively place parts of Austria, Germany, and Eastern Europe—previously out of range of the 8th Air Force—within easy reach. Italy also offered considerably better weather conditions than Britain. On November 1, 1943 the 15th Air Force was officially activated with a strength of 90 B-24s (and 210 B-17s), inherited from the 12th Air Force. Between December 1943 and May 1944, 13 new Liberator groups joined the 15th Air Force. The January 5, 1944 missions were the last under the auspices of 8th Bomber Command. It was decided to embrace both the 8th and 15th in a new headquarters called US Strategic Air Forces, Europe. On February 19, 1944 Operation Argument, a series of coordinated raids by the US Strategic Air Forces supported by RAF night bombing, went ahead. "Big Week" saw successive raids on the German aircraft industry and ball-bearing plants. By April, the powerful Mediterranean Allied Strategic Force was playing a vital role in the conduct of the war, which was by no means confined to Italy or the

Italian Front, and the 15th Air Force embarked on a campaign against enemy oil targets. From June 1944 onward they bombed railway networks in southeast Europe in support of Russian military operations in Romania. In July they began "softening up" targets in southern France in preparation for the invasion codenamed "Anvil." Marseilles, Lyon, Grenoble, and Toulon all felt the weight of bombs dropped by the B-24s and B-17s. Throughout the summer of 1944 Austrian aircraft manufacturing centers at Wiener Neustadt were bombed and oil-producing centers, too, were attacked. By late 1944 attacks on oil targets had assumed top priority.

In November 1943 South East Asia Command had been formed and Major General George E. Stratemeyer was appointed chief of Eastern Air Command, which effectively united the British and American air forces. Right up until the end of the war, the US and RAF B-24s worked in cooperation.

Early in the war the US Navy had recognized the need for a very long-range patrol aircraft. In the Liberator, the US Navy found the answer to this dilemma, and by July 1942 the USAAF had agreed to the Navy receiving a quantity of Liberators. In US Navy and Marines service the B-24 was designated the PB4Y-1. It was without doubt the finest patrol bomber of the war. In July 1943 Lieutenant-Commander Bruce Van Voorhis in charge of VP-102 (V being the code for heavier than air) during the Battle of the Solomon Islands was posthumously awarded America's highest decoration, the Medal of Honor.

Below: The Goon was a 308th BG Liberator in the 14th Air Force—the only B-24 group to operate from China in the war. For his actions in the South China Sea on October 25–26, 1944, Maj. Horace C. Carswell Jr. was awarded the Medal of Honor.

The air war over the enormous expanse of the Pacific Ocean, from Hawaii to the Philippines, and Australia to the Japanese mainland, was divided between three air forces: the 5th, 7th, and 13th. Major General Clarence L. Tinker, who in June 1942 was Commanding Officer of the small 7th Air Force, headquartered on Midway Island, realized the great possibilities in using the long-ranging Liberator and was determined to have it in his inventory. In a demonstration of the B-24's capabilities, Tinker put forward the idea of bombing Wake Island, 1,250 miles (2,011km) distant, using four LB-30s, which had landed at Midway after leaving Hawaii on June 5. They refueled at Midway and in the evening of the 6th took off again for Wake Island, loaded with every drop of gasoline the LB-30s could hold—and carrying six 500lb (227kg) bombs apiece. Thirty minutes after takeoff Tinker's LB-30 nosed forward into some overcast and was never seen again. The three other planes bombed Wake Island successfully. It was the first of many similar strikes. Tinker's crews did not share his regard for the B-24 and they were deeply

concerned when the 7th began equipping with the Liberator instead of the B-17. Tinker's successor had a difficult task in persuading his crews that accepting the B-24 did not make the 7th Air Force a second-class outfit. Gradually, the crews grew to accept the long-ranging bomber and Tinker's early enthusiasm was justified.

On December 22, 1942 26 B-24Ds in the 307th Bomb Group flew another mission from Midway to Wake. The B-24s bombed from 7,000 to 25,000ft (2,113 to 10,668m) and the only damage to the American formation was two small holes in the lead ship. Later, the 307th Bomb Group, better known as the "Long Rangers," were transferred to the 13th Air Force and some of their B-24Ds were taken on charge by the 11th Bomb Group. The 11th Bomb Group flew its first mission to Wake via Midway on July 26, 1943.

A line of longitude placed the 5th Air Force on the Southwest Pacific side and the 13th Air Force, activated in December 1942, on the South Pacific side. The 5th Air Force fought in the Philippines at the outbreak of the Pacific war and covered the retreat south to Java, playing a small part in the Battle of the Coral Sea. It really came to prominence late in 1942 when General George C. Kenney assumed command. Kenney had four B-24 groups by the end of the war: the 90th "Jolly Rogers," 43rd "Ken's Men," 380th "Flying Circus," and the 22nd "Red Raiders." The 90th Bomb Group had moved hurriedly to Hawaii in September 1941 and was assigned to the 7th Air Force while it completed training. In October 1942 it transferred to the 5th Air Force in Australia, thus becoming the first complete group to reach the Southwest Pacific. The Group flew its first mission on November 16, 1942 to Bougainville Island. By the beginning of 1943 the "Jolly Rogers" were flying long-range missions to Japanese positions in the Celebes and Java. The 380th, part of the 5th Air Force, was attached to the RAAF until January 1945 and among its regular tasks was training Australian B-24 crews for the RAAF.

The two B-24 groups in the 13th Air Force were the 307th "Long Rangers" and the 5th "Bomber Barons." Late in August 1943 a special unit of ten SB-24 Liberators, known as the "Snoopers," joined the 5th Bomb Group as the 349th Bomb Squadron and, equipped with new radar bombsights, they flew missions against Japanese shipping almost every night from August 27 onward. The strikes became known as the "Tokyo Express" and such was their success that a new squadron, the 868th, was activated in January 1944 and this unit operated independently in the 13th Air Force.

Right: B-24M Night Mission in the 30th BG, with nose art inspired by Vargas' April 1943 Esquire *centerfold. Lt. Winton Newcomb and his crew had been flying to Iwo Jima and Chichi Jima every other day when they asked for a night mission—in vain!*

Below: Mabel's Labels served in the 43rd BG at Le Shima in the Pacific in 1945 before returning to the ZOI (USA), where it was scrapped at Kingman, Arizona, in 1947.

On October 11, 1943 Hawaii was strengthened by the arrival of the 30th Bomb Group. Despite having had only a few weeks' training, the 30th was declared ready to participate, together with three squadrons of the 11th Bomb Group, from the Ellis Isles, in Operation Galvanic, the invasion of the Japanese-held Gilbert Islands (now Kiribati), 2,000 miles (3,218km) from Hawaii. Between November 14 and December 6, 1943 the 7th Air Force flew 29 missions to establish air superiority over Tarawa, losing seven Liberators. In January 1944, B-24s took part in Operation Flintlock, the 70-day pre-invasion bombardment of Kwajalein, the largest atoll in the world. The 7th rapidly earned a reputation for carrying out tough, specialist tasks and the next assigned to it was bomber support during Operation Catchpole, the invasion of Eniwetok and the Marshalls. The first heavy air strikes were made on February 17 and successive raids by Liberators of the 7th Air Force and Navy PB4Ys neutralized Japanese air bases in the Marshalls and the Carolines. The island of Truk in the Carolines became a regular mission for 7th Air Force

Above: B-24D-50-CO 42-40323 Frenisi in the 370th BS, 307th BG (note "The Long Rangers" on the tail), 13th Air Force, a veteran of 110 missions, on Los Negros, 1944.

crews and by late February 1944 the island had been largely neutralized. At the end of March 1944 all three army air forces had bombed Japanese airfields and positions on Ponape, Kusiae, Kapingamangari, and New Guinea. Navy PB4Y-1s had raided Palau, Yap, and Woleai. By April, the 11th and 30th Bomb Groups were based at Kwajalein and, together with the Navy and the 5th and 13th Air Force, they largely destroyed almost all Japanese air bases east of the Philippines. That same month seven 30th Bomb Group B-24s flew a shuttle bombing mission of more than 4,000 miles (6,437km) with PB4Y-1s on a triangular route from Eniwetok

Above: B-24M-20-CO 44-42151 Bolivar Jr., in the 431st BS, 11th BG based in the Mariana Islands, in June 1945.
Right: US Navy PB4Y-1 Lib commanded by Lt. Paul Stevens of VPB-104 ("Buccaneers of Screaming 104") strafing a Japanese vessel in the Formosa Straits on March 17, 1945.

to the Carolines and Guam in the Marianas. On May 15, B-24s of 7th Bomber Command, together with other aircraft, began round-the-clock bombing of targets in the Marshalls, ending with the destruction of all targets by the end of the month.

By July 1945 all the Pacific air forces had begun moving northward for the final assault on Japan. The European war was over and it was planned to send B-24 groups from England to the Far East; but when two atomic bombs were dropped on Japan in August, the Japanese finally surrendered. Had the war continued a little longer, the citizens of Tokyo would daily have witnessed thousands of Liberators flying over their capital. Thankfully, the B-24s were not called upon to do so.

Preparing for a Mission

"Early in the morning, before the break of day,
Along comes the Sergeant and pulls us from the hay.
We stumble to the mess hall to see what we can beg,
and what do you think we get boys, good old powdered egg.
Next comes the briefing, to answer to roll call.
Will it be Berlin or is it a No-ball?"

—*"Hard-Assed Luck Boys"* Lieutenants Neal, Constable, and Avery, 701st Squadron, 445th Bomb Group

By the time Edgar Spencer's crew were preparing to be shipped over to a combat outfit they were, according to the tail gunner Eddie Picardo, given the choice of where they wanted to go. Picardo wanted badly to go to the South Pacific to fight the Japanese Empire. The copilot wanted to go to Italy. The other eight crewmembers all wanted to go to England and join the 8th Air Force. They

Left: *A typical barrack room at an 8th Air Force base in England in 1944. The men are gathered around the ubiquitous pot-bellied, coal-fired stove to glean a little warmth.*

had a working democracy, so England it was. Picardo thought that the boys chose England because the living conditions there were supposed to be better than in other places during the war. Making the transition from training in the US to combat duty in East Anglia—or the Foggia Plain in Italy—was not easy. This was especially so in the early part of the war, when suitable equipment was often lacking, the weather was poor, and there were almost no escort fighters to keep the Axis at bay while the few Liberators and Fortresses available took the war to the continent of Europe. Freshly assigned "Greenhorn" crews soon discovered to their cost that what their instructors in the US had told them was true. There were no "easy" missions over Northern Europe, or the supposed "soft underbelly" in Italy either, but some were much less difficult than others, especially when no enemy action occurred.

Newly arrived crews spent several weeks in pre-combat orientation, theater indoctrination, and combat assignment training base. The arrival

"in theater" of Lieutenant John W. McClane Jr., navigator, and the rest of Charles Peritti's crew, having flown the South Atlantic route from the ZOI (Zone of the Interior—the US) and landed in Wales, is typical. Within 48 hours they were transferred to Northern Ireland for six weeks. Most of the orientation lectures draw a blank in McClane's memory. They were generally told about what to expect when they joined their Combat Group, or how to maintain good relations with their English hosts. One lecture was on the evils of VD, but the lecture that stood out was the one concerning the number of combat missions required to complete one's tour of combat duty. Some fool stood up and asked what were the odds. The lecturer responded thusly: "On an average . . . [flying missions over occupied Europe] the 8th Air Force loses four out of every hundred planes, i.e. 4 per cent. Of course some will be 'milk runs' with no loss but others will be a disaster due to very aggressive enemy action. Still, on an average a 4 per cent attrition rate could be expected." This being the case, the lecturer reasoned, "a crew that flies 25 missions has a 100 per cent chance of being shot down on the last mission." A great quiet fell over the room. For many, including McClane, this was the first time that it had dawned on them that they

Left: *Howard Courtney, copilot in Stan Winter's crew in the 714th BS, 448th BG at Seething, takes some "Sack Time" in his cold, cluttered hut late in 1944.*

"were not playing for marbles. Someone could get hurt." Up to now, they were just "big boys playing with expensive toys, not a care in the world nor a thought of danger." This was a sobering thought. How could anyone expect to survive such odds? The speaker quickly added that in reality many would go on to complete their tour due to the laws of probability. McClane estimated later that a third would. His crew kept a record of the 18 crews that trained together and went overseas together. Sure enough, six of them completed the tour, which by then was raised to 30 missions.

When combat time was at hand for Lieutenant Robert Tays' crew, North Pickenham, the home of the 492nd Heavy Bombardment Group, was to be their home—their next assignment. They were welcomed with open arms and the usual "You'll be sorry." Within a day, Tays noticed much tension and little talk from others. He thought it might be their newness or something personal. "It wasn't. Their combat losses caused this behavior. This group had been operational only six weeks and during these missions they had lost all but 11 of their original 77 crews. The losses were so great that within a week after we arrived, it was disbanded. Within a day or so, my crew was assigned to the 392nd Heavy Bombardment Group about 10 miles [16km] distant and [this] was to be our home for the next year—Nissen Huts for quarters, coke-fired stoves for heat, biscuits for mattresses, and a bicycle issued to each of the pilots."

At Hethel, Norfolk, Lieutenant Duane A. Hall's nine-man crew arrived at the 389th Bombardment Group (Heavy) base just outside Norwich and were directed to a barracks. The four officers went one way and the enlisted men another. Staff Sergeant Robert H. Sherwood, the top turret gunner, was appalled at the uninsulated tarpaper

barrack hut and the sinister silence which greeted them. No one yelled the usual, "I see they've lowered the standards again." Not a soul announced, "Here comes the fresh meat!" No one made a sound or looked at them. Looking around the hut Sherwood was disturbed to see an old and torn die-cut sign, which proclaimed, "Merry Christmas." In May? He looked closely at the men in the cots. He wasn't prepared for the green-tinged faces, the tired, listless eyes. His crew looked out of place, in their best uniforms and bright, expectant faces. Strangely dressed reclining figures, each more outrageous than the next, allowed themselves to be scrutinized and took no notice. They wore rumpled fatigues, assorted parts of summer and winter uniforms. Some had hats on, the knitted infantry wool cap, fatigue hats with the brims snapped up, fleece-lined leather caps. My God! There was one guy wearing a steel flak helmet. The whole picture was disturbing. The rest of the crew got it. He could see them tiptoeing around trying not to upset anybody. It was difficult moving around the narrow cots in the 3ft (91cm) space between each bed. Bob Sherwood felt his confidence slowly ooze away. What a bunch to live with—all in each other's laps. These men were all insane.

Both above: A Short Guide to Great Britain was issued to every GI on arrival in England. It had dos and don'ts, and sections on "Britain's Wartime Appearance" and "The People, Their Customs and Manners." This copy—Lt. Stanley Milberg's (448th BG)—doubled as a mission log.

Left: So You're Going to Fly in England, issued in June 1944, explained the procedures that crews would encounter in England. Diagrams and drawings included pre- and in-flight checklists, special procedure signals, and so forth.

Right: Gasoline-driven Unit 3 Homelite Auxiliary Power Plant Type C-10 Model HRU-28—known as the "putt-putt." It was used for recharging the batteries when ground crew were working on a bomber at night, and as a backup electrical supply in flight.

In England each combat mission would be set in motion at around 16:58 hours the day before, at the daily Operations Conference at the headquarters of the 8th Bomber Command at High Wycombe, and the bases in East Anglia would be alerted by the warning order. The Field Order, a yard-long message containing details of targets and aiming points, fighter support, aircraft required, routes out and back, bombing altitudes, zero hour, and radio procedure, was Teletyped to the Air Divisional headquarters for operational staffs to study. Colonel James J. Mahoney was impressed by the efficiency with which a long and complex Teletype-printed Field Order could be transformed, in a matter of a few hours, into an aerial armada. "It is still incredible to me how in the space of any ten to twelve hours, plans could be originated and carried out for the deployment of more than a thousand four-engined planes on a split-second schedule to attack multiple targets on the Continent. That was the end result of the overall planning at higher headquarters and the execution of those plans by the division and bomb groups." If the weather held, at around 23:30 hours the B-24 Combat Wings and their bomb groups would receive the Combat Order from the 2nd Air Division and bombs and gas would be loaded.

In Italy things were much the same, as William Carigan, an experienced instructor and combat pilot on B-24s and B-17s who studied everything he could about the B-24, recalls: "All night long, aircraft engines sang, snorted, roared, and made lullabies for sleeping crewmen. All night long, service vehicles added their sounds. After a while aircrewmen closed out these sounds, unless they were older crews who were going on the mission with the next light. But they, as a rule, didn't have too long to listen. Bomb-loading activity went on late at night or toward morning. Topping-off fuel tanks went on shortly before crews arrived. Charging oxygen systems could be accomplished the afternoon before the mission, as could ammunition supply for the .50 caliber machine-guns. Chaff [Christmas-tree tinsel to be dispensed by the waist gunners as the airplanes approached the target and cut to certain lengths to confuse the German radar] cartons were usually stacked in the waist section the afternoon before."

Above: A breakfast scene in the mess hall at Hardwick in April 1943, prior to a combat mission. Breakfasts usually consisted of unpalatable powered eggs— but on the morning of a mission, crews were normally treated to real eggs.
Right: Crewmen wish one of their buddies luck before a combat mission. He is wearing his parachute harness and carrying some Mae Wests and a parachute pack.

Ronald D. Spencer, a navigator in the 467th Bomb Group at Rackheath, Norfolk, recalls that "A sound I'll remember as long as I live was the wailing of the putt-putts all night long. All the airplanes had auxiliary power units located under the flight deck just forward of the bomb bay. They were always referred to as "putt-putts" and were fired up by the ground crews to provide electrical power when they were working on the airplane. Since they typically worked on the airplanes all night long, the putt-putts were almost always running. The sound of dozens of them running all over the field made a very distinctive sound that was very eerie; I'll never forget it."

Major Ralph H. Elliott, a 467th Bomb Group lead pilot, recalls: "Operations, briefing rooms, and squadron operations huts were all down on the flight line about a half mile from the billeting area, and we either cut through the woods or rode our bicycles to get there, except for combat missions when they sent trucks to the hut area for us. We never knew until the CQ [Charge of Quarters] opened the door and called 'Elliott' when the day would start. It could be anytime from midnight on, depending on the target and where we'd be in the bomber stream that day. Takeoff was as early as 05:00 and as late as 11:20. For a 06:00 takeoff for a major target where we were #1 lead crew, pre-pre briefing came about 01:00. This gave my bombardiers the first look at the target. Next came pre-briefing where all the day's lead crews saw the target. Breakfast would be at 03:00 and all the crews would be up. We could never divulge the target, but we did occasionally suggest that maybe they ought to eat an extra good breakfast or suggest that having fresh eggs that morning had a special meaning."

After stumbling through the blackout to the breakfast in humid mess halls that smelled of powdered eggs, stale grease, and wet wool the usual question was on everyone's lips: "Where are we going today?" Was it going to be a "milk run" over the coast of France or a deep penetration to the heart of Germany? On one mission Eddie Picardo saw their wingman on their left explode. He saw no 'chutes open. Earlier that morning, their nose gunner, Jim, had sat across from him at breakfast. Now he was gone.

Robert Tays recalls, "Breakfast would have to last us until supper and consisted of many substantial items and in great quantities, food being selected so as to cause little or no gas to form at [high] altitude. Our aircraft were not pressurized or heated, causing us to [with the pre-mission food, at least] prepare for this environment.

Above: *Col. Addison T. Baker, CO, 93rd BG, checks the Teletype machine in the HQ at Hardwick; a member of ground staff checks detail by phone. Baker was killed on the Ploesti low-level mission, and was posthumously awarded the Medal of Honor.*
Top: *B-24J-401-CF 42-50466* Ford's Folly *in the 578th BS, 392nd BG is loaded up with incendiary bombs for the Liberator's 100th mission, on D-Day. It did not return.*

"Pork chops with powdered egg omelet seemed to be the perfect breakfast with endless cups of coffee. Having been duly inspected and found qualified my crew was scheduled for its first mission. A Mission differs from a Sortie in that a Sortie is any flight; whereas, a Mission is a flight with a specific purpose. My crew was now a part of a team that had as its primary mission the destruction of Germany's industrial military complex and the transportation systems that supported it. Strategic targets were primary, with military and political targets—targets of opportunity—secondary. These were identified to us by higher authority and were selected in relationship to their impact on the German war effort. New as we were, we didn't know the night before our first mission that we were scheduled to fly the next morning. After three or four missions, everybody on the crew went by the orderly room each evening to check the battle orders and know if we were on or not. Awakened by a Corporal with a flashlight shining in our face at 2:30 in the morning with the message, 'You're flying a mission today,' gives you a bit of a start. Routine as this entire procedure became, the first go at it would call on much of our training so as to perform effectively, such as get dressed, go to the decontamination point, perform the morning ablutions, and don't forget to shave closely so the oxygen mask would fit snugly and not leak. Then it was on to briefing, where 'Target-For-Today' names such as Bremen, Brunswick, Ludwigshafen, Frankfurt, Kiel, and Emden caused one's breakfast to churn and sour.

"Then [we went] to the locker room at the flight line to change into flight clothing for high altitude. It was also necessary to deposit personal items in a bag for safekeeping until your return—wallets, jewelry, photos, letters, etc. Then to the blacked-out briefing room where secrecy and security demanded the black out on all buildings, and the guards at the doors were fully armed, allowing only light crews and command briefing personnel to enter. The building was made secure before any briefing began. The chaplain began the briefing with a prayer followed by comments by the Group Commander. A black curtain held our attention for it held the story of the day as planned. The briefing officer would step forward and pull the curtain back to expose the map identifying the target for the day. Emotions ran high as it soaked in on crews what might happen today. Routes in to the target and back

Above: A typical briefing room, with a map of Europe behind the platform, and a dais where the CO and group staff officers would explain details of the day's mission.
Above left: A mission map showing flak areas over the continent, and with the routes to and from the target outlined in red.

out were outlined, the specific target identified, enemy resistance estimated, weather briefing, codes of the periods, aircraft assignments along with positions in the squadron formation. Also included was a short classified briefing on what our ground forces were doing in Europe and [what] our ground and sea forces were doing in the Far East. This completed the general briefing, whereupon specialty briefing followed."

One morning Edgar Spencer's crew learned at briefing that B-17s had visited Hamburg the day before—but that they had missed the target. When the briefers informed them ominously that "The Krauts will be expecting you today," Eddie Picardo piped up, "If they're expecting us today, why don't we go tomorrow?" The strategists did not appreciate his suggestion. It was at the pre-mission briefing that crews would meet their day's destiny. Too many American flyers learned at those briefings where they were going to die but, recalls Picardo, "Somehow my crew avoided that fate."

Lieutenant Alvin D. Skaggs, a pilot in the 448th Bomb Group, adds: "The officers reported to one briefing room, while the enlisted men were briefed separately. This was because of the different types of information and data needed by each group. As we sat

Left: Nervous anticipation is apparent as these 491st BG crews at Metfield, Suffolk, are briefed for their first mission on June 2, 1944. Maj. Charles C. Parmele, CO, 854th BS (sitting, 2nd row, left) led the group's ill-fated raid on Misburg on November 26, 1944.

Both above: 93rd BG crews don winter B-6 jackets, A-5 trousers, and B-6 helmets before boarding their B-24D Lib in 1943; after briefing, crewmembers in the 453rd BG pile on a jeep at Old Buckenham for the ride out to the dispersal area.
Below right: B-24s of the 458th BG taxi out at Horsham St. Faith on Christmas Eve 1944. First away after the assembly ship has taken off will be Lassie Come Home.

Ronald D. Spencer recalls: "Then there was the setting of the watches at the end of the briefing; [this was] a very important ritual since timing of everything was of the essence. We all had 'Hack' wristwatches, which permitted you to stop the watch, set a time, then start the watch at a precise second. In practice, one of the navigators would be assigned to provide the time hack. Typically, he would say something like 'Coming up on 3:54 in 40 seconds.' You would then stop your watch and set it to 3:54. Usually he would call out 10 seconds, then continue with '5, 4, 3, 2, hack.' At hack, you pushed in the button restarting the watch. Everyone should then have had the time correct to the second. Some of the briefers, who used the baloptican [an early type of slide projector], made themselves popular with the troops by slipping in an occasional nude to get our attention. Even at 3 or 4am it never failed."

Robert Tays continues: 'When specialty briefings were completed, the crew assembled in the locker room for one last check to see if we had everything we would need. Anything forgotten, we would have to do without. A number of items were critical. Then [we are transported] by 6 x 6 [a GI truck with 6 wheels] to the aircraft, put everything on board, check with crew chief, and check out all systems on aircraft. A totally mechanically perfect aircraft is a real morale booster. Anything that didn't check out was immediately corrected by the time engines were to be started. Good crew chiefs are worth their weight in gold. They are the unsung heroes of an Air Force."

The moment of truth was at hand, there was no option but to go, and only God knew who would return.

waiting for the briefing officers to arrive, we could feel the tension building. When the cover, protecting the map marking the route of the mission, was raised, it caused every man in the room to groan. This reaction was to become standard regardless of how long or short the mission was."

At William Carigan's base the briefing officer would read out the instructions on the pilot's flimsy (very thin paper, almost like tracing paper, that could be destroyed easily in the event of being captured), then turn the briefing over to other briefers: "The weather officer gave a weather forecast and was followed by other special briefers, concluding with the chaplain's prayer for us. Then the operations officer called 'Attention' and the group commander dismissed us to go to our specialized briefings. The navigators and bombardiers went to target briefing; the radio operator was briefed to be sure he had the correct periods of applicability for certain codes. The flight engineer and the gunners went to the airplane, often helping the refueling men top off the gas tanks, then securing and safetying the gas-tank caps. The pilots and copilots walked around to the front of the group headquarters and met the commander at the flagpole. There he gave us any special reminders, such as, 'Long mission today. Keep the waist-window deflectors closed to save gas.' He wished us good hunting (I never felt I was hunting—more likely hoping the *Luftwaffe* didn't find me.) He'd look up at the flag intently and then add the one command he had to make independently of all higher echelons of command: 'Take off to the north.'"

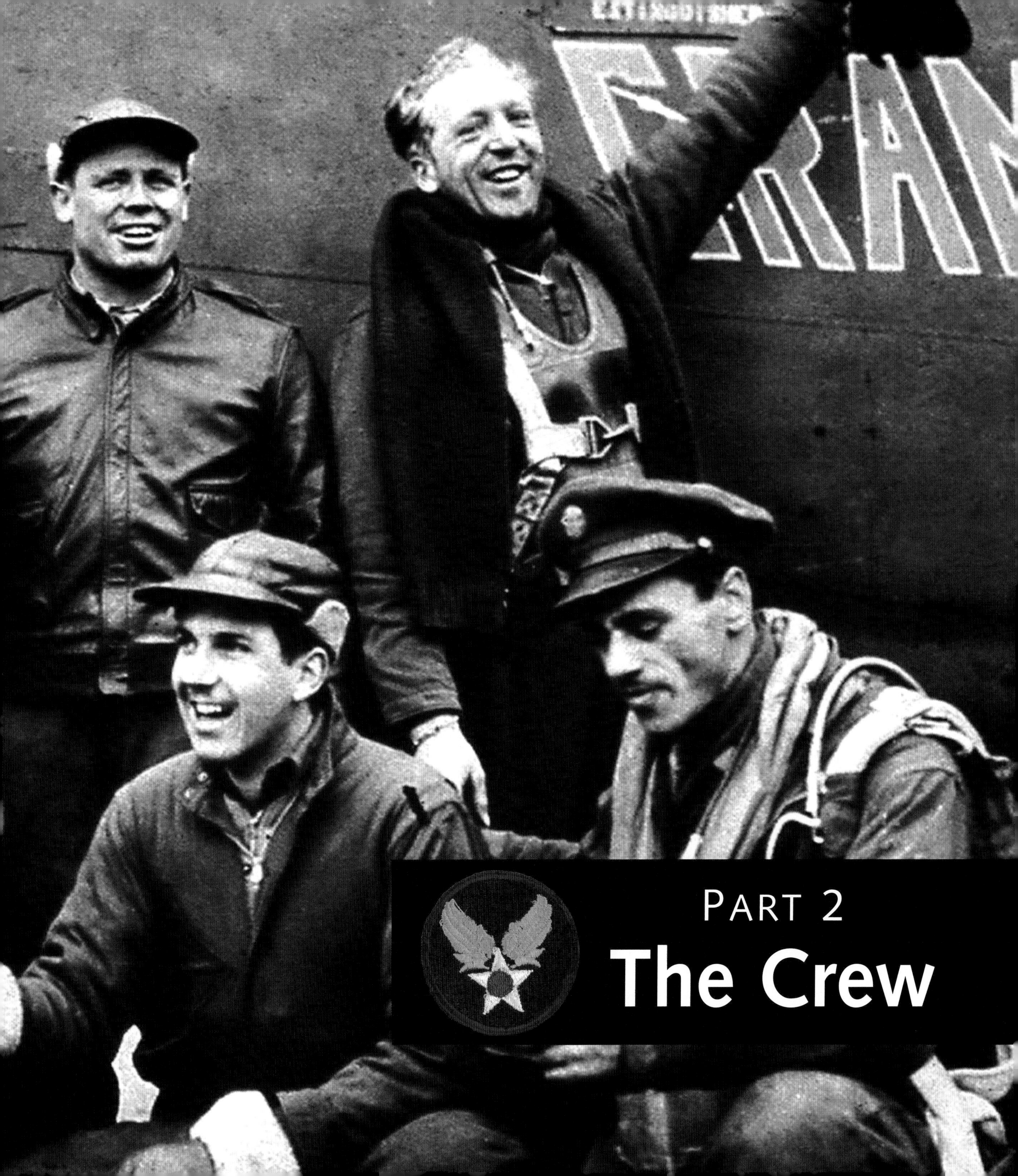

Part 2
The Crew

The Pilot and Copilot

"Ten men wearing silver wings thus came together to man one B-24. And those wings were date bait. The girls of the early 40s liked those wings; for Hollywood had also done its part in making the flyers seem glamorous. The girls also knew that those wings meant extra money in flyers' pockets. In my case, half of my base pay of $150 a month meant $75 [of] flying pay in my pocket every month. Whee. A short life but a gay one."—William Everett Carigan Jr., 737th Bomb Squadron, 454th Bomb Group

The pilot was in charge of the Liberator. Always. As such, his principal duty was airplane commander and his secondary duty was that of pilot. As an added duty, he was a navigation specialist. The copilot's principal duty was assistant airplane commander and his secondary duty was airplane engineering officer and assistant pilot. His added duties were fire officer and gunfire control officer. The aircraft commander knew that his best chance of building a supercrew was by knowing the strengths and weaknesses of his men, and, while acquiring this knowledge, he and his crew practiced the techniques that they knew they would one day have to face carrying out in combat. The pilot had to know as much as possible about the job of each man—how to determine the B-24's position by shooting stars with a sextant; how to aim and drop bombs; how to fill the fuel tanks; how to send a message in Morse Code; how to hit a target with a .50 caliber flexible gun; how to operate the turrets. Pilot (and the bombardier and navigator) positions were filled by graduates of flight schools who were usually commissioned as second lieutenants—occasionally as flight officers—upon successful completion of flying school.

Left: The pedestal of the B-24 flight deck had three sets of four engine control levers—superchargers, throttles, and mixture. The push/pull action on the control wheel worked the elevators, and required only minimal movement to have an effect.

William Carigan explains: "[The 1st pilot and copilot both] graduated from pilot's school, the pilot earlier. He'd gone through a B-24 transition school of about three months and had become fully proficient in flying the B-24. The copilot, usually, had just graduated from pilot's school, probably without any [hands-on] time in the B-24. But sometimes the copilot came from some other type of aircraft, voluntarily or involuntarily changing to the B-24. These pilots almost never volunteered to be copilots, but, ah, the country's need was paramount. Still, 'Why me, Lord?'

"Most young men, as soon as the message of Pearl Harbor reached them, thought favorably about the flying game. The Air Corps saw to it that they got the information about becoming flying cadets. As recruitment boomed along, the managers saw a need for classification centers, and these brought in the eager beavers who passed the physical examination and qualified under some other requirements—under 27 years of age, two years of college (later dropped), unmarried (later dropped), and various stipulations about good character—to be classified according to aptitudes and assigned to a flight-school program. The aptitude tests worked fine if you were selected for pilot school. If you were selected for some other school, you could see the faults in the system. Pilots used to say the classification tests sorted cadets into three bins: pilots were chosen from those who gave quick and correct answers; bombardiers were chosen from those who gave quick and erroneous answers; navigators were those who gave slow and correct answers. Being a pilot, I never knew what navigators and bombardiers said of the classification tests. In practice, I found all kinds in all the bins and the centers kept filling the schools with people who willingly served in all these honorable specialties.

"Whatever else the B-24 was, [it was] a man's airplane, sternly unforgiving and demanding sometimes super strength, always requiring considerable muscle. Heavy on the controls, the airplane tires the strongest teams of pilots on long missions. The wearer of the silver wings wonders why he ever took up flying.

"For its day the cockpit of the B-24 was spacious, the seating was good and fully adjustable. Pilots wore backpack parachutes, which formed the cushion of the seats on the B-24D. The Liberator was very 'nimble' at medium altitudes; at high altitude it got very 'sloppy,' more so when heavily loaded. The Liberator was not well suited to the European Theater of Operations [ETO], mainly because on missions it was expected to conform to the performance limitations imposed by the B-17E/F Fortress. The B-24D's operationally high wing loading made it a difficult aircraft to maintain in formation above 21,000ft [6,400m], although its service ceiling was put at 28,000ft [8,534m], about 4,000ft [1,219m] below the optimum Fortress altitude. Also, the B-24D's operational cruising speed of 180mph [290kmh] was between 10 and 20mph [16 and 32kmh] faster than the B-17's. This caused countless problems in mission planning, and usually the Liberators were relegated to the rear of the Fortress formations—where they consequently soaked up most of the punishment. The problem was that the Fortress was used in greater numbers and the B-24s had to adapt to the operational performance of the B-17, rather than the other way around."

Page right: Five plants turned out just over 18,000 B-24s in the war. They were operated by Consolidated at San Diego, California; Convair at Fort Worth, Texas; Douglas at Tulsa, Oklahoma; North American at Dallas, Texas; and the Ford Motor Company of Dearborn, Michigan. The famed Witchcraft *in the 467th BG was built by Ford, and by January 1945 had completed 100 missions without once turning back. Bottom left is the Flap Warning device and (right) the throttles operated by the pilot and copilot.*

Training for War

Primary and basic stages of a nine-week flying school course were followed by around 40 hours' flying time; then, after 120 hours' flying time, the reward was graduation, and gold bars. All just 11 months into active duty. Two months were then spent learning to fly the B-24 with an assigned crew of nine men, and—for the five who would have to defend the plane—bombing and gunnery practice.

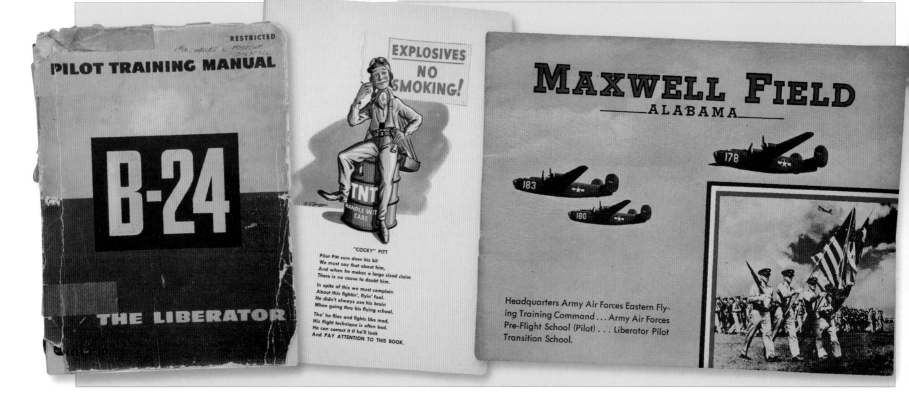

When I Saw Paris

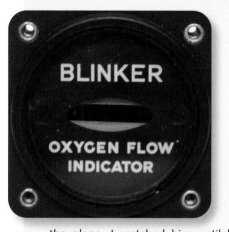

On December 20, 1942 twenty-one B-24Ds of the 44th Bomb Group set out for Romilly-sur-Seine, France. Captain Howard F. Adams, pilot of *Maisie* in the 66th Squadron, recorded the day's events in his diary:

"I was leading the second element of four planes while Colonel Taylor and 'Wild Bill' McCoy led the first element. It was bitter[ly] cold—way below zero—but in a few minutes we all forgot about that as we were attacked by some FW 190s. I closed in behind the first element until we almost touched wingtips, but all of a sudden an FW 190 came down in a screaming dive. This was my first sight of a German plane despite the fact that I have been in England almost three months now! He was so close that I could easily see the pilot and the beautiful yellow and silver markings of the plane. I watched him until he disappeared 5 or 6,000ft [1,524–1,828m] below us but it didn't take long as he was going close to 600mph [966kmh]. I was too busy to be scared but managed to call the crew on the interphone and told them to keep their eyes peeled for more fighters. My navigator had fired a quick burst on his .50 caliber nose gun at the first FW 190, to no avail. It took all my time and energy to keep in tight formation and so I did not see Paris as we passed almost over it. The Germans kept buzzing around us but I didn't see them. One of them dived on Major Key's ship just to my front and fired his 20mm, which hit one of the gunners square in the head—and that was the end of him. Now and again I would hear a short burst from one of our guns and would look over at my tiny copilot huddled underneath his steel helmet. I returned his weak smile and went back to flying, which was real work now as my fingers were like ice, and my oxygen mask was full of water and ice. Every once

in a while my plane would rock viciously and I knew that the flak was getting uncomfortably close. Being faster than the B-17s we flew back and forth over the top of them, finally working our way up so we were in the middle of the formation, which was lucky as the FW 190s were concentrating on the front and rear. We continued our running dogfight and after a wee bit I saw Paris spread out beneath us. The Eiffel Tower stood out like a sore thumb even from our altitude. It was not long before I saw several squadrons of RAF Spitfires cutting capers high above us. The white vapor trails against the blue sky were a beautiful and comfortable sight. *Maisie* roared along as faithful as ever, but I thought I never would reach the English Channel.

"We soon passed up the B-17s and headed for home feeling very happy and gay about our good luck. We chattered over the interphone like silly schoolboys, though when our radio operator told us that there was a wounded man on Major Key's ship we sobered up some. I peeled off and landed very cold and tired. Food and sleep were all we could think about after our five-hour ordeal. So ended our first real raid!" [Adams was Killed In Action (KIA) two months later, when enemy fighters shot down his B-24.]

Top left: The A-1 Oxygen Flow Indicator. The "Blinker" indicated that oxygen was flowing.

Left: The Type A-14 Demand Oxygen mask with microphone, which was standardized for USAAF use in July 1943. The oxygen supply going out could simultaneously supply several crewmembers. If a regulator froze up and the oxygen mask froze, too, it placed an additional burden on the already overstretched crew.

Above: *B-24H* Spare Parts *in the 453rd BG heads for home after a raid on a Luftwaffe airfield on February 21, 1944.*

Heavy bomber missions varied considerably in duration and intensity depending on the complexity, destination, and numbers involved. Assembly and formation procedures could consume an hour or more—meaning that even so-called "milk runs" to northern France took up four and a half hours of flying time. A round trip to Berlin could take nine to ten hours, sometimes more. A mission to the Ruhr could last seven hours, Brunswick eight, and Dresden nine. Often the chances of being killed or badly wounded depended on the position flown in the formation, and the level of exposure to flak and fighters. Pilot Robert Tays remembers:

"Long missions, [of] eight hours or longer, were extremely tiring and mentally fatiguing. I recall a long, deep mission into southern Germany, flak most of the way, some bad weather and the loss of several aircraft and crews. This was somewhere between my 25th and 30th mission. We came home exhausted, and something happened to me after landing. War, death, and destruction just didn't make any sense to me anymore."

If the Cap Fits

This red cap was worn by Lt. Paul Homan under his flak helmet for all his missions flown with the 448th Bomb Group at Seething, Norfolk. Homan bought similar red caps for all of his crew, and "Homan's Red Caps" flew their first mission together on February 6, 1945. Of the sweat stains on his cap, Homan added that however cold it was, you still sweated on the bomb run. Homan flew home from Valley, Wales, on June 5, 1945.

Right: *A smiling Paul Homan on his way back home to the US in B-24J 42-51075* Linda Mae.

Mission to Hell

Another 44th Bomb Group pilot, Colonel William R. Cameron, described by General Leon Johnson as "one of the best combat leaders we had in World War II," was awarded the DSC for his part in the low-level mission to Ploesti, in Romania, on August 1, 1943. Cameron, who flew *Buzzin' Bear*, recalls:

"The whole Ploesti episode began on a high note as far as I was concerned. After six months of combat operations in very cold and hostile winter skies over Europe, we were shifted, without explanation, to low-level formation practice over the green fields of England. We were told that for the time being, at least, there would be no combat—and it was springtime. There were new crews and new B-24s to replace those

that had been lost, and losses had been severe for our group. We didn't understand then that this relatively pleasant interval was preparation for an exceptional mission, one that would put it on the line for all of them.

"The day finally arrived. As we approached the target area, several B-24s were coming in straight for us from our left, but there was no time then to try to figure that one out! It was just one of several unexpected happenings that had to be accepted. As we raced toward Columbia Aquila, leveling off at our bombing altitude of 250ft [76m], my eyes were glued on the *Suzy-Q*. Her target would be almost exactly in line with the spot where our own bombs were programmed to go. We were expected to place our load into a low profile building some 210ft [64m] wide and 600ft [183m] long. I could not have lifted either wing during those few seconds without bringing sure destruction to the three of us. Even now, I can visualize the rivets of the bomber above us, which I could see all too clearly. I could occasionally glimpse the bomber below, but could only concern myself with the one above. Miraculously, both of our large neighbors slid away from us. We were now heading toward a point where the railroad disappeared into a great mass of smoke and flame—the Columbia Aquila refinery.

"It seemed to me that bombers were converging toward one small area that was free of flame and explosions. And then the *Suzy-Q* disappeared in that smoke and we were right behind. Below me in the nose section I could hear DeVinney and Clifford frantically trying to pinpoint our target. Then we were in the smoke—and then out of it. Bill Dabney maintained that our outside air temperature gauge reached its most extreme temperature reading as we sailed through the awful heat of those great fires that seemed to surround us! If you have ever flown an airplane through a lone fleecy white cloud, you will remember how suddenly you pop out on the far side. It was just like that, and, just as abruptly, I pushed hard on the control column and headed for the ground, all in a split second, and I am sure this near-spontaneous action saved our lives. Staring up at us were numerous shirtless antiaircraft gunners in gun emplacements with long, black gun barrels pointing directly at us. We leveled and began a flat turn to the right by pushing hard on the right rudder but keeping our wings from banking with opposite aileron control. It may be that the skidding turn threw the gunners off, but whatever the reason we escaped destruction. Unable to find our building in the smoke

Above: *Colonel William R. Cameron in the 44th BG next to* Buzzin' Bear, *which led the second wave to the Columbia Aquila plant at Ploesti on August 1, 1943. Bill survived this mission—his 27th sortie—and flew nine more as command pilot.*

(which was augmented by smoke pots), flame, exploding tanks, and the general confusion of that instant, our bombs were held too long. I can only hope that they fell in an area that contributed to the general destruction in the target complex. Few if any aircraft came off that target lower than we did—at least at that moment. Every Liberator I saw was above us. A B-24 ahead pulled straight up and then fell out of the sky. Two doll-like figures popped out of the waist windows, barely two or 300ft [91m] above the ground. I learned later that both men survived that fantastic jump. Eventually, we were well out over the Mediterranean and headed home. It had been a long day."

Small flak fragments typical of the deadly splinters that could pepper a B-24.

2nd Lt. James F. Gerrits, copilot of *Hitler's Hearse* flown by Captain Robert Mooney of the 567th Squadron, 389th BG, recalls:

"We headed down on a long glide into the target. There were a lot of orange blips appearing all over the target area . . . Suddenly there was a loud bang in the cockpit. It quickly filled with smoke. As the smoke cleared there was a horrible roar from a shell hole in the windscreen to the left of Mooney's head. He was leaning back. His hands were off the control wheel and blood was running all down his face. He wasn't conscious anymore. We were still in a shallow dive and maybe 200ft [61m] or so off the ground. I quickly grabbed the wheel and held the run for a few seconds. Then I pulled up and to the right and we went over the refinery structures a little to the right. I could feel something down the side of my face and my left arm hurt. I was alone. I thought it was all over for us, so I felt we should give them hell before we crashed. I pushed my intercom button and shouted 'OK, now give it to them, pour it at 'em. Let's go now. Keep those guns going!' The tail gunner had good shots at the refinery as we were pulling away. Then we were low over the trees, past the target and still in the air."

Left: Severe losses on the early low-level Ploesti missions resulted in the 15th Air Force using high-altitude bombing techniques against the Romanian oil refineries.

Mighty Close Shaves

Lieutenant William "Bill" Tinsman, copilot on the crew of Lieutenant Rockford C. Griffith, 44th Bomb Group, recalls the mission to "Big B"—Berlin, Germany—on March 22, 1944:

"This time we made it . . . the halfway mark for me since they raised it to 30 [missions]. Things went beautifully until 'bombs away,' when persistent contrails and poor formation flying raised hell with us. From there out it was every man for himself, just the way it shouldn't be. It was –40° [and] as my electric suit was out I got kinda cold . . . Flak ranged from light to heavy and accurate to inaccurate. Little over the target. Saw no enemy fighters as we had beautiful escort in and out, P-38s, '47s, and '51s. Five flak holes did little damage but narrowly missed several of the crew. Saw one B-24 have its tail blown off by flak, a '17 spin in and one dropped his bombs through his bomb bay doors, ripping the hell out of them . . . "

R. D. Russell in the 702nd Bomb Squadron, 445th Bomb Group and his crew in *King Kong* were flying their fourth mission on June 20, when the Liberators went to the Politz oil refinery at Stettin, Poland:

"What a day this was. Up at 01:00, briefing at 02:15, takeoff at 05:20 with ten 250lb [113kg] GPs [General-Purpose bombs]. Formed in a rush and climbed on course. The 389th was high right ahead of us and after we had passed Kiel [on Germany's Baltic coast] we saw two of their ships run together. One lost the tail and the other a wing tip. Both hit the water in a spin. We only saw five 'chutes. Later we saw another ship hit the water and blow up. We saw nine 'chutes this time. We had a good tight formation so the Ju 88s didn't bother us.

"At the IP [Initial Point], nine minutes from the target, we could see other squadrons dropping and hitting the target. Also we could see a solid wall of flak and rockets. I didn't have a chance to put on my flak vest. We finally got over the target and through the flak. It was bursting all around and the 'frump and crump' sounded as though each burst was hitting us. Just as 'bombs away' came, so also [did] a piece of flak. It hit our windshield and blew a hole in it about the size of a baseball. A piece of flak hit my throat mike, shattering it and lifted me right out of the seat and dropped me on the flight deck. The flak was so thick that the smoke filled the bomb bays and Jerry closed the doors to keep the sight away. Our bombs hit the MPI [Mean Point of Impact, or the planned center of destruction] directly and so did the bombs from the 20 groups ahead of us. That's one target we won't have to go back to. Mission ended with all ships home safe. Flight time: 7:55 hours."

Mittens were better than gloves as they retained more body heat.

Above right: *Figure dressed in an alpaca-lined B-10 jacket with mouton collar, heated electrical suit and B-4 Mae West, 50-mission crush cap and radio headset.*

Far right: *Rheostat for a heated flight suit. Electrically heated one-piece flying suits, developed by the General Electric Co., were standardized in 1941. The two-piece F-3A suit (from October 1944) was worn under the A-15/B-11 suit.*

Left: A B-24 in the 448th BG is cleaved in half by R4M folding-fin air-to-air missiles fired by Me 262 fighters on April 4, 1945.

second after the fuselage and seemed to help cushion the crash. The fuselage split on the right side and the crew was able to get out through the crack. No one was injured, though the engineer had some radio equipment fall on him. The force of the landing was so great that the No.1 engine was torn off completely . . . the last I saw of the plane, a large crane was trying to drag the wreck out of the way so they could continue the war! Next day we were back in England. The only clothes we had were electric-heated flying suits. We spent the night in London and were treated like Poles or some foreign air force."

Edward R. Glotfelty, a pilot in the 863rd Squadron, 493rd Bomb Group, recalls the June 25, 1944 mission to France:

"After we dropped our bombs we had a runaway [out of control—running away, or 'windmilling'] prop. I tried to feather [turn the propeller blades into the wind, against the airflow] but was unable to control it. The vibration was tremendous, shaking the whole plane. The noise was deafening. We lost speed and dropped out of the formation. My interest at the time was to hold altitude as much as possible but we were going down because of the great drag on the plane caused by the runaway prop. I started having trouble with the No.4 engine, the rpm surging, engine cutting out and the plane yawing because of the loss of power on the outboard engine. We were now down to 12,000ft [3,658m], and arriving over Normandy. I marveled at the panorama of ships and barrage balloons [below]. With the second engine in trouble I didn't think we could make it back to England and I saw two airfields below me, one obviously new, [a] one-runway fighter strip carved out of the countryside, and one paved, mature field that was farther from the beaches. I decided to go down and chose the field closer to the coast. I circled over the field, saw fighters on the strip, guessed at the wind direction and had another engine lose power! We were out of position; no power and dropping like a rock. I ordered wheels up and decided to land on the wide dirt strip alongside of the runway. We hit perfectly. The left wingtip hit a

Above: A 486th BG B-24 in the 3rd Bomb Division of the 8th Air Force passes over Allied shipping off the Normandy beach head near Caen on D-Day, June 6, 1944. A total of 2,362 US bomber sorties were flown on this momentous day with the loss of just three B-24s, two of them in a mid-air collision.

"Judas Goats"—the 2nd Air Division Assembly Ships

"On a mission to France Major James Stewart, movie star and 453rd Bomb Group Operations Officer, flew *Wham Bam*, our assembly ship, over the normal 'race-track' course around the group's homing beacon, 'Buncher Six.' Then he pulled out to the left about a quarter of a mile and flew on ahead to allow the lead ship to take over. However, contrary to procedure, he stayed in this position: all the way into France! Finally, the major turned *Wham Bam* around and came home. He said: *'If anyone breathes a word, I'll kill ya.'* Colonel Ramsey D. Potts, the Group Commander, probably wanted to know where he had been for the past six hours!"—Lieutenant Bernard H. Fowle, lead navigator.

The unusual concentration of bomber bases in East Anglia, and their proximity, demanded inviolate adherence to assembly procedure. Otherwise fatal accidents would result. Aircraft were required to

group had its own "Buncher" or "Splasher" beacon for control points. In this fashion they would sometimes climb through as much as 20,000ft (6,096m) of overcast (80 to 90 minutes of instrument flying) in order to form on top, since assembly had to be made under conditions assuring 1,500ft (457m) of clear air vertically.

Close-knit formations were vital if high concentration of bomb impacts and effective mutual defense were to be achieved. Gaudily painted assembly ships or "Judas Goats" (war-weary Liberators, stripped of all armament) shepherded their flock until the group successfully formed up on their tails. Monitor ships (normally P-47 Thunderbolts flown by high-ranking officers) were also employed to "ride herd" on the formation, using radio commentary instead of flares to direct operations. Some assembly ships had a line of bulbs forming the group identification letter on

Above: *Assembly ship used by the 448th BG; from January 1944 these assembly ships were painted a yellow and black checkerboard scheme for recognition purposes.*
Top and right: *Major James M. Stewart, who flew several combat missions in the ETO and, on at least one occasion, piloted* Wham Bam *in the 453rd BG.* Wham Bam *was repainted for use as the group's assembly ship; it was also given two large "J" letters in amber-colored lights forward of the waist windows.*

take off 30 to 45 seconds apart, sometimes in zero ceiling, with less than 500 yards (457m) visibility. Pilots knew beforehand the exact headings, speed, and distances separating each plane and the length of each leg in the pattern they were to fly. For self-protection, all climbed at the same rate to the briefed spot where the assembly pattern took shape. And each

both sides of the fuselage. Others had a line of lights along the centerline of the rear fuselage sides or an arrangement in a faired-over tail position.

The colors, size, and extent of the electric illuminations varied considerably. Flare ports were made in the rear fuselage of most aircraft and cargos of pyrotechnics were carried. Most operational groups had

Right: The Spotted Ass Ape *leads two B-24s in the 458th BG at the start of a mission in 1944. This war-weary formation ship was written off in a crash landing at Horsham St. Faith in March 1945.*

their assembly ships flying in garish decor by March 1944. Striping in various colors and widths predominated, probably because it was relatively straightforward to apply. Two groups used checkerboard patterns, four polka dots or discs, and one red zigzags.

In 1944 Major James M. Stewart, the famous movie actor, was the 453rd Bomb Group Operations Officer and he flew the yellow checkered assembly ship *Wham Bam* to form the group for the mission to Bordeaux. Stewart flew the normal "racetrack" course around homing beacon Buncher Six, until the group had formed up. The Judas Goats stayed with their groups because they were identified by their assembly ship. *Wham Bam* flew on ahead and higher to allow the lead ship to take over. Normally, the assembly ship would then break away and return to base but Stewart flew the unarmed and highly colorful B-24 all the way to the departure point at Selsey Bill, to the French coast, and in position all the way to Bordeaux and back again. On their return the Group

Commander would almost certainly have asked where on this earth they had been.

By the summer of 1944 second-generation assembly ships appeared in the 93rd, 389th, and 448th groups with different markings, all using yellow bands in different forms. With improved technique in assembling formations around "Buncher" radio beacons, the need for a distinctive painted assembly ship was considered superfluous by some groups and these brightly painted B-24s were less in evidence from late 1944 to early 1945. Some were pensioned off on communication and transport duties.

Above left and center right: Pete the POM Inspector *(formerly* Heaven Can Wait II *in the 44th BG), painted black with yellow discs circled in red, was the 467th BG's first assembly ship. Written off at Rackheath in October 1944, it was replaced by* Pete the POM Inspector 2nd *(formerly* Liberty Lib *in the 458th BG).*
Right: B-24J Tubarão *(Portuguese for shark) was the third 491st BG assembly ship, after* The Little Gramper *and* Rage In Heaven, *which crashed on takeoff in a snowstorm in January 1945.*

Frostbite and Flak

The cold was unbearable at high altitude, as Major Ralph Elliott, a lead pilot in the 467th Bomb Group at Rackheath, Norfolk, confirms:
"In winter flying, we wore nylon inner gloves; then a wool pair and finally a leather pair over that. I think the gunners had mittens with a separate trigger-finger, but, if a gun jammed, they'd take them off to work on it. If they took off the liners too, at 40 below zero their fingers would freeze to the gun. If they froze bad enough, the gunners would end up with gangrene and lose the fingers. I saw my first case of dry gangrene in the States where a man had frozen his fingers on a training mission. The outer joints of all of his fingers were black and the doctors were to decide whether to amputate or just let them fall off."

Above: Two B-24s in the 93rd BG pictured in flak-filled skies en route to Augsburg on March 1, 1945. Both are fitted with Carpet radio countermeasures to jam signals operating on the frequencies used by German fire-control radar.

Sometimes, though, the freezing temperatures could be a godsend. Lieutenant Norman E. Freidman, copilot, 493rd Bomb Group, recalls the mission to Merseburg on October 7, 1944—his 24th, and the first since returning from the "flak shack:"
"No enemy fighters were seen; but the flak over the target was the most intense we had ever experienced. It looked like a solid black cloud. We dropped our bombs with no difficulty and hit the target. After turning 90 degrees off the run-in heading, our plane was struck by a burst of flak near the No.3 engine. I was hit directly on the bridge of the nose between the eyes. The leather on my sunglasses was cut and each glass flew in a different direction without breaking. The flak missed my steel helmet and after hitting my nose, hit my flak suit near my lap and landed on the floor of the plane. The entry hole was above my head. Just then, No.3 engine quit running and the propeller was feathered. I slid out of my seat and tore the oxygen mask off my face. At 32,000ft [9,754m] it does not take long to pass out from the lack of oxygen. I dropped down between the two pilot seats and made my way to the nose compartment. [One of the crew] immediately put the spare oxygen mask on me. I was starting to turn blue. I was given a shot of novocaine to ease any pain and the nose area was covered with sulphur powder to prevent infections. The bleeding stopped because of the low temperature at that altitude, –68°F [–55°C]. Later, doctors at the hospital sewed the bridge of my nose and straightened it up. It was broken and lying over on the right side after 12 days in hospital! I was presented [with] the Purple Heart and another cluster to my air medal, which made three. I was unable to fly combat missions because I could not wear an oxygen mask on the bridge of my nose. I returned to the States in January 1945."

Meanwhile, Lieutenant John White, a pilot with the 448th Bomb Group at Seething, prayed that his crew's August 24, 1944 mission would be uneventful—and their last. Uneventful, though, it would not be:
"Today we flew what I hope is our last mission. It was plenty rough and I don't want anymore like it. Briefing was at 04:00 and our target was an airfield just north of Brunswick, Germany. In fighter country. We ran into a little flak going in but it wasn't bad. However when we went over Brunswick we really got a lot of it. A kid by the name of Morse was shot down somewhere and we saw a fighter blow up in the target area.

"I've never seen the sky filled with so much flak before in all my life. Everywhere we looked we saw dirty flak smoke—no wonder tho, [as] we went near Hamburg, Bremen, Magdeburg, Hanover and Osnabruck and a few other choice spots. The 8th Air Force was out in great style and were raiding targets all over the place. The sky was really filled with planes. Our bomb load was 32 clusters of frags [fragmentation bombs]—about six bombs to a cluster. 'Bombs Away' was a welcome sound to me . . . these frags are mighty damn touchy. For some reason, which I don't know, we dropped our bombs right in the middle of Brunswick, so I suppose we killed off a lot of people with them. They [the frag bombs] are damn wicked.

Above: *Flak has torn a large piece out of this B-24 Liberator near the starboard waist position, but the ship still made it back to base. Ground officers inspect the damage, while the crew confer and reflect on their lucky escape.*

"One boy in our group had quite an experience today. Somebody dropped a 500lb GP bomb thru' his wing between No.1 & 2 engine. It went on thru' without exploding and it took the landing gear on that side along with it. The kid brought the ship back and made a belly landing with it here on the field. He really did a good job and was plenty lucky.

"I guess our group won't be flying many more operational missions. We're supposed to go home in October sometime, according to Colonel Mason [the CO]. We should be all done by then, though. Maybe this one today will be our last mission. Please God it will."

Left: *The mangled remains of* What's Up Doc? *in the 825th Bomb Squadron, 484th BG in the 15th Air Force. It crashed at its home field in Italy after the pilot managed to nurse the stricken Lib back from a mission to Germany and then belly-land the plane, which, remarkably, did not catch fire.*

Fighting for Survival

Various types of First Aid kit were issued. The Parachute First Aid kit was originally issued to paratroopers, while the Aeronautic First Aid kit, issued on the basis of one kit to two crewmen, or one per man at a remote station, was fixed at crew stations. The large zipper-closed pack contained three field dressings, compresses, tourniquet, eye dressing and burn injury sets, morphine syrettes, sulfadiazine powder or tablets, halazone tablets, and scissors.

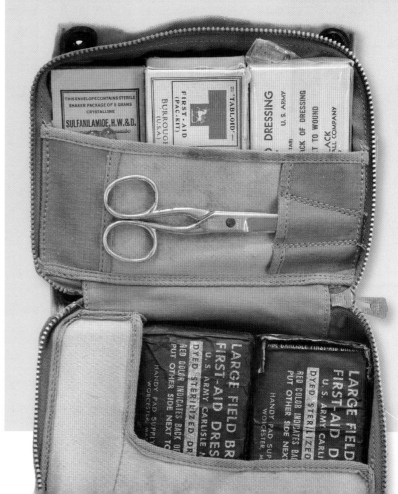

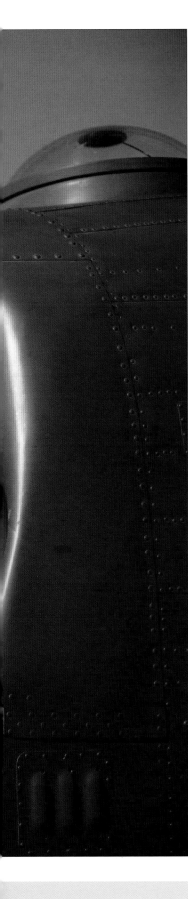

The Navigator & Nose Gunner

"One could walk into a room full of airmen and in a short time pick out with considerable accuracy who held what position just by observing the mannerisms of those present. Navigators were easy to sort out. Just look for a hypersensitive guy, someone who can't hold still one minute, an eager beaver asking questions unrelated to the interest of anyone else. It helped to be a little odd, but I loved the job."

—2nd Lieutenant John W. McClane, navigator, 68th Bomb Squadron, 44th Bomb Group

The navigator (and bombardier) were usually newly graduated from their respective training schools. Many of them had taken an unsuccessful shot at pilot's pre-flight school and their keen interest in flying caused them to accept their second choices. Navigation was, naturally, the navigator's principal duty, and a trainee would have spent many hours learning codes, mathematics, maps and charts, aircraft and naval recognition, principles of flight, aerophysics, and altitude equipment training. As a secondary duty, the navigator was qualified as a nose turret gunner. Added duties included assistant bombardier, oxygen and equipment officer, and First Aid specialist. Occasionally, two navigators would ride in one ship; one would get into the nose turret and help in early location of the bombardier's aiming point, or would man the guns to give him something to do with his hands.

Navigator school was a 20-week course, and all the students would also have to complete six weeks at flexible gunnery school. Trainees spent 104 hours airborne in Beechcraft AT-7s learning dead reckoning using compass, wind drift, and airspeed to calculate positions, and practiced navigating by radio bearings and night navigation techniques. Another 782 hours were spent in ground

Left: The all-electric Emerson nose turret was introduced into the B-24H in June 1943. The B-24G/H/J series were the first Libs to have a nose turret, but installation affected aircraft performance.

school learning pilotage navigation (observation of the ground and its features and comparing them to a map), instruments, dead reckoning, radio, celestial navigation, meteorology, and codes and recognition. Trainees were awarded navigator's silver wings, appointed flight officers or commissioned as 2nd lieutenants and sent on to unit training. By VJ Day more than 50,000 students had graduated from the specialized navigation schools.

Lieutenant Harold Dorfman, a lead navigator in the 712th lead Squadron, 448th Bomb Group, based at Seething, Norfolk, describes the different roles that a navigator could be assigned to: "A typical Group Mission [involved] four squadrons of 12 aircraft in each squadron, [making] a total of 48 aircraft. Occasionally, there were considerably less because of wounded aircraft. Toward the end we occasionally put up a 'maximum effort' of up to 55 aircraft. Two aircraft from the 712th squadron specially equipped with high-precision radar and other good stuff were set up as squadron lead and backup deputy lead. All ten, more or less, planes in the squadron would salvo their bombs on a signal from the lead plane. With four squadrons flying there would be eight lead planes from the 712th lead squadron.

"A lead plane, above and beyond the normal crew, which had only one navigator, was manned by three equally qualified [and] experienced navigators with a lot of missions behind them, working as a team. The Dead Reckoning, or DR Navigator, plots the course on a map, directs the pilot on a compass heading, and directs and calculates all changes to course to and from the destination. He has the final decision and responsibility as to all instructions given to the pilot. The Lead DR Navigator is responsible for all aircraft behind him. This may be anywhere from a squadron of 12 planes to a wing (four groups of 48 planes each) with up to 200 planes. You don't dare screw up. The responsibility was awesome.

"The Pilotage Navigator (PN) manned the nose gun turret, which was specially equipped with basic navigation instruments such as a compass and an air speed indicator. A major significant addition to the gun turret was a brass azimuth ring immediately under the clear plastic dome. The clear plastic dome dominated the entire upper half of the turret providing the PN with a fantastic view for hundreds of miles. The azimuth ring converted the nose turret into a giant, extremely accurate, easy to use pelorus (direction finder) when used in conjunction with the turret's optical gun sight. The PN could sight a known landmark many miles away and provide the DR Navigator with an extremely accurate relative bearing or 'line of position' (LOP).

"Even with a solid cloud under-cast an experienced navigator might pick out a distant mountain peak or high tower that sticks up through the low clouds, such as the Eiffel Tower. In addition to all these good things the nose turret was the most comfortable position on the aircraft, where you could sit for hours basking in the sun reading a comic book, occasionally inconvenienced by a three- or four-minute interruption to provide an LOP or to fire a few bursts at an enemy aircraft which might be interrupting your nap. All navigators were gunners. I had the fifth highest marksmanship score in a class of 500.

"The Radar Navigator (RN) operated the most sophisticated air-to-ground systems available in 1944–1945. During that period any new improved system, would, when available, be immediately installed in the lead planes. The earliest system was called 'Mickey' [named for Disney's Mickey Mouse], a nickname that was applied to all future radar systems such as Pathfinder (PFF) or the most advanced H2X. The RN would function as a navigator/ bombardier. The RN provided the DR Navigator with LOPs, and, when the primary target was obscured by cloud ground cover, would direct the group to a secondary target selected for PFF bombing."

Thumbing his Nose at the Enemy!

Advertisement from the Van Dorn Iron Works Co., Cleveland (left), with a pun on "thumbing his nose," and a Sergeant Flakbaite cartoon from *Short Bursts*, published by the 8th AF Headquarters Operational Analysis Section to improve all aspects of aerial gunnery. In combat, nose guns were rarely a match for the *Focke Wulf* 190 and *Messerschmitt* Bf 109 fighters making head-on attacks.

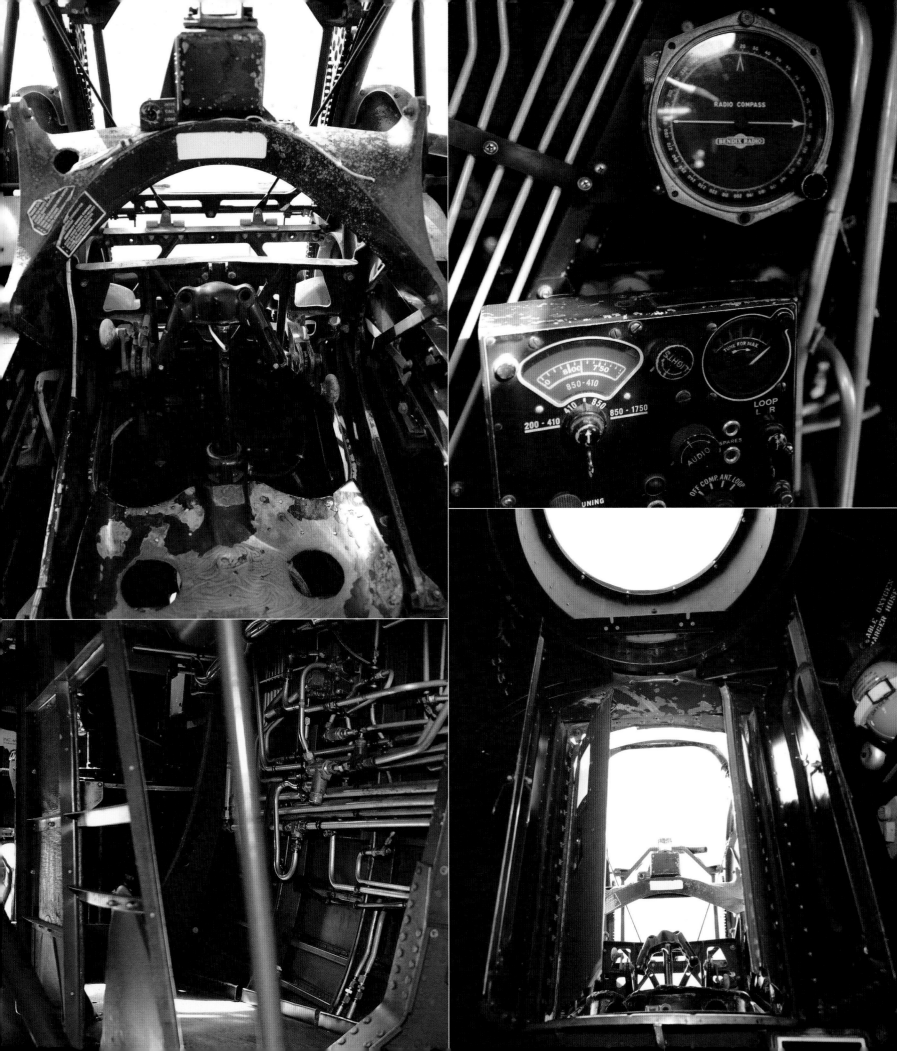

Navigational Dangers

Ronald D. Spencer, a B-24 navigator in the 467th Bomb Group, recalls the great disparity between being a classroom navigator and performing the function in the real world:

"For starters, the navigator's accommodations in the B-24 were rather poor; a small cramped space between the pilot's feet and the nose turret. Visibility to either side wasn't too bad, particularly with the local modification, which replaced the standard small flat windows with larger Plexiglas bubbles. These provided a somewhat restricted and distorted view down, forward, and aft, much inferior to the spacious accommodations in the B-17 . . . In the B-24, the navigator also stood up and faced to the rear since his desk was mounted at the rear of the compartment. Thus, you rode into combat backward, which made pilotage difficult since everything was opposite from what you'd expect. You had to consciously reverse everything you saw on the ground. Desk space was also small, with the left

Above: *8th Air Force 734th Bomb Squadron, 453rd Bomb Group (E8) and 565th Bomb Squadron, 389th Bomb Group (EE) PFF Liberators en route to their target. Each of the two PFF aircraft has an H2X scanner in its ball turret opening.*
Left: *B-24D navigator, wearing his parachute harness, pictured at his fold-up table.*

side obstructed by the Gee Box, which was mounted above it. We typically used at least two types of map; the gridded, small-scale Mercator projection, and the larger-scale sectionals, with several of these needed for a long mission. Invariably, it seemed that the course cut across or along the edge of two or more maps so that you were constantly shuffling from one to another as you moved along. The extremely cold temperatures of –40 or –50 degrees [–40°C to –45°C] resulted in moisture dropping from the oxygen mask falling on the maps and instantly freezing. Thus you had to periodically pick up the maps and break off the ice so you could see what you were doing. After 35 missions, the poor sectionals were in pretty sad shape; all tattered and torn. Drawing and erasing countless courses didn't help any either . . . [and] wearing two pairs of gloves did nothing for good penmanship in filling out the log and doing calculations.

"The bulky clothing, oxygen hose and radio, and heated suit cords restricted your movements and required care to preclude accidentally disconnecting them. Undetected, disconnecting the oxygen hose could map or do calculations. I used goggles with a couple of dark lenses when looking outside, then had to raise them to read anything inside. Thus, I was often constantly raising and lowering the goggles as we flew along.

"Navigation tools were pretty rudimentary, consisting of a so-called E6B computer, a hand-held and rather clever device that enabled you to make calculations considering airspeed, ground speed, wind, aircraft heading, and course in various combinations. We also had a Weems plotter—a clear plastic ruler/protractor combination. In addition, we had a pair of dividers to pick off distance measurements on the maps, plus pencils and erasers. All of the gear was carried to and from the airplane in a briefcase. For instrumentation, we had a repeater for the gyro fluxgate compass—a pretty good one compared to the old alcohol-filled, aperiodic compasses that we struggled with in navigation school . . . We also had an airspeed indicator, altimeter, outside air temperature gauge, and a drift meter. In the wing ships, i.e. those not leading, the navigator was also the bombardier, in that he had to set up the bombing panel. In the lead ships, the bombardier did this. At the Initial Point, you set up the panel by cranking in airspeed, altitude, temperature, ground speed, plus the desired intervalometer setting [a device that let the bombs out one at a time], i.e. the spacing between the individual bombs as they struck the ground. When properly set up, a whole series of indicator lights came on representing each bomb station in the bomb bay. When the nose gunner hit the toggle switch in the turret, the bombs began training out individually with each light going out as the associated bomb left its shackle. The navigator watched the lights as they went out with his hand on a large salvo handle on the left side of the compartment. As long as the lights went out in sequence, you would just watch. But if there was a pause, or the sequence stopped completely, you then immediately salvoed the whole load or whatever was left. You had to do it quickly since you were usually moving along at a ground speed of 400ft [122m] or so a second. Any delay and you could be a considerable distance from what you were aiming at.

"In sum, the navigator was kept quite busy if he was diligent about his job . . . [Although we were] often called 'naviguessers'—or worse—we all did our thing as best we could under the conditions."

Above and right: *B-8 Flying Goggle case and colored lenses, which were plastic, flexible, and "shatter resistant." Instructions to remove dust and finger prints were "by breathing on the lenses and wiping with a soft clean cloth;" a US Army Air Forces Computer, Aerial, Dead Reckoning, Type E6B.*

be fatal in short order. For that reason, the navigator had the additional chore of calling for an oxygen check about every ten minutes or so when at high altitude. Each crewman had to respond to make sure he was okay. Anoxia was insidious in that you could quietly pass out without knowing it was happening. I accidentally disconnected my hose a couple of times, but felt lightheaded enough that I quickly noticed it. Not everyone was that lucky.

"Our crew was very lucky in not having any major problems like so many others. Thus, I wasn't called upon to perform any great feats of navigation when all shot up and all alone a long way from home. While at times I didn't have the foggiest idea where we were, we were able to stay in formation until I got located. A classic case of the old adage, better to be lucky than good. Words to live by—literally.

"One problem we all had was the brilliance of the sun at high altitude. This was a real problem for the pilots when flying formation into Germany. The low sun in the winter was directly in their eyes. It was also a problem for the navigators trying to do pilotage navigation since it was extremely bright when looking outside, and relatively dark inside trying to read the

Leading From the Front

2nd Lieutenant John W. McClane, who went on missions as both a navigator and, later, a lead navigator, experienced the full gamut of dangers, and emotions, during his 1944 tour:

"One of my duties was to wait a few seconds after I heard 'Bombs Away,' and when I felt the last bomb leave our plane, to reach under my navigation desk with my right hand in order to push a red salvo handle. The purpose of this was to mechanically release any bombs still hung up in the bomb bay that were not let go by their electrically operated

Above: *A navigator wearing his oxygen mask (but not his gloves) and bending over his fold-up table with pencil in hand. Note the bubble window to his left, which was usually modified in the field to improve outward vision fore and aft.*

shackles. We always took off with the bomb bay doors open. Water could be splashed onto the latches and would soon freeze as we gained altitude because the temperature was always far below zero. I never failed to watch the bombs fall as I had the best view to see in all directions of any crewmember. My bubble windows on either side of my navigator compartment afforded full visibility straight down as well as

forward, outward, and to the rear. On one mission just a split second after I had moved my head from the bubble window a flak shell exploded just outside the left front of our plane. A large jagged hunk of metal tore through the window, passed over my head and neck and then tore a large ragged hole through my wooden navigation desk, splintering it all to pieces. The extremely cold air came rushing through the hole in the Plexiglas (not a scratch was on the metal window frame). This blast of air sucked up my maps and charts, throwing them through the maze of pipes and wires that separated my desk from the pilot and copilot's feet then tore them to bits. By the Grace of God I was spared. Had I moved one second later, my whole head would have been torn from my body. I sat up to survey the damage. When I saw I had nothing left with which to navigate, my desk was destroyed and I had been scared out of ten years of growth, I became so angry that I guess I went into shock.

"It was not my duty to man a gun but I certainly did like the nose turret as it gave my navigation compartment much protection from frontal attack . . . As lead navigator I had a great responsibility. It was a complicated and exacting task. [As when] the 8th Air Force dispatched about 1,200 'heavies' to various targets in Germany, on October 2, 1944. The 44th Bomb Group launched 25 aircraft and we were to lead the 14th Combat Wing, which led the whole 2nd Division. My H2X Mickey radar navigator [see page 51] and I were to be put to the test. Of the two positions, I had much the better job. I was the senior lead navigator working at my desk with full visibility out of the plane. The radar navigator sat in front of his cathode ray tube [radar scope screen] in semi-darkness plotting our course by observing a very fuzzy reproduction of the ground below. But don't underestimate the value of his work. At times, we could see nothing on the ground in the target area. He then worked with our bombardier to determine when the bombs were to be dropped."

Delmer Wangsvick, navigator in the 732nd Bomb Squadron, 453rd Bomb Group (based at Old Buckenham, Norfolk), meanwhile, commented on the Lib's cramped accomodations:

"I always think they almost forgot the navigator when they developed the B-24—and then slotted him in between the bombardier and the nose wheel. A navigator has maps, papers and needs plenty of space to work. In the B-24 he got a narrow table fixed to the nose compartment

Above: *B-24 Liberator* Red Ass—*for PR purposes, renamed "The Buckaroo"—which led the "Bungay Buckaroos" on D-Day behind a 389th Bomb Group PFF ship.*

bulkhead, where he sat on a skimpy seat facing the pilots' feet and plumb in the way of the bombardier or nose gunner whenever they went back to the flight deck. There was always enough air whipping in around the sides of that darn nose turret to make it necessary to pin down any papers or they'd be blown way back to the bomb bay. A single bulged observation window on either side of the nose provided the only places

the navigator could look out to make ground checks. These windows were far too small, and because visibility was so limited the navigator's job was made harder. In visual conditions he was back and forth to the side windows craning his neck for most of the mission. A lot is said about B-24 pilots having a heavy time on the controls and being mighty tired after a mission, but I can tell you [that] a navigator was just as ready for the sack. For takeoffs and landings I went back to the flight deck and sat near the liaison transmitter [a radio]. This was for safety in case the nose wheel collapsed. The nose was no place to be in a crack-up. Although the compartment was a cold, shaky place my only real complaint about the navigator's position was the poor lookout. I did at times get a change when I flew the 'Command Navigator' position. As such, I did no 'commanding' but operated the nose turret and assisted the crew navigator, primarily in picking out visual checkpoints and occasionally making recommendations to the pilot. A different matter of concern in this position was the possibility of having trouble in making a hurried exit in case the turret got stuck on 'Azimuth' for some reason or other. Otherwise—provided there were no enemy fighters —this position could be almost pleasant and relaxing."

Below: *Navigator's Dead Reckoning Type A-4 Case. This one held Edward "King" Schultz's (448th BG) navigator's log, bombing grid, flight plan, computers, protractor/dividers, weather card, code data sheets and pencils.*

Right: *Joe Nathan, a navigator in the 715th Bomb Squadron, 448th Bomb Group in the 8th Air Force, pictured here at his work station with his navigator's briefcase propped up beside him.*

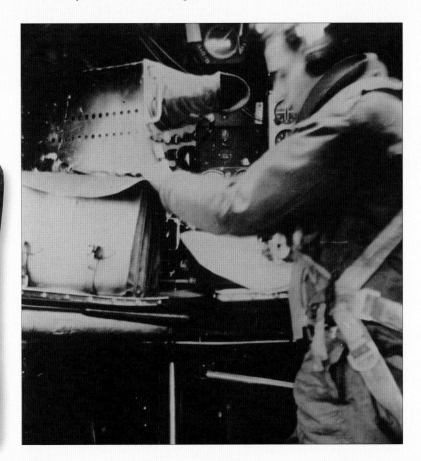

Through Stormy Weather

When the weather played havoc with combat missions H2X was used, as Quintin R. Wedgeworth, a navigator in the 392nd Bomb Group based at Wendling, Norfolk, recalls:

"A mission to the Altenbekin Viaduct near Paderborn [Germany] in January 1944 was aborted due to poor weather and the secondary [Hamm marshaling yards] was the target. The bombing had to be done with H2X and the results were unobserved. This mission turned out to be a milk run. The flak was moderate but inaccurate and all ships returned safely. Clouds continued to mask the British Isles and most of the Continent for much of the next two weeks. It cleared briefly on February 3, permitting the group to accomplish mission No.233. They had been assigned to the oil complex at Magdeburg but wound up bombing [by H2X] the marshaling [secondary] yards. The flak had been moderate and

fairly accurate, with six ships having been hit. The results were again unobserved but evidently considered poor since it was reassigned again on the 6th. Mission No. 234 turned out to be a carbon copy of the previous effort. Plagued by bad weather, they were once again forced to use the H2X system against the secondary . . ."

Before nose turrets were used for pilotage navigation or by the navigator to keep himself occupied in flight, aerial gunners used the Emerson and Motor Products installations (two different makes of nose turret fitted to Libs). This account by Staff Sergeant John W. Butler—who was flying as nose gunner in *Naughty Nan* when the 93rd Bomb Group attacked the

Above: *A wonderful mural with an American eagle and Liberator painted silhouettes, which still decorate a wall at the former ground officers' mess at the 392nd Bomb Group, 8th Air Force base at Wendling (Beeston), Norfolk.*

buzz-bomb construction works at Siracourt, France on February 11, 1944—reveals how cramped and draughty they were:

"The temperature was minus 30. I didn't go in the turret until we were at 14,000ft [4,267m]. You needed help getting in and out of the nose turret, as they had to close the turret door behind you. When you wanted to get out you had to call them on the interphone to let you out. Well, I threw my heated and heavy gloves up on the ammunition box and then I climbed into the turret. The navigator then closed the door for me. The four little windows were open and the guns were elevated so the wind was blowing in quite fast. It was very cold. I got my oxygen mask connected. I then tried to close the windows, but my hands were frozen. I couldn't reach my gloves because my guns were elevated. The main line was off and it had to be turned on from the outside. I plugged in my heated suit but I had no gloves on and they were beet red. I had no feeling in them. I finally got my throat mike on and I yelled over the interphone to get me the hell out of this turret. The navigator opened the door and pulled me out. I went up to the flight deck for heat. When my hands began to thaw out I really suffered. We shot a red flare as we came in for a landing. The pilot called for a meat wagon, which met us at the end of the runway and took us to the hospital."

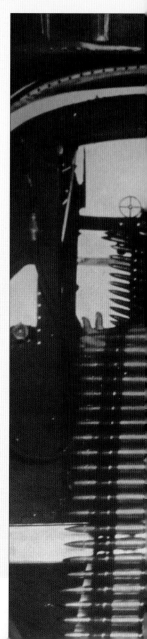

Blind Bombing/Navigational Devices

Gee This British navigational device involved a special aircraft radio receiver working on pulsed signals received from three ground stations. It was limited to a range of about 400 miles (644km). By late 1942 Gee had been rendered almost ineffective by German jamming, and it was replaced by Oboe. Gee-H was a development of Gee, giving more precise fixes to aircraft, and Micro-H was a further development of the Gee system using ground stations' signals, but combined with H2X for bombing.

Oboe This British technique adopted by the USAAF got its name from a radar pulse, which sounded like the musical instrument it was named for. Two ground stations were used, but in contrast to Gee, an aircraft's position was assessed at the ground stations, which operated on re-radiation of radar signals directed at the aircraft. Its range was 280 miles (450km).

H2S This British airborne radar provided a map-like image on a cathode ray tube. It employed a revolving scanner antenna in a radome (protective housing) beneath the nose of a bomber or in the position once occupied by the ball turret on heavy bombers. City areas on coastlines or estuaries were chosen as targets when using H2S because of the clear distinction between water and land on radar screens. This technique allowed a large increase in raids during the

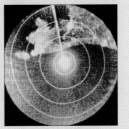

Left: Map-like image on an H2X radarscope as fitted to 8th Air Force B-24 Liberators and de Havilland Mosquito aircraft in the 25th BG, commanded by Col. Elliott Roosevelt.

test period in late 1943 and early 1944. About 80 per cent of 8th AF missions in the last quarter of 1944 used some type of radar bombing devices, either for navigation or targeting. The 8th AF Analysis Section estimated that bombing in good visual conditions was six times more accurate than with Gee or with a beacon combination with H2X called Micro-H, and 150 times more accurate than with H2X through complete overcast conditions (the 8th AF dropped 49.7 per cent of its bombs with non-visual methods, the 15th AF 18.5 per cent). By 1945 bombing accuracy in Europe had risen to 44 per cent of all bombs falling within 1,000ft of the target and 73 per cent within 2,000ft (609m).

AN/APS-15 (H2X, or "Mickey") Usually known as H2X, this was a US-developed version of H2S. The first use of H2X was made on the mission to Wilhelmshaven in October 1943. Sets were available in sufficient numbers by late 1943 to mount the first major raids to test its effectiveness, and it became the standard device for bombing through overcast conditions. Using H2X on D-Day, June 6, 1944, 1,365 8th AF bombers dropped 2,798 tons of bombs through cloud behind the beachheads 30 minutes before the landing.

Above left, center, and right: H2X "Mickey" operator at his table. H2S was a British invention; so named, reportedly, because Prof. Lindemann, Churchill's scientific advisor, said: "It stinks!" The US-developed version was re-named H2X.

Banana Boat or S.O.B?

"The B-24 Liberator was my friend and respected companion; as ugly as a whistling shit house and yet truly a magnificent lady."—Lieutenant Robert H. Tays, 578th Bomb Squadron, 392nd Bomb Group.

Ronald D. Spencer, a B-24 navigator in the 467th Bomb Group, recalls that "The B-24 was considered by many to be the ugly duckling of the heavy bombers, sometimes referred to as the 'box the B-17 came in' and 'a ground-loving S.O.B.' Nonetheless it had certain attributes that endeared it to its crews—some, but certainly not all. It was a bear to fly, particularly in formation; not benefiting from boosted controls as in the B-17. It was said that you could always tell a B-24 pilot by his calloused hands. Its Davis high-efficiency wing gave it excellent range; one reason for its extensive use in the Pacific Theater, where long-distance missions were the norm. A fully loaded B-24 could not get as high as a B-17; the B-17 typically operating at about 27,000ft [8,230m] while we were pretty much limited to about 23,000ft [7,010m]

Left: A rare "Pratt & Whitney U.S.A. Dependable Engines" motif, which, in this instance, refers to engines built by Buick.

for the average airplane. You could get higher if you had newer engines, but the dogs had trouble making 23,000 [feet]. I considered this an advantage, since the B-17s were given the rougher oil targets because of their altitude advantage. Merseburg and Leipzig were typical of the targets reserved for the '17s. A favorite ditty at the time was *'Don't send my boy to Merseburg'*—and for good reason."

The Davis wing resulted in the Liberator being faster than the Fortress but it provided far less lift than the Fortress wing. Also, the shoulder wing configuration and the weight of the wing made heavy crash landings risky, and crew casualties were greater than in aircraft with low-set wings, which absorbed much of the shock. Though the B-24's accident rate was not much greater than the B-17, the casualty rate for the Liberators in accidents was almost double that of the Fortress. Fatalities were about five B-24 men for every three B-17 men.

There were several comfort and control features that were superior to the B-17. For example, the pilot's seat was adjustable—up, down, back, and forth, and angled back or forth. The B-24 had a tricycle landing gear, which made taxiing the plane, taking off, and landing easier.

Below, from left: B-24 Dumbo *in the 453rd BG at Old Buckenham in 1944. Not every Liberator crewman liked the plane—a state of affairs reflected in disparaging names such as* Consolidated Mess, *given to at least a dozen B-24s in England. More respectful were B-24H* Old-Faithful, *in the 446th BG, and* Never Mrs., *in the 734th Bomb Squadron, 453rd BG, lost on November 11, 1944 on its 70th mission.*

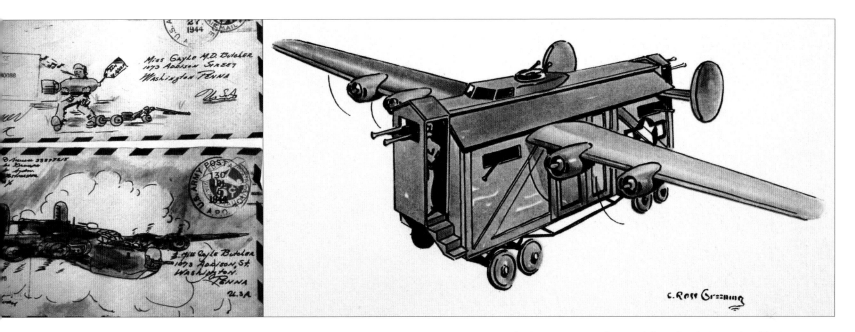

Above, left and right: *Airmail envelopes sent with letters from ground technician Jake Krause to his girlfriend Gail were illustrated with cartoons of life at Horsham St. Faith (now Norwich Airport) in 1943–45. The B-24's appearance led to it being dubbed the "Flying Box Car," and, by B-17 crews, as "the crate that ours came in."*

There were other differences, too, as Spencer continues: "The B-24 could carry a heavier bomb load than the '17. A common slur at the time was that the B-17 huffed and puffed, climbed to 30,000ft [9,144m] and dropped a hand grenade. As expected, a considerable rivalry developed between the B-24 and B-17 crews; each making nasty comments about the capabilities of the other's aircraft. The B-17 with its broad wing got off the ground much quicker than the B-24. We had 6,000ft [1,829m] runways, which were normally used for all mission takeoffs. It was not uncommon to see a '24 take the whole 6,000ft plus some grass [at] the end. A lot of pilots wanted as much airspeed as possible in case they lost an engine, and held it down as long as possible, then horsed it up at the last minute. Because of its tricycle gear and low stance, it looked as if it were never going to leave the ground, thus the oft-used term, 'ground-loving S.O.B.' At least the B-17 would get its tail up, and at least [it] looked like it wanted to fly. A very big plus for the B-24 was its excellent P&W [Pratt and Whitney]—much superior to the Wrights on the '17. We used to say that it was a good thing that the '17 could fly so well with one or even two engines out since it had to do [so] so often."

Abandon Ship!

On October 14, 1944 eleven hundred B-17s and B-24s bombed marshaling yards and targets in and around Cologne, Germany. *Jolly Roger*, piloted by Lieutenant Klusmeyer in the 458th Bomb Group, took a direct flak hit in the nose. Lieutenant Robert L. Ferrell, the lead navigator, remembers the incident:

"With his eye glued to the Norden sight, Ernest Sands, the bombardier, shouted, 'Bombs Aw . . .' The Plexiglas of the Emerson nose turret turned red with blood and the bombardier was blown from over the bombsight back into the nosewheel well. My left hand showed blood through my gloves from three shrapnel piercings and the smell of cordite seeped through my oxygen mask. [Ferrell then went to the aid of the second navigator, Millard C. Miller.]

"I slipped my hands under his armpits and pulled on him. His head fell back against my right shoulder. I looked at Miller and vomited into my oxygen mask and nearly drowned from it. I had never seen a human head hit by a shell. I laid him on the floor of the navigator's compartment. Sergeant Pohler, the engineer/upper turret gunner, dragged Miller through the tunnel and toward the flight deck, where he

was thrown out the bomb strike camera hatch opening after Pohler secured a 25ft [7.62m] static line clip to his [parachute's] 'D' ring." [With a macabre touch, Ferrell made an entry into his navigation log using the blood lying on his table. Three rings on the bailout bell ordered the crew to abandon the aircraft. A fire in the bomb bay forced the men back to the front compartment. Ferrell pulled the emergency handle on the nosewheel doors, but they failed to open.] "This was our only way out now [he continued] . . . Sands stooped over and jumped up and down on the nosewheel doors. They began to part and fly away. He dropped through the opening until his outstretched arms held him momentarily. He looked at me and shouted: 'This sure as hell pisses me off!' Then he dropped out and away." [Ferrell quickly followed. Klusmeyer, copilot Fred Wright, and Ferrell landed in Boppard, Germany, near the same farmhouse and were taken prisoner. Miller also survived but although one or two of the enlisted men initially managed to avoid capture, they were eventually caught.]

On March 3, 1945 the 8th went to Magdeburg, Germany. For Sol Greenberg, a navigator in the 453rd Bomb Group, it was his second mission to the city—and almost his last:

"The 453rd was after the oil refineries and I recall it was a rather clear day above the clouds. We were crossing over the northern part of the Zuider Zee when . . . suddenly all hell broke loose with the most accurate flak I had ever experienced. The guns evidently had a very good track on us. I could hear the shells bursting all around me, and when you hear that, you're in trouble. I just made the silly remark that 'I have but one life to give to my country and I might as well give it now.'

"At that instant the moment of truth arrived. The entire bubble came up into my face and a piece of shell fragment, about one and a half inches wide by eight inches long, tore against my forehead. Blown down against one of the ammunition storage cans that served as seats on each

Above: The Emerson nose turret on the B-24H was not for the faint hearted. With few windows in the nose to allow for scanning, when the turret was unmanned it would often be the mount for the toggling bombardier or lead crew pilotage navigator.

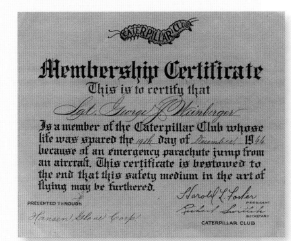

Right: Parachute First Aid kit ("Frying Pan Insert"), issued with the B-2, -3 and -4 parachute pack emergency kit assemblies. The emergency supplies were housed in a small OD painted, circular, flat metal can.

side of the navigator's compartment, I attempted to take stock of my situation. Obviously I could not see. I was naturally furious at having been treated to such an indignity. The metal continued on through the plane skin just under the left foot of Bryson, our pilot, and the plane rocked rather uncomfortably. Bryson recognized that this was not the usual type of peppering and asked if anyone had been hit. I replied in the affirmative and he then asked if I wanted to return to base. In true heroic fashion I bellowed down the microphone 'No, no—go on with the mission, we are going in to the target.' Actually I am not that much of a hero but my reactions were

somewhat hazily through one eye as the tears washed out the Plexiglas. Naturally that was the eye that Gehrt bandaged. By then I was really furious at what had occurred and ripped off the bandage, instinctively attempting to return to my navigating. After all that was my job. We had the silly sight of Al still attempting to bandage me and me fighting him off as I recorded the compass headings, altitudes, airspeed readings, and tried to pick up the next landmark to ascertain our position. It must have been five or ten minutes of insanity up there in the nose. Finally Gehrt left me to do what I wanted although I am certain he had misgivings about leaving me in such a mental state. Instant flak happiness.

"The navigation all the way into the target was extremely poor as we wandered from one major flak area to another . . . The flight back was just as poorly navigated and we unnecessarily took a good deal of flak.

"From the French coast on, we left the formation and went in by ourselves. Upon landing at our field we were met at the end of the runway by an ambulance and I was placed on a stretcher, my left eye giving me some sight but the right one absolutely nothing. I had been so busy that I had not pondered the possibility of blindness on a partial basis until that moment. As I was placed in the ambulance I suddenly felt something very cold and

Above: S/Sgt Virgil "Rudy" R. Heddlestone of the 704th Bomb Squadron, 446th BG, after his capture on July 31, 1944, having bailed out of his B-24 Hula Wahinna.

Above: Caterpillar Club certificate presented to Sergeant George J. Weinberger in the 448th Bomb Group at Seething, who bailed out of his B-24 on December 19, 1944.

instinctive and had I taken a few seconds to think the situation out, I might well have elected [to do] otherwise.

"My bombardier, Al Gehrt, who had been in the bomb bay de-pinning the bombs, came up forward and proceeded to apply a bandage. The slight cut from the flak had stopped bleeding and I was beginning to see

sticky on my hands and placed my finger on my nose. No doubt about it, it was blood. It suddenly occurred to me that I must have been hit elsewhere and had not noticed it when the medic told me that they had just returned from taking a wounded gunner from another crew down to the hospital and apparently he had been badly wounded in the intestines. I must say it was at that point I had my first true fright and was relieved to find I was no worse than I had surmised."

The Radio Operator

"As I straddled the catwalk during the bomb run and pressed the bomb bay anti-creep lever, a chunk of shrapnel ripped through my blue bunny, nearly making an instant soprano out of me as it shorted out my suit. It was a cold flight home. The two-ounce shot of 86-proof was especially welcomed at the end of a difficult day. It hit my empty stomach like an exploding star."—Technical Sergeant Donald V. Chase

The radio operator was a key position in the ten-man crew of a B-24. It was his job to service, maintain, and operate all radio communications equipment, tuning units, frequency meters, radio compass, emergency flare supplies, Verey pistol, telegraph key, the SCR522 radio transmitters and receivers, and radio navigation aids. On some early models, the radio operator was stationed aft of the copilot. Behind the pilot, a lounge bench ran fore and aft where the bombardier, navigator, and nose turret gunner stayed during takeoffs, landings, and ground operations. Aft of the bomb bay, where a catwalk in the center ran back to the rear fuselage compartment, four crewmen operated, with the radio operator usually in the area above the rear portion of the bomb bay, sometimes laughingly referred to as the command deck. The radio position was cramped, but not unduly so. The simple backless stool that he sat on—at a small metal table, which had the receiver on top, and the transmitter underneath—was not very comfortable for long flights, but men got used to it. Flexes to the earphones were sufficiently long to allow him to stand up and look into the cockpit during takeoffs and landings, and at other times he could also act as another pair of eyes for the pilots and gunners. Apart from being able to look up ahead through the cockpit

Left: The BC-348-Q radio receiver in situ on a B-24 Liberator. Manufactured by Wells Gardner & Co., the receiver was used in conjunction with a BC-375 transmitter and tuning units.

Perspex, he also had a small observation window in the fuselage side, against the radio. There was always plenty of radio noise, especially W/Y (Morse). However, if he tuned in on purpose to the various American radio programs that could be picked up at random, then he could fail to receive important messages affecting the outcome of the mission. On long flights the radio operator's lot could be monotonous, but he did have other members of the crew close at hand, and knew just what was going on by way of the intercom and visual observation.

The radio operator was also qualified as top turret gunner and nose turret gunner, and he would also man one of the waist guns if needed. Among his other duties were assistant airplane engineer (if he had the most maintenance experience), turret specialist, and assistant to the armament officer or the armorer. He also had to know First Aid and be able to help the wounded when needed.

Staff Sergeant Forrest S. Clark was the assistant radio operator as well as tail gunner in Rocky Griffith's crew in the 44th Bomb Group. Clark describes his training and induction into the USAAF in 1942—and his first experiences of combat missions: "My induction into the Armed Forces took place at Fort Dix, New Jersey, in October 1942. My crew training took place at Clovis, New Mexico, and Biggs Field, Texas. We flew many practice missions over the deserts of New Mexico but none more memorable than one of those designed to test our night navigational and radio skills. Abe Sofferman, a typical street-smart kid from New York City, was at the radio. I was in the waist. Over the pitch-dark desert we nearly collided with another B-24. It would have been the end for us as a crew. Abe stayed calm throughout this incident and he and Bob Weatherwax, our cheerful, outgoing navigator, formed a close bond.

"We used the old Morse code message system and the standard code signals. However, the radio equipment was primitive by today's standards and was later often rendered inoperable by enemy fire. Some equipment was inherited from the old Signal Corps and dated back to the 1920s. Radio operators had no gun position but when there was no flight engineer, they took the top turret gun. Most of the time Abe Sofferman and me sat in a cramped space near the front of the plane behind the cockpit. Abe took his job seriously. [After training, they flew to England via the 'Iceberg Route'—by way of Labrador, Greenland, and Iceland]. The 'Iceberg Route'. . . was dangerous and we were to report any enemy submarines' positions. The radio operator was also to send reports of any suspicious ships or planes in the vicinity. [At one point] Abe took a break in the waist leaving me at the radio controls for a couple of hours. It was snowing when we took off from Goose Bay for Greenland. Soon we were lost in a blinding snowstorm and tried to turn back in what was by then a whiteout. Weatherwax pressed on and turned us on a new course for Bluie West 1, Greenland [Bluie West 1 was one of the USAAF's airfields in Greenland]. Our troubles were just beginning as we faded out of Goose Bay's radio signals and we could not pick up a signal or beacon from BW1. [Approaching BW1] I was getting only static on the receiver from the Greenland station. I had the trailing wire antenna out for the frequency. Suddenly there was a tap and then a bang. I had forgotten to reel in the antenna. It hit the runway and the 'fish,' a lead ball at the end [of the trailing antenna] broke off and went flying toward one of the Quonset huts of the base officers. I got hell for this. Griffith and

Sofferman stepped up and smoothed things over for me, explaining that I was a novice at the radio. 'I think I'll handle the radio,' Abe said to me after that. In late January 1944 I was just recovering from a bout of sinusitis when Abe Sofferman was in a B-24 that was shot down over Belgium. I found out later that he was killed fighting with the partisans."

Trailing Wire Antenna

Type MT-5E Antenna Reel, made by Bendix Radio, Baltimore, Maryland. The trailing wire antenna, essential on long over-water flights such as the "Iceberg Route" from the Eastern United States to Great Britain, would be reeled out of a B-24 Liberator to help the radio operator obtain radio signals and beacon frequencies. But as Forrest Clark found to his cost (see story, left), forgetting to reel the antenna back in could prove embarrassing, if not disastrous!

The Kiel Debacle

On May 14, 1943 *Scrappy* in the 66th Squadron, piloted by 1st Lieutenant John Y. Reed, became the sixth and final 44th Bomb Group loss as a result of the Kiel mission. Reed recalls his radio operator's attempt to help his wounded top turret gunner on the mission:

"We came under very heavy fighter attacks in the target area and were quite vulnerable because of our spread-out bombing formation. Just prior to dropping our bombs, I saw an FW 190 peel off at us from about 1 o'clock and slightly high. As the puffs of bursting 20mm ammo came toward us, it became apparent that the line of fire would put the successive bursts right into our cockpit. Purely reflex action alone caused me to hit the wheel in a dive to try to get below the line of fire but, unfortunately, the bursts did not quite clear the plane, hitting the top turret directly behind the cockpit. The resultant explosion tore the top turret canopy completely off and the shrapnel severely wounded Technical Sergeant Adam Wygonik about his head, neck, and upper body. The inside of the turret and the gun barrels were pitted from the force of the shrapnel. Either the force of the explosion or Wygonik must have reflexively dumped his seat lever, as he immediately fell out onto the flight deck.

Technical Sergeant Alan Perry, radio operator, immediately sized up the situation, left his own oxygen supply and attempted to give Wygonik—who was bleeding profusely from his head and body wounds, and had no oxygen supply— some first aid. Perry snapped Wygonik's chest pack onto his harness and put his hand around the ripcord ring, inasmuch as Perry intuitively concluded that Wygonik would die before we got back to England and medical attention. He intended to roll Wygonik out of the ship as we were still over the target area; [if he survived the landing] there was at least the possibility of immediate medical attention.

"Perry was suffering from lack of oxygen [by this time], and returned to his oxygen supply to keep from blacking out—but when he was able to turn back to Wygonik, Adam was gone! Apparently, intentionally or otherwise, Adam had rolled off the flight deck, onto the catwalk in the open bomb bay. The bay doors were still open as we were on the bomb run. No one could say for sure that Adam's 'chute had opened since all attention was on fighting off the attacking aircraft. We had no way of knowing whether Adam reached the ground dead or alive, though the odds seemed stacked against his survival due to the severity of his wounds

and the resultant loss of blood, and the fact that he was without oxygen even longer than Sergeant Perry.

"The plane, as we came away from the target, was severely damaged, with one engine smoldering, loss of top portions of one vertical stabilizer and rudder, and multiple hits from 20mm fire, including the blown-away top turret canopy. Unable to maintain position in our formation, I dove toward a group of B-17s that were ahead and below us in a shallow dive toward the coast and managed to hold position behind and below their rear flight. This protected our top with their bottom and rear turrets. After the fighter attacks broke off, we flew pretty much back to England." [*Scrappy* was abandoned over England after being headed back out toward the sea by the pilot, where it was shot down by RAF Spitfires— effectively counting as a loss caused by combat action.]

Communication Systems

As far as equipment was concerned, B-24 Liberators used three main aircraft communications sets:

The Command Radio (SCR-274-N) provided for short-range voice contact with ground stations or B-24s nearby and was also used for communication with control towers to a maximum of 30 miles (48km). The Liaison Radio (SCR-287-A) provided for long-range, two-way voice and Morse code communication between B-24s and a ground station, though in England the apparatus was normally used purely for coded signals by W/T (wireless telegraphy). The set was used to send mission progress signals or distress calls when at long range. The VHF Command Radio (SCR-522-A), finally, was the principal operational set for verbal communication with bomber and fighter aircraft; it had a range of about 150 miles (240km) for an aircraft at 20,000ft (6,096m). If a Liberator got into

distress, the radioman would send out distress signals and position fixes if over the sea. The radioman was also responsible for the Radio Compass (SCR-269-G), which was used in direction finding with "Buncher" and "Splasher" systems for assembly and undercast conditions. In spring 1943 the 8th Air Force began making use of the dozen or so RAF Splasher medium-frequency radio beacons, and crews were given a list of call signs and frequencies for the Splashers selected for the day's mission.

Left and below: In the control tower at Hardwick—watching B-24s return was a tense job; a microphone used to put out Tannoy and other messages.

Above: On May 14, 1943, on the mission to the shipyards of Kiel, Germany, the 44th "Flying Eightballs" BG flew above and behind the Flying Forts for the first time in the ETO (European Theater of Operations). Flying a scattered formation on a longer bomb run than the B-17s to drop incendiaries, they lost six B-24D Liberators (shot down).

Far left: The shattered Martin top turret of a B-24D Lib.

Above: Hardwick Control Tower; the rooftop bristles with antennae for communicating with wing and group HQs, as well as bomber crews.
Left: A radio operator at his post, communicating with other radio and crew personnel via his microphone.

"Timb-a-a-ah"

Technical Sergeant Donald V. Chase, a B-24 radio operator-gunner in the 44th Bomb Group, had flown the Ploesti low-level mission on August 1, 1943. His pilot, Lieutenant Charles Whitlock, had been forced to abort the mission 125 miles (200km) short of the target, due to fuel transfer problems and oiling difficulties, which forced them to shut down No.1 engine and feather the propeller before No.4 lost power also; they eventually put down safely on Cyprus. While he and three other crewmembers were grounded with respiratory and ear infections on August 16, six of their fellow crew and four replacements failed to return when *Timb-a-a-ah* was shot down over Foggia. Chase wrote:

"Long after the last ships returned and the sun had set we mournfully trekked back to our tent area. It was a night of anguish. Eight of our group's aircraft had failed to return. If I had been older, instead of 22, perhaps I might not have searched for a symbolic reason which governs fateful events. But regardless, I picked up my Gurkha Kukri that I had been the custodian of since our crew were presented with it in Cyprus, walked into the desert and threw the curved 10-inch blade across the sand into the darkness. It had brought only bad luck. More than half my crew were gone, probably dead. I cried. It was difficult to find an experienced crew in need of a radio operator. I felt like a wandering Bedouin searching for an oasis. I considered leaving a conditional 'goodbye' letter in my footlocker, thanking my parents for 23 good years, but I couldn't summon the courage to tempt fate."

[For the next three months, in England, Chase flew no combat missions, but in mid-December he took the place of a radioman on Lieutenant James Hill's crew who had fallen, or been blown, from the foot-wide bomb bay catwalk during the bomb run and had parachuted into France. He flew his next

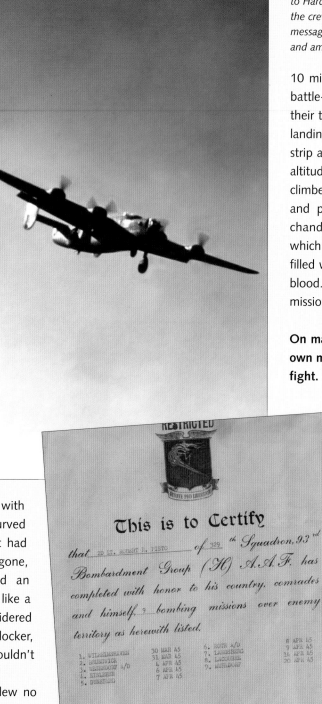

Left: A B-24 in the 93rd BG on its final descent to Hardwick airfield. If wounded were onboard, the crew would fire red flares to back up radio messages from the radioman to the home tower and ambulance crews would be alerted.

10 missions with Lieutenant Hill and his battle-experienced crew, who completed their tour on February 25, 1944. Prior to landing, Hill buzzed the base perimeter strip at Shipdham "with full power at an altitude too low to estimate." He then climbed at a steep angle, rocked the wing and put the B-24 through a modified chandelle, "the resultant G-force of which made my body feel as if it were filled with cement instead of thin, scared blood." At that time Chase still had eight missions to fly before ending his tour.]

On many missions Forrest Clark saw his own men and the enemy die in the same fight. Yet the mission to Bernberg, Germany, in April 1944 stood out above all others as a lesson in this overwhelming feeling of disgust with war:

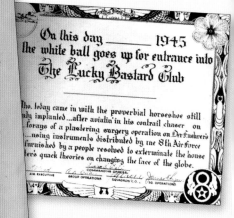

Above and left: "Lucky Bastard" certificate (above), plus a "Mission Completed" certificate belonging to Lt. Robert R. Pisto in the 329th Bomb Squadron, 93rd BG.

Left: *44th Bomb Group "Flying Eightballs" personnel play cards at Shipdham. On the Bernberg mission in April 1944 Forrest Clark witnessed the death of crewmen with whom, a few hours earlier, he had been playing cards at the barracks at Shipdham.*

Below: *1st Lieutenant Leroy L. Engdahl in the 713th Bomb Squadron, 448th Bomb Group, dressed in striped pajamas and a top hat after completing his 30th and final combat mission at Seething. He is holding a cardboard replica of a DFC ribbon.*

plane before it exploded. Bill Tinsman said he saw one burning body go dangling through space with no 'chute. In many cases crewmembers did not have time to attach their parachutes, or forgot them in their panic to get out of burning planes. Many of them jumped to their deaths this way. The cockpit of the burning bombers was filled with flames and the crew never had a chance to survive this inferno. It was later said that the fire and explosion came because the bomber dropped its bombs through its bomb bay doors. Contact with bomb bay doors was enough to ignite high explosive bombs and there were other reports of similar incidents. I knew the crew of that doomed bomber. Some had been with us a few hours before back at the base, playing cards, and singing in the barracks and then they were gone, burning in the skies over Germany. Such was war. There were no heroes, only the lucky ones, only those who survived and carried the guilt to their graves. Years later my copilot told me, 'I am not a religious man but I still pray and remember those who didn't come back.'

"I recall sitting in minus 30 degree temperatures at altitude seeing our planes and those fighters of our enemy bursting in flames and going down and thinking to myself in the next instant—'Would I follow them in some blinding explosion?' I would sweat under my flight suit and my hands would get wet from sweat, the sweat of fear, and a bone-chilling type of fear. Some men vomited into their oxygen masks from fear and sickness and this could be dangerous and fatal by cutting off their oxygen supply."

"We had one strong and fierce attack by seven Me 109s straight on and through our formation. You could see the enemy gunfire ripping through our group. As fearsome as this was it was nothing compared to what happened to one of our own planes and crews. Flying near us in the formation, we saw one of our bombers catch fire and then the tail blew off. What was left of the plane did a loop before exploding right in front of us. It was a miracle that we were not taken down with it. It was a sickening sight. Three 'chutes were reported coming out of the burning

A Few Hundred Holes

Rudy Acosta, radio operator on Lieutenant Norman "Buck" Rogers' crew in the 449th Bomb Group flying *Buzzer*, recalls the mission to the Ploesti marshaling yards on May 5, 1944 when it was bombed by 38 of the group's B-24 Liberators:
"It was uneventful until we reached the IP. Then all hell breaks loose . . . I can still see a B-24 blow up like a giant ball of fire. Are we ever going to get the hell out of here?! It's like a lot longer over this target than the previous times. No wonder, we fly over this target twice. For some reason the bombs were not dropped on the first run. By the time we are out of flak range we are flying by ourselves. We pick up a bomber here and another one there. Six of us flying by ourselves!

"Fighters jump us. First attack I see one bomber go down with a wing on fire. I count six 'chutes before I get busy again firing at fighters coming low at 7 o'clock. Second pass of fighters, another bomber going down on fire—too busy to look for bailouts. It seems like forever before we get to the Danube, and Yugoslavia. At least if we bail out we will be in Partisan country. We get to the Adriatic Sea and feel better, except we freak about how the

hydraulic lines have been torn apart by flak. Damn, look at the size of the hole on our right wing; you can crawl through it.

"Over the base now—Rizan has to crank the [landing] gear down by hand. We check the yellow lock markers to see that the landing gear is down and locked—it's okay, we hope. Rizan, and I can't recall who else, are trying to plug hydraulic lines with rags as we land. We have barely enough fluid to brake at the end of the runway and get off a little bit to one side. We all jump off and a truck picks us up and takes us to debriefing. Later that night, we go to see the damage to the ship. I remember I started to count the holes in the ship. A few hundred holes later I give up. It takes six weeks to repair the ship."

Above: *Neutral Switzerland was a safe haven for Libs and Flying Forts in trouble. Many damaged bombers or those low on fuel on missions deep into southern Germany landed at Dubendorf, shown here.*
Right: *Turbo supercharger, driven by exhaust gases to ram more air into the cylinders and produce added power at altitude.*
Left: *View of walkway from near the navigator's position, looking aft toward the bomb bay. Note the hydraulic lines, to left.*

Right: *B-24H Dual Sack in the 714th Bomb Squadron, 448th BG. It crash-landed at Bultofta, Sweden, on June 21, 1944. All of the crew were interned.*

Fred Aldrich, radio operator with the W. Snavely crew, 712th Squadron, 448th Bomb Group, based at Seething, had his work cut out on his third mission on July 12, 1944—though the mission began well enough . . .

"If our first two missions could be termed 'milk runs,' mission no. 3 was to be dramatically different indeed! It was a repeat trip to Munich. Targets the same. Flak was expected to be heavy, and there was the possibility of opposition from enemy fighters based there. Everything went as scheduled and we hit the marshaling yards. The flak was heavy and as I stood at the head of the bomb bay, holding the doors open on the bomb run, the flak was bursting directly beneath us. (It was on the bomb run that a formation was most

susceptible to damage as no evasive action could be employed—you had to stay on course during the bomb run.) We got hit on the left wing tip but it did not cause a problem for us.

"We were about one-and-half hours away from the target on our way to home base when it happened. A supercharger on one of our engines acted up, perhaps from battle damage. This caused the engine to consume an excessive amount of fuel. As a result, the pilot had to feather the prop on the engine, reduce speed, and drop out of formation. We could not reach England and [so] there we were, flying over Germany alone, unprotected, and expecting enemy fighters to attempt to finish us off at any moment—but we were lucky!

"The pilot called us on the intercom and gave us two choices. He could either head for neutral Switzerland, where we would be interned for the remainder of the war, or try to reach the newly established beachhead and a temporary auxiliary landing strip in France. We chose the beachhead. I worked my radio for three hours trying to get information to help guide us. My head ached and my ears rang from the static and squealing coming through my earphones, but to no avail, as I never reached England. (I later learned that my receiver was inoperative—a tube too weak to amplify a C.W. signal.) The pilot instructed the others to jettison all detachable equipment and ammunition to lighten the load to help us keep airborne and conserve fuel. They were working to the utmost, some without oxygen, at 16,000ft [4,877m] altitude.

"While we were still at it, the navigator had succeeded in getting us to the auxiliary field. It was a British Spitfire and Hurricane landing strip just behind Caen, France, taken two days previously by allied ground forces. It was simply a bulldozed strip covered with portable steel sections, adequate for fighter aircraft, but not for a four-engine B-24 bomber! With fuel tanks on empty and sweating with fear, we approached the runway, but our pilot 'Bill' Snavely and copilot 'Roy' Morris rose to the occasion and made a successful landing—we had made it thus far! We rested in a nearby bunker, listening to the war going on about us while the pilot successfully negotiated with a tank commander for enough fuel to get us home.

"As we took off, fear gripped us again. Could we get airborne off such a short strip? We did, but it took us quite a while to gain altitude, and we could see the water in the English channel below us. We made it and successfully got back to our base at Seething. We were congratulated. We learned that six planes were already missing from our base. One landed in Switzerland, three crash-landed in England, and one was presumed to be shot down, and we had made it home! Altogether, the 8th AF had lost 26 bombers that day. Only 27 more missions to go!"

The Carpetbaggers

"We dropped some agents in the foothills of the Alps near Munich. It was a 'hairy do' because the only possible withdrawal maneuver was a 'chandelle' to avoid slamming into the mountains. A few nights later we made 'S' Phone contact with the agents on the ground and asked what other supplies they might need. The answer we received was *'We want a bunch of bananas and a few packets of condoms!'*"—Lieutenant Colonel Robert W. Fish, Carpetbagger CO.

The 801st (P) Group—later 492nd Bomb Group—was activated at Harrington, Northamptonshire, in the summer of 1943 using crews and B-24D Liberators from the disbanded 479th Anti-Submarine Group at Dunkeswell, Devon. The Liberators received a series of modifications to enable the Carpetbagger crews to fly at night to occupied Europe, where they dropped supplies and agents, or Joes, to the underground armies in France and the Low Countries. Late in the war missions were extended to include Scandinavia, when a team headed by Bernt Balchen, the famous Arctic explorer, mounted "Sonnie" operations from Leuchars in Scotland. In total, 3,016 people were evacuated, including Norwegian aircrew trainees and 965 American internees.

For Carpetbagger operations, the B-24s were painted black overall and the ball turret was removed. The "Ball" project (which got its name from this) in July 1944 saw crews make supply drops to the Norwegian Underground. The ball turret opening became the "Joe Hole" through

which agents wearing parachutes were dropped. Late B-24 models had their nose turret removed, to be replaced by a "greenhouse" which permitted the bombardier an excellent view of the drop zone so he could assist the navigator in spotting landmarks. Suppressors, or flame dampers, were fitted to the engine exhausts and the two waist guns were removed. Only the top and tail turrets were retained. Oxygen equipment was also removed because of the low altitude flown, and a variety of special navigational equipment and radar was installed.

The Carpetbaggers came under Special Operations, 8th AF, while OSS (Office of Strategic Services) directed operations and handled the reception grounds in the occupied countries. Carpetbagger missions contributed hugely to the success of the invasion of Normandy in the run

Below, left to right (this page): Colonel Cliff Heflin, Carpetbagger CO in 1944, studies a map of France before another drop to the French Resistance; the crew of Screwball (an ex-467th Bomb Group B-24), flown by Sam Goldsmith (1st Lieutenant Edgar F. Townsend, navigator, is far left in the back row); paratroopers prepare to board a Carpetbagger Liberator at Harrington, Northamptonshire, in 1944.

Right: B-24D Playmate, *pictured in India in November 1944, served in the 389th "Sky Scorpions" at Hethel prior to joining the Carpetbaggers.*

Opposite, above: 788th Bomb Squadron badge; in May 1944 11 crews and aircraft from this squadron were transferred to the Carpetbaggers.
Opposite, below: Another ex-389th BG B-24D to join the Carpetbaggers was Fightin' Sam, *pictured at Hethel, 1943.*

Below, left to right (this page): The modified rear area with plywood-covered floor near the Joe Hole in a Carpetbagger B-24; blackout curtains in the waist section for night operation; a Carpetbagger B-24 on a training flight over England in 1944.

up to D-Day, June 6. That month the 801st BG flew no fewer than 424 sorties, of which 347 were successful; in July, 397 sorties were flown.

Lieutenant William B. Dillon, a Carpetbagger pilot, remembers: "In all the flights we made over the Continent, there was only one time we actually saw a Jerry nightfighter. Evidently he was on radar because he missed us by only about 50ft [15m]. We saw his exhausts as he went over the top of us. I think that one of the most exciting missions we flew was when we took a French paymaster for the FFI [French Resistance] from England to east of Bordeaux. He had over a million dollars in francs. We found the IP and the target but on our first run over the target we had a wrong identification signal. We tried again. But again a wrong

signal was received. Our agent was very enthusiastic and really wanted to get out of the airplane and down on the ground again. I told the crew we would make a third pass. This time we got our third different identification signal. I told the crew that we had been here long enough. We were getting out. We got to about 5,000ft [1,524m] and were bracketed in searchlights. Evidently, the Germans were there. I was mighty scared at the time."

When the final Carpetbagger mission was flown on April 16, 1945, a total of 82 agents had been parachuted into Germany by aircraft of the Dijon mission set up in France. In all of the operations to France, the Low Countries, and Scandinavia, 26 aircraft and 208 crewmen were lost.

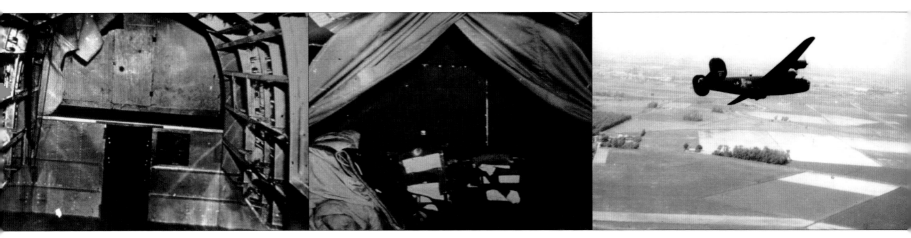

The Numbers Game

Technical Sergeant Donald V. Chase flew his 20th mission on March 22, 1944:

"Six of our squadron aircraft participated in what was a mammoth raid on Berlin. It was a long day. Up hours before dawn; breakfast; briefing; pre-flight; takeoff at 08:15 hours; [then] eight hours in flight, dodging our own aircraft on climb-out through the clouds (and on the return, too); sucking in your breath as shards of 88s and 110s pierced our ship's thin, olive-drab skin; checking the configuration of fighters to determine if they were bandits or 'Little Friends;' hoping that the oil pressure of No.4 engine didn't drop any lower and possibly force your ship to be a straggler for enemy aircraft to prey on—all that kept the adrenaline surging. Those 'Little Friends' looked so good, shuttling back and forth like protective Border Collies shepherding their flock. The flak over Berlin was intense and accurate of predictor-control fire and barrage fire type. Many of the group's aircraft received flak damage. [Returning from Berlin] fighter support was excellent, and no enemy aircraft were sighted. Squadron Operations now passed along the news that each crewman must now fly 30 missions, not 25, before his tour of combat was over. Instead of four I now had nine missions to go. It was disturbing news. I didn't think I had enough luck to take me through nine. Operations called me in and said I'd only be required to fly a total of 28,

Below, left to right: 491st BG crews being debriefed by an Intelligence Officer on their return to Metfield after a combat mission in 1944; Liberators in the 493rd BG taxi out at Debach in Suffolk in 1944 ("Helton's Hellcats," as they were known, made their combat debut on D-Day, June 6, 1944); a Lib goes down over the Continent after taking a flak hit; a crashed Liberator in Normandy, just after D-Day.

based on the number of missions I'd already flown. Okay, fine, but that still meant three extra missions . . ."

Claude M. Basler, a radio operator-gunner on Lieutenant John S. Wise's crew in the 827th Squadron, 484th Bomb Group near Cerignola, Italy, recalls:

"We flew 19 combat missions. The first was in the last plane of the last formation over the target. This meant hundreds of planes had already gone by and they [the enemy antiaircraft gunners] were getting good target practice. Not good. In both the first and last mission, we lost exactly half of the planes sent up by our group. On the bomb run, which was at full throttle, it was like driving a Model T at the Indy 500. By the time we dropped our bombs, there was no American plane to be seen. All you could see were clouds of smoke, planes on [the] ground on fire . . . We had two engines knocked out; oil pouring and splashing back on the windows, partially blocking the view. A very lonely, desolate, desperate, defeated feeling as we flew over an enemy airstrip. I felt like a sitting duck. At one point ditching in the Adriatic became a possibility. After many calculations, and crossing our fingers, we decided to get back to our landing field, and we did."

Paul W. Pifer, radio operator on *Battle Dragon* in the 446th Bomb Group, was shot down on New Year's Day, 1945—less than a month after his 19th birthday:

"We were assigned two extra crewmembers who were flying their 34th 'makeup' mission in order to fly number 35—the last—with their

PRINT THE COMPLETE ADDRESS IN PLAIN BLOCK LETTERS IN THE PANEL BELOW, AND YOUR RETURN ADDRESS IN THE SPACE PROVIDED. USE TYPEWRITER, DARK INK OR PENCIL. WRITE PLAINLY. VERY SMALL WRITING IS NOT SUITABLE.

Right: *V-Mail cartoon by Technical Sergeant Harry L. Tower in the 409th Bomb Squadron, 93rd BG, sent to his wife, Loris, to show the pre-mission routine. The censor's stamp is empty.*

regular crew. One [crewmember] requested my regular position as radio operator; so I went to the waist as observer. The IP was Trier, Germany, a small medieval town just east of Luxembourg. For some reason the formation circled tiny Trier for a second directional bearing to our target. One of the three flak guns found our range on that second pass. No one was seriously concerned with three antiaircraft guns until our ship shuddered from a sickening thud as No.3 engine was shot off its mounting. We could observe fuel being whisked back over the starboard wing—very frightening because of the great fire hazard. The pilot headed southwest and shortly thereafter our load was jettisoned over a forested area. With parachutes strapped on we awaited the inevitable bailout signal, which came when the

fuel gauges revealed minimal gasoline remaining. At 22,000 feet [6,705m] we jumped. When the others had gone out the floor hatch, I called my pilot on the intercom to notify him that the waist was clear and that I was jumping [too]. He acknowledged by saying, 'Good luck, I'll see you down below, kid.' Four of us experienced 'failed parachute openings' upon pulling the ripcord. It was presumed the 'chutes froze at altitude. The navigator sustained crushing fractures of his right heel upon landing. I had an incomplete fracture of the right pubic bone. He and I were conveyed to hospital and he was returned to the US for further treatment. [Once recovered] I rejoined my crew. February 25, 1945 we bombed Aschaffenburg from the *Dragon Lady* . . . we were hit by flak and had to feather No.2 engine. There were no casualties but we were becoming leery of B-24s associated with the name 'Dragon.'"

The Bombardier

"Down a lonely road on a cold black night
A miserable beggar trudges into sight
And the people whisper over their beers
There goes the last of the bombardiers.
What is a bombardier?—No reply
But men grow silent and women sigh
As a death-like silence fills the place
With a gaunt grey ghost of a long-lost race."

—The Last of the Bombardiers (Anon.)

The bombardier bore a heavy responsibility. Before a mission began, ordnancemen would have toiled around the clock loading the bombs, screwing in the nose or tail fuzes and "safetying" them with a pin and wire to prevent the arming vane spinning, and arming the bomb while the aircraft was still on the ground. A bomb bay was a cramped, poorly lit, and dangerous place, especially in darkness or in flight. Injuries were not uncommon—so quite often fuzes were fitted before loading. Early in the flight the safety pins would be removed. Then it was all down to the bombardier at his station directly behind the large Plexiglas nose, his bombsight mounted in front of him. Either side of his seat, levers and panels of dials and switches fed data to and from the sight. When the US entered the war, the standard precision bombsights were the Norden Model M series and the Sperry S-Series, but in very high altitudes, enemy activity, cloud cover, and atmospheric conditions, especially wind strength and direction, and drift and bomb ballistics, affected dropping time, trajectory, and accuracy. In time visual bombing was

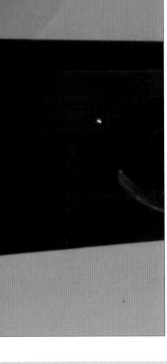

Left: *Outwardly, the B-24J was similar to the B-24H. Internally, the H had a C-1 autopilot and Sperry bombsight, while the Norden M-series bombsight with C-1 autopilot was used on the B-24J.*

reduced by the use of equipment that enabled bombing through overcast. By 1945 USAAF bombing accuracy in daylight in Europe had risen to 44 per cent of all bombs falling within 1,000ft (305m) of the target.

In the US, bombardier training originally had been based on the lead aircraft of each element or small section sighting for range and deflection, while all the other planes sighted for range only, but in the ETO this could result in collision. By late 1942 bombing was therefore being carried out on the squadron formation leader's aim, and element leaders set their sights for range only so that from the IP squadrons maneuvered to approach the target in train. Large defensive formations dropped on a group box leader's aim so that squadrons would not have to separate at the IP. (Squadron formation leaders sighted for range only.) In theory, this concentrated a pattern from a single formation, but in practice the fractional time delay between the release of the lead plane's bombs and those of the rest of the formation could result in some or all missing the MPI (Mean Point of Impact, or the planned center of destruction). To achieve a good pattern around the MPI, the Aiming Point for the lead plane was thus set short of the MPI, to allow for the delay in releases by the other aircraft.

Nearing the target, the bombardier's desired changes in course made by manipulation of the bombsight were conveyed to the Pilot's Directional Indicator (PDI) on the cockpit instrument panel for the pilot to follow, or to the automatic pilot (A-5 or C-1 models), which was known as Automatic Flying Control Equipment (AFCE). AFCE allowed the bombardier to take over flying the aircraft from the pilot, giving him lateral control through the bombsight's connection to the autopilot. Once the bombardier had picked up the actual aiming point he would ask the pilot to confirm that the automatic pilot was engaged, as he needed to integrate the AFCE and bombsight to control the heading, turns, and drift while the pilot maintained a constant altitude and airspeed. Any deviation at this time could upset the mechanism and affect accuracy of the drop. The bomb run began at the IP. Once the cross hairs of the bombsight had been set, the bombardier would remain hunched over the aiming device making final adjustments for corrections until "bombs away." During those next few minutes the bomber was like a "sitting duck" in a shooting gallery.

Bombardier school was a 20-week course. There was no shortage of candidates and those who washed out of pilot training swelled the numbers. During 1941–45 no fewer than 45,000 bombardiers graduated from AAF schools. Every bomber crewmember had to be an expert gunner, so their training included six weeks at a flexible gunnery school where they were taught everything about the weapons they would use, as well as ballistics, turret operation and maintenance, and gun repairs. They also shot at air and ground targets from a moving base and from a turret. At the end of the course, bombardier trainees were awarded silver wings, appointed flight officers or commissioned as 2nd lieutenants, and sent on to unit training.

Robert Tays recalls, "The word was out to both friend and foe alike that with the Norden bombsight we could drop bombs with such a high degree of accuracy that we could put them down a smokestack. Accuracy we had, but the concept of saturation bombing did prevail using the group formation as the basic flying unit. This provided for a rather large margin of error and still was effective. Most bombs would fall within a radius of 1,000ft [305m] of the target making a destructive pattern great enough to cause an acceptable reduction in industrial capability. Men and machines are not infallible when working in this medium [. . .] The many variables and uncontrollable unknowns will come into play and cause targets to be missed, targets not to be found for whatever reason, or the ever-present pilot or crew error. This caused some of our critics to refer to us as the '8th Agricultural Air Force.' Yes, Switzerland was bombed twice by mistake. Cruel weather conditions with limited technical devices could mislead the best navigator or bombardier."

Page right, clockwise from top left: The bombardier's position, below the nose gun turret; close-up of the position, with the Norden bombsight at front; the bombardier's Electric Selector Panel with four sets of indicator lights (with a column for each vertical rack, and an indicator light for each bomb station. Unit 4 below the panel is the Intervalometer, used to release bombs singly or in groups); the Norden M series bombsight. The Mk.9 was introduced late in 1943 and by the end of that year, about 2,000 Norden bombsights were being produced each month.

Bombs Away

This publicity photo shows the intensity of instruction during the bombardier course; the *Bombs Away* commemorative book is for graduates of the Carlsbad, New Mexico, training facility (45–5B).

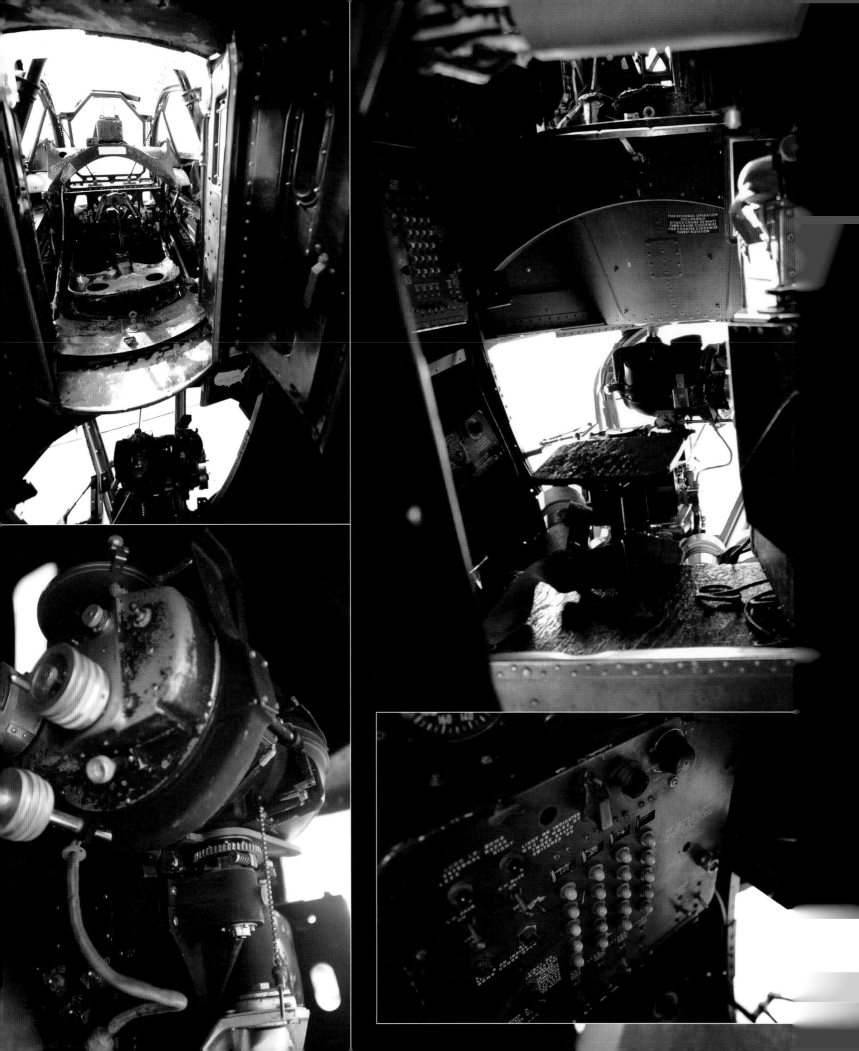

Tales of Vienna Woods

Bombardier Charles Freudenthal, of the 489th Bomb Group, described what it was like to fly on a combat mission:

"The bombardier's station in a B-24—the models with a nose turret—was pretty tight. With flak suits, parachutes, steel helmets, and other equipment and the navigator [as well], you could get tangled up nearly every time you moved. It was far from the ideal workplace for setting up a run on a target. The nose turret made it

necessary for the bombardier to crouch way down to operate the Norden sight. He normally knelt on his right knee. Since all the knobs of the Norden sight were on the right side, he would reach across with the left hand to operate the 'Turn and Drift' knob (deflection). The right hand operated the 'Mirror drive clutch' (rate knob), which determined whether you were over, short, or on target. In this position the view down and directly ahead through the Plexiglas was sufficient for the task, once the plane was lined up for the target, but there were nowhere near enough windows to allow for scanning. Finding the target was always the problem and even when visibility was good both bombardier and navigator had to work hard pinpointing to ensure a successful approach. As I usually flew lead, the problem of watching for the release of bombs by other planes in the formation didn't often arise. For bombardiers who were toggling (releasing their bombs on sight of the lead's drop) the fact that the nose turret obscured vision above the horizontal plane was a headache. Toggling bombardiers would ride the nose turret when not at their sight. Usually a lead crew would have a 'pilotage' navigator in the nose turret. Concentrating on setting up the run you'd forget the man in the turret and if he fired a burst, being just above your head, it really made you jump. The seal round the front turret never seemed to be effective and an icy draught was nearly always present,

although this troubled the navigator most. Actually, the biggest discomfort I personally found was that in the first electrically heated flying suits we had—the one-piece 'Long John' types—it could get very warm behind one's knees when kneeling or sitting, since the wiring seemed to bunch up."

For William E. Carigan, who was with the 15th AF's 454th Bomb Group in Italy, unforeseen "gremlins" combined with the usual operational "difficulties"—such as hung-up bombs—to make accurate bombing even more of a challenge:

"In those critical days of the war, the ten-ship box satisfied the demand for squadron integrity, since one squadron could put up ten airplanes. One group could put up three or four boxes, and thus satisfy the absolute requirement for group integrity. The whole combat formation could form in trail, staggering assigned altitudes by group, going up and down by 1,000ft [305m] increments for a total variation of say 3,000 or 4,000ft [914 or 1,219m], enough to keep the German antiaircraft fire directors at some uncertainty about our altitude. They couldn't just find us and keep pouring it to us at that altitude. The whole group usually bombed on the lead ship's cue, thus using the best bombardier to give us our best chance at the highest effectiveness. The lead and deputy-lead bombardiers aimed at the target; all other crews dropped on the first bombs out of either of those two planes. The bombardiers in following planes had set their intervalometers as prescribed for the mission, then pushed the toggle switch when they saw the first

Above: *Bomb shackles in the bomb bay of a B-24J Liberator. Often these would freeze in flight; or, if they didn't freeze, the bombs sometimes failed to release and had to be kicked out of the bomb bay by the bombardier or armorer.*

bombs come out. To save bombardiers the danger of going on the mission at all, we led a toggle switch to the pilot's wheel and let the pilot toggle the bombs out when he saw the bombs from the lead ships start falling. The armorer knew how to use the screwdriver in case the bombs hung up.

"The whole 15th Air Force formation took two hours or more to fly over a target when all wings and all groups flew over in trail. People in the churches of Budapest had to strain for an unbearable period of time to hear the service. Antiaircraft gunners could do a lot of bracketing to find exactly where we were in the sky. To cure our objections about accurate flak, some 15th Air Force operations type ordered that we drive group formations across the target from all points of the compass at once. The drawbacks with this procedure became apparent as we crossed Vienna one fine Sunday morning from all directions. Quite dismaying to the combat crews was the sight of all these formations flying at each other from right, left, and front. More dismaying: the bombs falling from higher groups through the formations assigned to lower altitudes.

"In the early spring of 1944 we were using the standard of six seven-ship boxes for the group effort, setting the formation in two waves of three seven-ship boxes. In this two-wave, 42-ship formation, all bombs

were dropped on the lead or deputy lead. The prescribers of this toggling-on-the-leader method recognized the delay in getting the whole group's stick of bombs out; thus the group leader aimed slightly short to make the main groups of bombs fall on the center of the target. We still had bombs from following planes going out quite late, so the pattern stretched to the local village, or church, or hospital. Compound all this with heavy flak and terrified crews to make a very long pattern. Furthermore, bombs sometimes hung on the bomb shackles; the bombardier or armorer went back to the bomb bay and kicked out these bombs with a screwdriver. Any spot of grease at 40 below zero congealed to the consistency of firewood, all too frequently causing the bomb to stick. Gremlins abounded in the super-frigid sky, causing strange electrical-current shorts that defied reasoning. Anyway, bombs fell long on nearly every target, so there were some wild tales in the Vienna woods. May you always be absolutely elsewhere when the Americans bomb."

Above: *Armorers in the 785th Bomb Squadron in the 466th BG at Attlebridge, England, in 1944. They are loading blue-painted 100lb (45kg) M38A2 practice bombs filled with some 80lbs of dry sand, for a practice bombing flight over the Wash.*

Bomb-Run Stresses

In England as in Italy, bombardiers (just like other crewmembers) had their own ways of dealing with the stress of combat missions—as John McClane recalls:

"As soon as we took off, our bombardier John Warga would curl up in the passageway between the forward compartment and the tunnel to the rear. When necessary, Warga manned the gun turret; otherwise he dozed at my feet. As we would gain altitude, the atmospheric pressure decreased until at 10,000ft [3,048m] we were required to put on our oxygen masks. Needless to say, we were glad to breathe pure oxygen again. How could Warga be so relaxed as we approached the target area? When we were close to beginning our bomb run, usually about 15 to 30 miles [24 to 48km] before bombs away, I would kick him with my

Above: *Bombs dropped by the 492nd BG in the 8th Air Force Second Bomb Division explode on a rail junction at Angers, France, in a raid on August 6, 1944. Five aircraft and engine factories and seven oil refineries were also hit; 25 aircraft were lost.*

left foot and say, 'Warga, wake up—we are coming to the IP [Initial Point].' At this he would become alive. He had to be one of the best bombardiers in the Air Force. He almost never missed. The flak would be exploding all around us and I'd be a nervous wreck, but not Warga. He was completely calm. He stayed alert just long enough to see the bombs hit the target and [would then] promptly relax on the floor again. Planes could be burning and exploding all around us but who cared? Not Warga. The truth is that he was ideally suited for his job, [but] certainly not [for being a] navigator or pilot.

"Why our bombs were set to explode as soon as they left our bomb racks [on one mission], I do not know. All other times the bombs had a small propeller on the nose that would unscrew as it fell through the air, thereby arming the bomb on its way down. The sight of bombs leaving the nearby planes always fascinated me. We reached the drop point and the bombardiers released the bombs. As they fell, it would appear as if the bombs were stacked one above the other suspended in space in a long stream, especially when they were stacked 52 high. I was looking directly at *Northern Lass* when flak set off the bottom bomb. It exploded and set off the one above it which in turn set off the next higher and so on until the last exploded in or very close to the bomb bay. The plane fell out of formation and began to go down with the men bailing out.

"Usually the Germans jammed my Gee Box with spurious radio signals as soon as we crossed the enemy coast. This resulted in a multitude of blips on my screen to the point where I could not tell the true course from all this 'grass' (so called because the phosphor on our cathode ray tube emitted a bright green color). For some inexplicable reason [on one mission], the Germans were not jamming our signals and my Gee Box was working perfectly. Warga had no idea where to drop the bombs. I asked him to calculate how far in advance of the bomb drop that would be required in order to hit the target from our 23,000ft [7,000m] altitude. He made this calculation, which I plotted on my map. I then set the Gee Box controls to these coordinates. I watched the blips come closer and closer. When they got exactly one over the other I said,

Right: *A yellow regulator and cylinder assembly-diluter demand oxygen assembly, also known as a "Breathing Oxygen Low Pressure Oxygen Cylinder."*

'Bombs Away,' at which time he released our load of explosives. Only 'Heaven Above' knows where those bombs went. Once, when Peritti [the pilot] ordered Warga to release our bombs to lighten our ship so we could keep up with the others, he picked out a German farmhouse in the middle of nowhere. The bombs started walking across the barnyard, through the barn and into the house, coming out the other side of the yard. No one on the ground could have survived this completely unexpected disaster. When questioned at interrogation why he picked this target, his reply was, 'What's the difference in destroying a farmhouse or a city house?' I never have had a bad conscience about it, as the Nazis had no qualms about sending V-2 rockets into England that plummeted out of the sky at 3,000mph [4,828kmh], exploding with no warning whatsoever. This was war and we were just young boys playing the game."

On May 28, 1944 Lieutenant William Bailey's crew in the 448th Bomb Group at Seething were flying their first mission, to Zeitz, Germany. Ben C. Isgrig, the bombardier, vividly recalls it:
"Our particular target was the ammonia section of [a manufacturing] plant. We were carrying 48 100lb [45kg] GP bombs and were in the first section over the target. I guess we were all pretty scared and nervous. I

Above: The foot-wide catwalk in the bomb bay of a B-24J—precarious, to say the least, for aircrew with no parachute at 20,000 plus feet.
Right: A green H-2 emergency low-pressure, continuous-flow, walk-around oxygen cylinder assembly. The wooden ball allowed mittened aircrew to turn it on.

watched the lead plane's bombs begin to drop and started to toggle ours out but, instead of falling clear, seven bombs in the right rear rack hung up. I went back into the bomb bay and was scared to see that the propellers on the fuzes of three of the bombs were turning rapidly, which meant they were probably fuzed and liable to go off at the slightest jolt. I got Kovalcheck, a gunner, to help me and was able to get them out by lifting them up one at a time and dropping them out. It was a wonder that one or both of us didn't fall out of the bomb bay. It's no joke to stand on a foot-wide catwalk with no parachute at 22,000ft [6,705m] in a 200 below zero breeze and no support and throw out bombs one at a time. Kovalcheck was using our one walk-around oxygen bottle; I had none. As we turned to leave the bomb bay I stumbled and nearly fell from the plane, but Kovalcheck caught me and pulled me through the door and to the nearest oxygen outlet. The trip home was uneventful."

The Unlucky Group

Lieutenant Lyle E. Day, bombardier on *Superwolf* in the 859th Squadron, 492nd Bomb Group, piloted by Lieutenant Elmer J. Smiley, recalls the mission to an aircraft assembly plant at Bernberg on July 7, 1944:

"About 05:30 we took off on our 19th mission. In our bomb bay were six 1,000lb [453kg] demolition bombs. We formed over England and left the English coast about 07:30. As we crossed the enemy-held coast of Holland, we were met by light but accurate flak. Several previous trips over the same area had shown this area to be flak-free; however, mobile flak batteries had been moved in. Several ships were hit and forced to turn back; we were untouched. On the way to the target, we were fired on several times by flak. We reached the IP and started our bomb run; we were in extremely intense and accurate flak along the bomb run. The

I saw our nose gunner shoot a German down who was attacking us. Sergeant Young shot one down from his position in the waist. It was impossible for me to see what was happening in the tail. The last I heard from one of the gunners was 'fighters at 6 o'clock' then his guns fired a long burst. He called 'fighters' again and fired again. About two passes later I could hear 20mm shells bursting inside our plane. Then our ship went into an immediate spin. No effort was made to control the ship. Both pilots must have died a quick and merciful death. Centrifugal force caused by the spin held me in the fire. After a turn or two, the gas tanks exploded and blew me out of the bombing window. Then I 'chuted into Germany—and prison." [The 492nd Bomb Group lost 12 B-24s shot down that day.]

Left: B-24J Hairless Joe *in the 493rd BG in formation with P-51B Mustangs.* Hairless Joe *was the maker of "Kickapoo Joy Juice" in Al Capp's legendary* Li'l Abner *comic strip. The Lib was written off in a crash landing in late 1944.*

George M. Collar, a bombardier in the 702nd Bomb Squadron, 445th Bomb Group, recalls his first combat mission, on June 29, 1944:

"We went to the Junkers engine works at Kothen [in Germany] and they split us up. I was flying nose turret navigator in the deputy lead ship. As we made landfall over the Dutch Coast up came the flak and they all had yellow centers. Luckily, we

flak was both predicted and barrage. We received a few pieces of flak in the wings, but no one was hurt. A few seconds after I dropped the bombs, enemy fighters were reported, and then our gunners called 'fighters' from most every position. As I watched our bombs land squarely on the target, incendiary bullets caused a raging fire in my compartment. While I was fighting the fire, our gunners were all firing. Roughly 300 planes were attacking the bombers and our fighter escort.

got through this okay and didn't see any more until we got on the bomb run. We were on the bomb run for 12 minutes and the flak was really thick. I glanced off our wing and saw a burst under a B-24. I saw them feather an engine and then they dropped down and I lost sight of them. About that time, we were hit and a piece of flak tore a hole in the side of the nose compartment, and passed between me and the navigator and out the other side. After all this terror and excitement, we passed

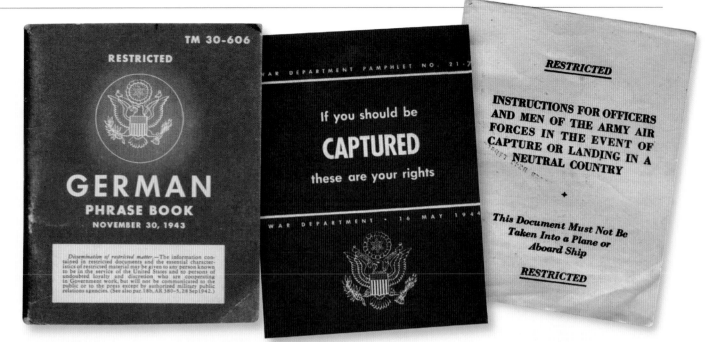

Right: Aircrews downed on combat missions over Europe often relied on Resistance groups to help them avoid capture and imprisonment. Apart from escape equipment and silk maps printed on both sides, they were issued with French and German phrase books and War Department pamphlets on their rights if captured, or in the event of landing in a neutral country.

over the target without dropping our bombs, due to the target being obscured by low clouds. We next flew to the secondary target and again didn't drop the bombs. We headed back west and found a target of opportunity where we dropped on the railyards and did a creditable job. We all got back safely.

"On July 24 we participated in the famous St. Lô [France] raid. This was the largest raid in history up to this time. Everything that the 8th and 9th Air Forces combined could put up, plus all the RAF bombers and fighter-bombers (3,000 planes in all) took part. We dropped 260lb [118kg] fragmentation bombs, which were about the same overall size as a 100lb [45kg] GP bomb, except that the walls were about an inch thick and were serrated. When they exploded, they scattered 1in [2.5cm] square chunks in all directions and were deadly anti-personnel weapons. We went in at 15,000ft [4,572m] and bombed the front lines along a 10-mile [16km] stretch of road that runs between St. Lô and Perrier. The artillery laid down pink smoke markers as a guide, but unfortunately the wind drifted the smoke and one group dropped short, killing 400 American troops including General McNair. I am happy to say it was not our group."

[Two months later Collar had finished his 28 missions and was supposed to leave on a three-day pass on September 27 but he had to take the place of another bombardier who failed to show. Collar, who was aboard one of the 25 Liberators lost on the Kassel mission, survived and was taken prisoner.]

Left: The Germans went to great lengths to shroud cities and other Allied targets in the Reich with smoke screens, as seen here at Erkner, a suburb of Berlin, photographed from 21,000 feet on March 8, 1944.

The Ploesti Missions

"Above us we could look into Stan's open bomb bay doors . . . we could see the bombs hanging ready, willing, and able. Tracers . . . red . . . white . . . were streaming up at the boys ahead . . . hitting them, too! Then our cockpit exploded with sparks, noise, and concussion . . . tracers spat out over my head. Luckily, George and I crouched down, making ourselves as small as possible. The tracers melted away into the smoke and fire of the refinery. Murphy cut loose in the top turret with the twin .50s . . . I wanted to shoot him . . . he was ruining our bomb run!"—Lieutenant John McCormick, pilot, *Vagabond King*, August 1, 1943, (KIA November 18, 1943).

Early in 1942, twenty-three B-24Ds commanded by Colonel Harry H. Halverson, codenamed HALPRO and en route to the 10th Air Force to bomb Tokyo from the Chinese mainland, were held at Fayid in Egypt to raid the oilfields at Ploesti in Romania on June 11. Thirteen Liberators proceeded individually to Ploesti and destroyed an oil depot and damaged the port of Constanta. It was the first time that American heavy bombers had bombed a European target.

Left and right: White IV, the Unirea-Orion and Astra Romana refineries, burning from bombs dropped by Colonel John "Killer" Kane's 98th BG formation. The 389th Bomb Group provided Kane's Pyramiders with eight complete crews and 16 individual replacements for the raid.

In May 1943 the 44th, 93rd and 389th Bomb Groups trained for Operation Tidal Wave, a daring low-level raid on the Ploesti oilfields. Early in June they joined the 98th and 376th—the two 9th Air Force B-24D groups—in the Libyan desert and on August 1, 1943 177 Liberators set out for Ploesti. Malfunctions and accidents en route reduced the effectiveness of the force and navigational errors caused severe problems in the target area, forcing some groups to bomb each other's assigned targets. Delayed-action bombs from preceding groups damaged or destroyed Liberators in the following groups; 167 actually attacked their targets and dropped 311 tons of bombs on the refineries. "Red I" was destroyed by bombs dropped by 26 B-24Ds of the 389th Bomb Group. Some 54 B-24Ds were lost over the targets and three more crashed into the sea. Seven B-24D crews were interned in Turkey; 19 landed in Cyprus, Sicily, or Malta. Of the 92 that returned to North Africa, 55 had suffered battle damage. Five Medals of Honor were awarded for actions on the Ploesti mission, three of them posthumously. All five groups received Presidential Unit Citations.

Lieutenant Dahl, a pilot in the 93rd Bomb Group, recalled: "Arrived over the target at approximately 14:55 hours and due to faulty navigation

Below, left to right: Colonel Jack Wood, CO, 389th BG and staff gather in North Africa to plan the "Sky Scorpions'" part in the low-level mission to Steaua, Romania; Captain Kenneth M. "Fearless" Caldwell (center) discusses plans for the Ploesti raid; arming a B-24D Lib; B-24D Bomerang in the 93rd BG, flown on the raid; Ploesti veteran B-24D Joisey Bounce in the 93rd BG; inspecting a Ploesti-damaged B-24D.

Above: *Col. Leon W. Johnson, CO, 44th BG, one of five men awarded the Medal of Honor for actions at Ploesti. He became commander of the 14th Combat Wing at Shipdham.*

Above: *Lieutenant Lloyd D. Hughes, pilot of* Eager Eagle *in the 389th BG formation. He was awarded the Medal of Honor posthumously for pressing home his attack after his Lib was set on fire.*

on lead group's part we were led into our oil refinery target right over flak corner. They threw so much flak the sky was black with it. We were flying at about 50ft [15m] all in tight formation going 220mph [354kmh]. Saw Colonel Baker and Lieutenant Porter with whom I was first going to ride, both go down in flames and explode in front of us. Every haystack was a machine-gun nest. We got our bombs into a cracking plant. An exploding tank missed us by seconds. It got the plane right behind us. Bombs were 30-minute fuzed. Somehow we managed to get out, going like hell. In all I saw seven planes go down in flames and explode. On [the] way home two more collided and spun in. Saw no fighters on return flight. However, fuel was a big problem. Sweated it all the way home. Touched down at 21:00 hours, exactly 13½ hours after takeoff. Only 12 planes of 32 dispatched returned to home base. Some may be safe elsewhere. God was with me on this one. Amen."

Though 42 per cent of Ploesti's refining capacity and 40 per cent of its cracking capacity were claimed destroyed, most of the refineries were soon repaired and, within a month, were operating at pre-mission capacity again.

Throughout 1944 the 15th Air Force flew high-level bombing missions to the refineries at Ploesti. During the oil campaign, on July 9, Lieutenant Donald Puckett, a pilot in the 98th Bomb Group "Pyramiders" was posthumously awarded the Medal of Honor; the last of seven awarded to crewmembers during raids on Ploesti.

Squat "n" Droppit

On June 12, 1944 Lieutenant William Bailey's crew in the 448th flew their ninth mission from Seething, to Rennes, France—but their B-24 developed electrical trouble and they were given a replacement ship called *Squat "n" Droppit*. Bailey took off late and tagged on to the 446th Bomb Group. Ben C. Isgrig continues:

"At the IP the mission turned into a disaster. No fewer than four bomb runs were attempted and on the fourth *Squat 'n' Droppit* was hit by flak. Enemy fighters attacked the lone aircraft and [I] heard Ken Zierdt, the radio operator, repeat over and over in a steady voice: 'Fire in the bomb bay, Fire in the bomb bay!' In a few more seconds someone said: 'Get the hell out of here.'"

[Vic Fleishman, navigator, and Leslie Fischer, engineer, bailed out and Isgrig quickly followed. Meanwhile, George Cooksey, the pilot, and Zierdt, the radio operator, had opened the bomb bay doors and also bailed out. Zierdt was hit by machine-gun fire from a Bf 109 and died later on the ground. Isgrig continues:] "A Mustang circled lazily above me while another followed the German down. The Bf 109 cut to the left, passing within 50yds [45m] of me and began to climb. The P-51 was right on his tail. I screamed and cursed the German, waving and offering all my moral support to the American as he passed. The German didn't have a chance. Within ten seconds his ship began to fall apart and burn. The German bailed out and he landed 300yds [274m] from me. After shooting down the Bf 109, the P-51 climbed toward Fischer, circled him and waggled his wings before roaring away." [Long after the war Isgrig and Fischer discovered that their savior had been Major George Preddy of the 352nd Fighter Group. Preddy, who was killed on Christmas Day 1944, finished the war as the number two US air ace in Europe. Bailey's crew, meanwhile, were rescued by the French Resistance and were returned safely to England after D-Day.]

Right: B-24H Squat "n" Droppit in the 448th BG. The crew thought the name a bad omen; and they were right.

Top right: A 389th "Sky Scorpions" Lib explodes after taking a direct hit over the target.

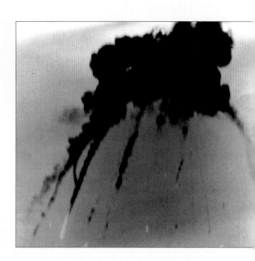

On November 26, 1944 the synthetic oil refineries at Misburg in Germany were the target for the B-24s. But, as Lieutenant Don F. Ferguson, navigator in Lieutenant James K. Wenzel's crew in the 491st Bomb Group recalls, the day went from bad to worse, ending with the loss of 16 Libs:

"[It was] a beautiful, clear flying day and the stage was set for a great sky battle. Our crew was flying deputy lead and [with] the usual nine men aboard. We'd flown a mission just the day before to Bingen, west of Frankfurt on the Rhine. Misburg would be our 15th mission and the crew had become rather 'flak happy' at this stage of combat . . . Once we came to the IP and made the turn for the target, the battle was on. Dense, heavy, black flak was seen straight ahead and the intercom was full of comments from the entire crew. I was taking notes like mad and trying to log anything of importance.

"This was the beginning of the bomb run. Each squadron, with their radio-controlled bombsights, was assigned a frequency whereby the lead bombardier's 'flick of the switch' automatically released all the bombs in

every plane in the squadron to blanket the target. Through some fault of the lead bombardier, or malfunction, a premature release of all the 854th Squadron's bombs occurred 15 miles [24km] before the target was reached. Our bombardier was horrified at such a result and disgustingly announced the 'bombs away' message. One plane over the right side and slightly behind us did not have its bomb bay doors open in time and the bombs fell through the doors leaving them flapping in the breeze and causing the plane to fall behind.

"Our squadron began taking a beating from the FW 190s, with some starting to shoot down our stragglers. Our gunners were firing by this time at the enemy fighters that were seemingly coming from out of the southeast and low—four and five o'clock low—as the intercom chatter stated. Things seemed in a bedlam with planes all over, in and out of formation, taking evasive action.

Combat Bombing Flight Record 1 by 2nd Lt Joseph Feingold, 93rd BG (left); review photo of the Erkner ball-bearing plant, January 16, 1944 (below).

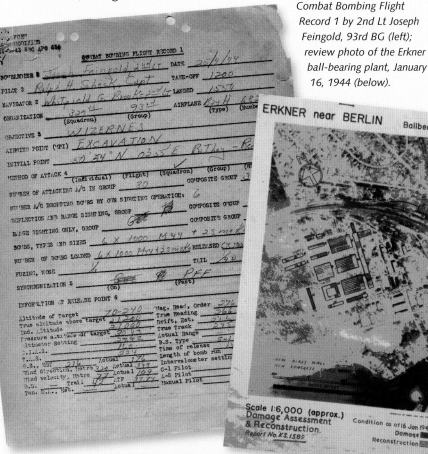

"Our aircraft had only four small hits, all about the size of a 50-cent piece. We were just plain lucky or divinely favored and were thankful for that. When the attacks subsided, no less than 16 Liberators had been blasted out of the sky—in the space of just 15 minutes."

Death on the Bomb Run

Above: *The wing of B-24J 42-110187* Belle of the East *in the 467th BG breaks off after taking a direct hit in the fuel tanks over the Ju 88 plant and airfield at Oschersleben, Germany, on June 29, 1944.*

On Thursday June 29, 1944, Lieutenant William H. Counts and his crew at Rackheath were supposedly "standing down" but at the last minute were called to fly the mission to the Ju 88 plant and airfield at Oschersleben, Germany:
Over the Channel, Counts left his seat to take a leak; on his return to the flight deck he reconnected his equipment but forgot to fasten his safety belt and shoulder straps—a lapse that would save his life when blown out of the aircraft. Eight crew were killed. (Staff Sergeant Thomas J. Hansbury, tail gunner, had the night before been on guard duty; Counts had decided he would be in no fit shape for a mission so told him to stand down, but that he would credit him with the mission. Sergeant Robert Fisher, engineer, flew the tail turret position on the Oschersleben raid and the ball turret, unmanned, was retracted into the aircraft.) A German major who interrogated Counts after his capture drew a picture of the fuselage of his Liberator, showing the location of six bodies that the Germans had recovered. Counts was told where the other two bodies had been found. One man had not opened his 'chute; the other had been thrown out 'chute-less. Counts was incarcerated in *Stalag Luft III*.

The Engineer/ Top Turret Gunner

"The aerial engineer—the flight engineer—with his wide knowledge of the airplane ranks highest of the enlisted crew. The crew will not be successful without him. I believe I need him most because he is nearly always the most experienced man on the crew, and when he has this experience and knowledge I always develop affection and respect for him. Flying the B-24 becomes miserable work if you have a weak engineer."—William Everett Carigan Jr.

The top turret gunner was usually also the flight engineer; as such, he had received additional training in maintenance and related tasks. Many engineers had been to flight school, which they had failed, for one reason or another, to complete. The engineer was also qualified for copilot duties—but although he knew what to do if required to assist the pilot, he was not qualified to fly the B-24, though in combat emergencies the engineer was known to take over the flying. His added duties included parachute noncom, First Aid specialist, and assistant radio operator, and he was also the leader of the crew's six enlisted men. In the B-24A and early Liberators, the flight engineer occupied the right side of the aircraft. Flight engineers had their work cut out. Prior to takeoff the flight engineer would carry out an external and internal inspection. The hatch in the top of the fuselage behind the pilots' seats provided access to the top of the fuselage and wing and, when taxiing, the engineer was supposed to stand with

Left: *The first B-24s were armed with a Martin A-3 dorsal turret. With the arrival of the computing gun sight, this was redesigned as the A-3A "High Hat" with a replacement center Plexiglas window.*

his upper body half out of the hatch to make sure that the wings cleared other airplanes or any other obstruction. After landing it was usually mildly exhilarating to stand in the hatch out in the breeze. On the mission the engineer stood for most operations, aft of the pilot's pedestal.

Ted Parker, a top turret gunner in the 858th Bomb Squadron, 491st Bomb Group, remembers that . . . "When out of the turret [the engineer] sat on a jump seat on the right side of the flight deck and monitored the fuel gauges and operated the transfer system. He also checked on the engines and generators during the early stage of a mission. It was usual to climb up into the Martin turret once over the sea and fire a test burst. The gunner's head was low in the turret so you didn't have much of a view below the horizontal, and parts of the turret mechanism blocked your view at that level on both sides. Apart from that there was excellent visibility as the Plexiglas was frameless. I found the seat and footrest gave a fairly easy position, and from the point of view of gunner comfort it was the best defense position to fly on a B-24. The sun on the curves of Plexiglas made glare that could be a nuisance, even with tinted glasses. Constantly swinging the turret around with the sun beating down could make you drowsy after a few hours, and it became difficult to stay keyed up for a possible fighter attack. With the guns so close to your head the noise and kick when they were fired was terrific. Smoke tended to stay in the top of the turret and could be troublesome. It was important that the bomb bay hatch was closed when firing to prevent spent links and cases falling down and jamming the bomb bay doors. The Martin turret generally had no problems, was easy to operate, and [was] a pretty effective defense point."

Bill McCullah, a gunner on the crew of Lieutenant Paul Helander in the 448th Bomb Group, observed Staff Sergeant Gerald "Jerry" Carroll (the first engineer and top turret gunner) in action on several missions, and had reason to appreciate the additional training he had received: "On takeoff he stood in the doorway—his normal takeoff position—behind and between the two pilots. Carroll's was the third set of eyes scanning the multiple clusters of instruments on the front instrument panel. As an emergency measure in the US we all were given wheel and rudder training to acquire some 'stick-time.' This certainly paid off once, when we were hit by fighters and flak [and] the pilot was badly injured. Carroll, sitting in the top turret, took a hit in the oxygen bottles beneath his turret seat. The four oxygen bottles exploded, slamming his head into the top turret dome, cracking the Plexiglas. Carroll, [although] momentarily dazed, was not seriously injured, and he had to perform copilot duties from the left seat after the copilot took command of the plane.

"On takeoff one day something was dreadfully wrong. The pilots were standing on the rudder pedals, backs arched and straining, trying to horse the B-24 to a higher altitude. We were 50 feet [15.2m] off the deck—about to go into the ground! 'Jerry, give us a hand,' Helander quietly said to Carroll. Carroll calmly grasped both control wheels, pulling rearward, but the B-24 would not budge. Helander, seemingly resigned, said to Carroll, 'Jerry, stand by to cut the master shut-off valve.' Carroll stopped pulling, calmly placing his right hand on the red knurled knob above the cockpit entry door. Calm as a rock, he watched and waited for the command to spin the knob to

the 'OFF' position that would cut fuel to all four engines. If Carroll closed the master shut-off valve we were dead! If we went in at all, our ass was grass and the B-24 was the lawnmower! The lock that held the B-24 let go, and we climbed hard. The 'G' force of the climb slammed me to my knees, holding me to the floor of the plane . . . Only then did I hear the source of trouble. Our No.2 engine, revved to its limits, had run away. The danger was that the prop would shear its shaft, flinging the propeller through the side of the plane. A runaway engine on takeoff, fully loaded with fuel and bombs, was a bad scene—far worse than an engine with a feathered propeller. Helander banked the B-24 into its two good engines and landed downwind."

All American

Early B-24s had four neatly cowled Pratt and Whitney R-1830-33 mechanically supercharged Twin Wasps. In 1941 turbo-supercharged Twin Wasps replaced the 33s; the oil coolers were relocated to each side of the radial engines instead of below, giving the elliptical cowling characteristic of all later models. When not in his turret, the gunner would monitor fuel gauges and operate the transfer system

Quit-yer-Bitchin'

Bud Markel, engineer on Ben Guisband's crew in the 827th Bomb Squadron, 484th Bomb Group at Torretta, Italy, talks about "the deal" that flight engineers struck with their Liberators to coax the best from them:

"Every throttle jock and gunner knows that sooner or later you learn to accept and then eventually to love the equipment assigned to you—it's not romance, but survival that triggers the match. The B-24 was a cantankerous, lumbering, draughty, unforgiving son-of-a-bitch, heavy in the controls, over-grossed and difficult to fly in formation, with an ancient boiler-gauge-style fuel quantity system that was almost useless. The heaters never worked when you needed them, and were removed by many combat groups as being too dangerous to operate because of the fuel lines on the flight deck necessary to feed them. Nose steering, such as power steering in an automobile, was nonexistent and throttles and brakes maintained headway. The famously weak nose gear had a mind of its own, often collapsing of its own volition, so the flight engineer would have to sit astride the mechanism, waiting with a heavy foot to kick the stubborn thing down to lock. Familiarity breeds self-confidence, at least in this case and you soon learned not to take off with the cowl flaps open as this caused too much drag. You learned to keep the generators

Above: This view of a 389th BG B-24D—from the the ship above—shows the potential dangers of flying in formation over an enemy target when bomb bay doors were opened at the IP just before "Bombs Away."

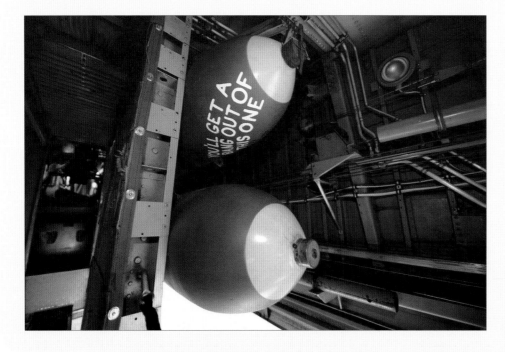

parallel and to plot cruise control charts to calculate fuel consumption, or how to transfer fuel without starving the engines or pumping it overboard. Many would call this becoming professional, but we called it accommodation, a deal struck with the airplane, like a standoff between two boxers who respect each other's strengths. With this out of the way, the war could be attended to.

"The airplanes were cold, and systems grew sluggish and bomb shackles would freeze, especially the lower ones nearest the draughty bomb bay doors. Some bombs would release and fall free from the arming wires causing the propeller to spin off, so that the slightest jar might cause the bomb to explode: so there you were, the bomb bay a confusion of wires, cables, and hydraulic lines being

Left: Eight 1,100lb [500kg] bombs—twice that of the B-17 Flying Fort—could be carried vertically in two sides of the bomb bay of the B-24 Liberator. The bomb bay was behind roller-shutter doors.

distorted and swollen by 500lb [227kg] of instant destruction. The catwalks were narrow, so that you couldn't move about with a parachute pack—one slip or a fraction of a second's lack of concentration and you 'bought the farm' [were killed]. On some ships the bombardier freed the bomb shackles with a skillful foot or the deft use of a screwdriver, thus letting the bombs fall from the airplane."

There were downsides to being located near the top turret gunner—although, as radio operator Technical Sergeant Donald V. Chase remembers, he was nevertheless always grateful when the turret was functioning correctly:

"Once [on one combat mission], off in the distance, about 2 o'clock level, I spotted a '24' that had had its top turret plastic bubble shot completely away. I kept thinking, 'Headless Horseman . . . Headless Horseman.' The crippled ship continued flying but slowly fell behind the Group's formation. When our top turret gunner, flight engineer Charlton Holtz, a Minnesota lad, got off several

Above: The Load Adjuster calculated with mathematical precision.

bursts [in combat], the empty casings clinked against one another as they fell onto the cabin deck. [Chase continues that the same thing happened when, en route to a target, all ten .50 caliber guns would be test fired.] When Holtz test fired, spent shells cascaded out of the turret onto the cabin floor next to my radio position. Occasionally a shell or two would bounce off his leg and land on me. The casings were hot. One landed on my neck and left a burn welt. However, I preferred ducking hot shells to flying in a ship with a malfunctioning turret. I crouched behind the armor plate that protected the copilot's back, only my helmet and eyes above the armor as I watched the action. Oh, how I wished I could shoot back . . .

"After 28 missions of varying intensity and the loss of many friends I was through with combat. And I wished that nobody, anywhere, ever had to go to war again."

Death at Dawn: The Crash of *Hookem Cow*

On April 14, 1945 two Liberators crashed near the base at Horsham St. Faith, Norfolk, shortly after takeoff. Sergeant Don C. Neville, top turret gunner in one of the planes—*Hookem Cow* in the 55th Bomb Squadron, piloted by Lieutenant David R. Totten—was one of the two survivors:

"We [had been] awakened around 3:30am . . . Our mission was to Bordeaux and the cargo was four 2,000lb [907kg] bombs . . . A few minutes after becoming airborne I noticed that the inboard engine on the left side was 'flaming' regularly and did not appear to be functioning properly. I called several times on the intercom 'waist to pilot,' but received no answer. The plane was having trouble gaining altitude. Our landing lights were still on and I could see the tops of the trees below. Suddenly there was a flash and an explosion and I was thrown against the interior of the plane and knocked unconscious. When I came to, I was laying on the ground on my back in a wooded area, surrounded by a large fire. The entire area had been drenched with aircraft fuel and the fire was quite intense. Oxygen containers were exploding periodically in the fire and I found myself unable to move. Various pieces of the plane were scattered around me, one part being the landing gear sticking up in the air with the wheel still turning. I heard something moving close by and discovered it was Lavonsky [Michael C. Lavonsky, the bombardier]. I called to him and he crawled over and lay down beside me on the ground. Shortly afterward, an English gentleman who lived nearby arrived and sat down on the ground next to me. He assured me he would stay until help arrived. He inquired as to how many bombs we had on board. He said he had seen two. None had exploded. He placed something under my head for comfort. His presence was heaven sent, for I just knew that my time was near. At the base hospital I learned that only Lavonsky and I had survived."

Top: These burned goggles are one of the few items to have survived from Hookem Cow, *pictured right.*

Hitting the Silk

On May 11, 1944, the 44th Bomb Group—the "Flying Eightballs"—were part of the bombing effort directed against the marshaling yards at Mulhouse, France, but the primary target was obscured by clouds, so several targets of opportunity were hit instead. The Liberator flown by 2nd Lieutenant James H. Walsh Jr., however, was singled out northeast of Châteaudun by Lieutenant Addi Glunz, CO 6./JG 26, who set the No.1 engine afire. The B-24 left the formation "in difficulty" but still under control, as Sergeant Joseph O. Peloquin, engineer, remembers:

"The time of day was very close to 14:20. It's always been a habit of mine to look at watches when things occur—and I do recall that very well. We were shot down by Me 109s. Our position in the formation was Purple Heart Corner [so called because it was the most vulnerable position]. It turned out to be just that! As an engineer, my position was the top turret, and that is where I was just before it

PULLING THE RIPCORD

LOOK AT RIPCORD

USE BOTH HANDS

LEGS STRAIGHT

FEET TOGETHER

was flak banging around us as well as fighters firing at us. One Me 109 hit us in the No.2 engine, setting it on fire. Another shell exploded in front of us and blasted my headgear off just as I was scrambling to get my chest 'chute. Sergeant Puksta helped me to snap it on and that's when I could see that he had been hit also. I opened the escape hatch and told him to jump. He looked at me and said, 'You go first!' The plane was going down and he didn't look too good, so I told him to be damned sure to follow me. Puksta bailed out, [was injured by shrapnel], was captured, and became a PoW.

Left: Page from an instruction manual showing the correct position to adopt before pulling the D-ring.
Below left: Attachable chest-type parachutes (QAC Group 1 and 2 Assemblies) could be put on quickly. Type A-4 had a single-point, quick-release harness.
Below right: Graph showing the rate of speed in free fall versus a parachute drop from 40,000ft.

all started. Things were rather quiet and as we had a fighter escort, Walsh suggested that I go back and transfer my fuel. It would seem to be a good time as we had used enough from our main tanks to transfer in from the outer cells. And the fuel would be out of the way in case we ran into trouble later and couldn't spare the time. So I went back to the waist section and told Sergeant Lawrence Richards to cover my position while I was doing my job of transferring the fuel. I could take his position if anything happened. Well, I had just had time to finish and was on my way back to the waist position when all hell broke loose. There

RESTRICTED
T. O. No. 00-25-13

RATE OF SPEED *in* FREE FALL *and* PARACHUTE DROP *from* 40,000 FT.

THE FASTER YOU FALL THROUGH *this* AREA, THE BETTER FOR YOU!!

INTENSE COLD *and too* LITTLE OXYGEN!

ALTITUDE IN THOUSAND

2min

3 MIN. 4 SEC
(free fall)

24 MIN. 32 SEC
(parachute)

RESTRICTED

Left: B-24H in the 763rd BS, 460th BG on fire on the mission to Vienna on June 16, 1944. One crewmember can be seen exiting the escape hatch behind the flight deck. Cuddles, in formation above the doomed B-24, was written off just a few days later, on June 23. **Below:** *Crew 41 with Joe Hollywood (foreground), after its return from a mission to Hamm, Germany, on October 2, 1944.*

"My experiences are ones that I still have nightmares about. When I jumped, I counted to about ten—enough to clear the plane. We were at about 15,000ft [4,572m] at that time and I pulled my ripcord—and nothing happened. No 'chute came out! So I was falling free at 120mph [193kmh] and I tugged and pulled at the flaps on my 'chute—and finally pulled out a little of the silk or nylon. As I kept pulling, the pilot chute came out and it, in turn, released the main 'chute. All of this took so long that when it finally blossomed out, I was about 300ft [91m] from the ground! This is one of the reasons why the Germans did not spot me coming down. When I landed, I injured my left heel and I, too, had been hit by the shrapnel from that exploding shell that had hit Puksta. I had one in my arm above the elbow and several small ones in my face and another one in my neck, which just missed my jugular vein.

"I met up with Richards a couple of weeks or so after we bailed out—on a bus, along with our Free French escorts, going to a farm camp in the Forest of Freteval, where the Germans had an ammunition dump and these men all hid out successfully, right under the Germans' noses. When the camp was started, there were only about eight or ten of us, but things changed rapidly and soon there were several hundred of us evadees."

The same month that Sergeant Joseph O. Peloquin was shot down—May 1944—Joe Hollywood, top turret gunner-engineer with Crew 41, 714th Squadron, 448th Bomb Group, arrived in the ETO from the US. He flew his first combat mission from Seething, Norfolk, on June 3, 1944, and his fourth on D-Day—June 6. In his diary Hollywood recorded seeing the invasion fleet, and remembers the horrific events of his fifth mission, four days later:

"Had a good idea something was going to pop. All passes pulled, shows closed, and everyone was ordered to stay around their barracks. The whole field was on alert. We were on guard at the planes. About midnight they loaded up and took off later. Maximum effort. We were called for the third mission of the day. Took off at 11:05 and landed at 5:00. The Invasion was well under way [as they approached the French coast]. There were hundreds and hundreds of ships in all sizes and shapes heading toward France. It was a wonderful sight. A few warships were shelling the coast. Couldn't see much of France as there

was an overcast. [On] the first run we could not see our target, Caen [and as] . . . our deadline to bomb was up at 1:05, we just didn't make it. Had to bring all our bombs back. No flak at all—no enemy aircraft.

"Fifth mission. June 10, 1944: Bombed airfield at Evreux, France . . . Got accurate flak about 15 minutes before target. Just before 'bombs away' [there was a] terrific explosion under the ship. Plane flying next to us got a direct hit as far as we know. Black smoke came from under the ship. One of his bombs might have gone off. It caught fire in the rear bomb bay and burned past the waist windows. Flew along for a short while and they broke up in half. I saw one 'chute, but there were more I couldn't see. The front section fell like an autumn leaf and the rear went right down. Too close for comfort. Got us all a little rattled for a while. Our ship was hit pretty bad. Concussion blew out the waist windows and shattered the bombardier's window. At least 25 holes in all parts of the ship: wings, bomb bay, rudder, and fuselage. Nothing was hurt but one small hydraulic line to the bomb bay doors; however they worked alright. No one was hurt but some close ones . . ."

Ditching in the Med

Ray A. Nichols, flight engineer in Lieutenant Henry Dionne's crew in the 825th Bomb Squadron, 484th Bomb Group in Italy, flew his first mission on August 13, 1944, when the Liberators attacked marshaling yards near the capital. Nichols recalls:

"The flak was very heavy. Intelligence estimated that 450 AA [antiaircraft] guns protected the target but we suspect there were a lot more as the flak was really thick. We came through this with flak holes scattered throughout the forward end of the plane. Spent flak bruised the bombardier and ripped through the copilot's flight suit near his calf. Our engines, flight controls, and flight surfaces were not damaged and everything was normal when we peeled off for Tortetta Field near Cerignola to line up for landing. While waiting for our turn to land we saw a plane touch down hard on the runway and one of its 500lb [227kg] bombs, fully armed, fell out of the bomb bay. It bounced and blew off the tail of the plane, causing it to roll end-over-end. When we landed we passed the control tower and a mass of rubble in front of it—no sign of a tail, and with broken off props, hydraulic fluid, and flight jackets strewn all about.

"We flew our second mission on August 24, to a railroad bridge at Ferrara in Italy. We lost No.1 engine a few minutes before reaching the IP. I was in the bomb bay trying to change a turbo amplifier when the bomb bay doors opened on the bomb run. We were hit by heavy flak. No.2 engine quit immediately and the No.3 engine developed a large plume of oil, indicating a punctured oil tank and siphoning it empty in three or so minutes. This left the plane with one full operating engine, which ran away, the bomb doors were stuck open and one 1,000lb [453kg] bomb was stuck on one

hook in the bomb bay. I toggled this one out. There was also indication of an engine fire. I was still in the bomb bay and out of contact by interphone when Dionne gave the order to bail out. We landed in a 10-mile [16km] circle 45 miles [72km] north of Ancona in the middle of the Adriatic. Our navigator was never seen again after we plunged into the sea. We assumed that he hit a bulkhead on bailout and was knocked out. The tail gunner was pulled from the sea six hours later in total darkness in a very poor condition, due to exposure. At about dusk we were picked up and taken to a British Army hospital in Ancona where we were looked after for about four days."

Above: B-24J-5-FO 42-51564 (foreground) and another Liberator, both in the 449th Bomb Group in the 15th Air Force, over the Alps en route to their target.
Below: *The demise of B-24H* Extra Joker *in the 451st BG, hit by Fw 190s.*

was caught in a drift on the bomb run and being under the lead plane he couldn't slow by lifting his nose, at risk of the two planes colliding. At this moment the time came for 'bombs away' and an unarmed 500lb [227kg] bomb fell on his nose just forward of the flight deck. It crushed the control cables and pulleys and disabled the plane, which fell off in a tight spin into a 90 degree bank, wing tip down. This generated an overwhelming spinning force pinning anyone inside against the plane and thus preventing their effort of escaping and bailing out. Because of this the plane fell over into a tight spin and disappeared into the clouds below. We saw no parachutes and no flak, and all were presumed dead."

On March 22, 1945, the 484th Bomb Group attacked oil refineries at Vienna again; for Ray A. Nichols and the rest of the crew, this completed their 33rd and final mission of their tour. Nichols recalls:

Above: *Hydraulic failure caused these parachutes to deploy from the waist positions of Pegasus, a 466th BG B-24H, slowing it down on landing at Attlebridge, Norfolk.*
Right: *HQ frowned on crews using parachutes for brakes, urging them to use the 3,000ft-long emergency runway at Woodbridge.*

"We took near misses from several 88mm shells over Vienna. Our No.1 and No.2 engines and our hydraulic system were knocked out. We flew to Hungary on the right engines, crabbing all the way. Not all of the shells were misses. I cranked down the landing gear by hand and kicked out the nose gear, and tied my 'chute and harness to a waist gun mount to stop the plane on the ground at the Russian airbase at Kecskemet, Hungary."

[Nichols logged 255 hours' combat time during his 33 missions. Two days later, on March 24th, the 15th Air Force bombed Berlin for the first time, while on March 25th, 650-plus heavies from Italy raided targets in Prague, and on the 26th, more than 500 planes pounded the marshaling yards at Wiener-Neustadt in Austria. By the end of March the strategic offensive was almost over. The Germans in Italy finally surrendered on May 2. The 15th Air Force had made 151,029 heavy bomber sorties and had dropped 303,842 tons of bombs on enemy targets in 12 countries during 18 months of operations. Of the 3,544 B-24s assigned, 1,756 were lost in combat.]

Dionne's crew returned to mission status on September 1 and flew their third mission, again to the railway bridge at Ferrara, Italy. Two days later their fourth mission was to a rail ferry crossing on the Danube at Srnederevo, Yugoslavia. Nichols continues: "We were flying planes delivered to us from the 8th Air Force. They were much heavier than our own planes and flew awkwardly due to tons of armor bucket seats and flak armor around the flight deck. For instance, when power was decreased, their own momentum drifted them forward and the only control for speed was to slow down by raising the nose. Of course this strategy was sometimes impossible due to the position in the formation to which a plane was assigned, because it could have rammed the plane above, which might have been fatal to both planes, and possibly others close by. One of these types of plane flying 'brown-nose' position [intimately close to the formation's lead plane]

The "Groundpounders," or "Paddlefeet"

"The bomber base is the striking arm of the 8th [Air Force]. Although less than a third of its men fly the planes, everyone on the field, whatever his job, shares in the victories and losses of heavy bombardment. The tough jobs, which didn't work out so well, disappoint the men on the line and the office workers as well as the combat crews. When the returning fliers grin from ear to ear as the planes taxi to their hardstands, everyone brightens up. The ground crews swell with pride at a bull's-eye job and the Group, from the control tower to the bomb dump, catches the spirit."—*Army Talks* for the 8th Air Force.

"Groundpounders" or "Paddlefeet" (the non-flying members of a group) are the unsung heroes. "A bomb group," recalls James J. Mahoney, "encompassed two distinct and very different populations. Of about 3,000 personnel, roughly 700 were 'flyboys' and the remainder, excepting a few command and staff flying personnel, were non-fliers, or 'paddlefeet.' They were the permanent party. They had been there since the start-up of the base and would be there for the duration of the war. They had time to form friendships on base and in local villages. They kept our planes flying and made the base and its equipment run.

They worked hard and long, but never heard a shot fired in anger, except from an infrequent intruder."

Everyone in Ed Barr's barracks in the 490th Bomb Group at Eye, Suffolk, was a mechanic of some sort— shop specialists, electricians, and general mechanics assigned to an airplane. What made the biggest impression on Barr on arrival, apart from drawing three biscuits, two blankets, and two sheets, was the cold. "I thought I would never get warm again. One time I stood only 18in [46cm] away from the small stove in the barracks dressed in long underwear, my woolen winter dress uniform, coveralls and my sheepskin-lined suit—and the date was July 13! In the early days maintenance personnel had a pretty easy time of it. As long as the daily inspections and routine maintenance were done we could read or lounge about. Even though the aircraft was the property of the AAC, we felt like we owned it; if the aircrew treated us okay we might let them borrow it for a short time."

Center top: *An Aerial Mechanic's badge.*
Above: *Ground crews of the 467th BG work on the Pratt & Whitney radials in the open at Rackheath airfield, near Norwich, in 1944.*
Right: *Engine specialists work on the port engines of a bomber at Seething. The groundpounders had to work at night, too, and in all weather conditions, in order to ready the bombers for combat missions.*

Ronald D. Spencer recalls: "I never ceased to feel sorry for the poor mechanics out there in the dark and the cold. I wouldn't have traded places with them for anything. If there were any unsung heroes around it was those guys. Fiction has it that the ground crews sweated out missions until their airplanes returned. I'm sure a lot, and probably most, did. However, if they had to maintain some of the old tired airplanes, I think they'd have been happy if you dumped it somewhere. I'm sure they would have hoped that the crew got out in most cases. We found the ground crews very good and quite responsive to our gripes about the airplane."

Forrest Clark says: "It was said that the ground crews did not want to get too friendly with the aircrews because they knew that sooner or later they might go down and they would lose friends. I liked many of the ground crewmen but we had little time to build a strong friendship because we were flying so much of the time."

Above: *Figure in the clothes of a ground crewman; he is carrying a bore sight to clean out the machine guns aboard the Liberator.*
Above right: *Closeup view of the bore sight.*

Above top: *A smiling Corporal James Atkinson poses on his Light Bomb Cart, which is transporting a 500lb (227kg) General Purpose demolition bomb at Hardwick.*
Above: *The groundpounders were the unsung heroes of the air forces. As they did the dirty work, the view was that only a tough-working soap could get these men squeaky clean. They had an opportunity to hold their own, though, when there was a USO party on the base and the local girls were invited.*

"Probably the greatest difference between paddlefeet and flyboys," adds James Mahoney, "was fear. A 'flyboy' was in constant fear of being killed. The 'Paddlefeet' had no reason for such fear. Despite their different situations there was no rivalry, resentment, or lack of respect between the two groups. One might liken the situation to boxing. The paddlefeet were in the corner doing all they could and cheering for their man out there taking the punches."

I Thought I was Dead

On January 16, 1945, more than 550 heavies bombed oil plant and engineering centers in the Reich. The 448th Bomb Group was among those units, which bombed a synthetic oil plant at Dresden from 22,000ft [6,705m]. Dick Dugger, the top turret gunner in *Rosie's Rivets* in the 448th BG at Seething, who was flying his second mission, recalls: "We were hit over the target area and began to lose gasoline. The bomber had been hit in the tanks. We made it to Lille [in northern France], but could not cross the Channel. Finally, the fuel gave out, the engines quit and we had to land in a park just outside Lille. [The crew got back to Seething and were given a new B-24, which they christened *Windy Winnie*. On January 28 *Windy Winnie* was also hit, over Dortmund. *Winnie*'s pilot nursed the bomber back across Germany and France as the crew threw out everything that was not screwed down. Dugger continues the story:] We were hit many times. *Winnie* had so many holes in her, it was like flying outdoors. A Liberator does not fly well with three engines at treetop level, but we kept in the air by throwing out everything we could—radio equipment, supplies, and even the guns. [*Winnie* finally crash-landed in Luxembourg. Dugger concludes:] Small trees were cut down and with her wheels up *Winnie* did some skating. I thought she would never stop, but finally she hit a ditch. Then it was very quiet. I thought for a moment I was dead. I crawled out of the bomber on the side where it had split open. None of the ten aboard was hurt, just bruised very badly—but no blood or anything. Later, the RAF flew us to London and we made our way back to Seething and yet another new bomber."

Above: Rosie's Rivets *in the 448th BG, which crashed at Lille, France, on January 16, 1945. On the left is Richmond Henry Dugger, the top turret gunner.*
Top right: *B-24J* A Dog's Life, *an Azon Lib in the 753rd BS, 458th BG, crashed after takeoff from Horsham St. Faith during a training flight on February 13, 1945.*
Center right: *A column of smoke signals the end of a 448th BG Lib at Seething.*
Bottom right: *Ambulances and GI trucks at a snowbound Seething, 1944–45.*

When top turret gunner and flight engineer Jack W. Earnshaw was transferred from Hardwick to Seething in January 1945, the end of the war in Europe was only months away—but, as Dick Dugger was finding out, that didn't make the missions any easier:

"When we arrived in England we were assigned to the 93rd Bomb Group, 330th Squadron as a replacement crew, and occupied the beds and hut of a crew just recently shot down. It wasn't a very pleasant way to get started. Above my bunk was a calendar for the year, on which the former occupant had circled his missions and crossed off each day. I continued circling the dates of our missions and crossing off the days. Due to heavy losses and crews completing their tour of missions, the 448th BG desperately needed replacement crews and we were sent on detached duty to the 715th Squadron, 448th BG from January 14, 1945 to March 24, 1945 . . .

"All [that] winter the weather was extremely bad, especially for fliers. We would be alerted for missions, go to the briefing room and even get out to the plane—only to learn the mission was scrubbed. Over and over.

"When we did fly we would take off in fog and freezing rain, snow, and mist that would freeze on the wings, windows, and runway. On one occasion one of our aircraft, heavy with fuel tanks of gas and a heavy bomb load, crashed at the end of the runway and burned—the mission [was] scrubbed for fear of exploding bombs destroying other B-24s taking off over it. Returning from a mission was even more dangerous, as England was covered by low clouds, rain, mist, freezing rain, or snow. We would be letting down from 22,000ft [6,705m] in bright sunshine, and [would] clear white clouds hoping to come through the cloud cover to use visual aids to find our base. During that winter it was seldom the case and we would find ourselves breaking through the clouds at a few hundred feet above the ground—and seeing terrified faces as the local people hoped the descending bomber would not crash on them or their loved ones.

"Perhaps my most remarkable experience during the war was on a dangerous mission. The flak was thick and black all around me. I was scared and all alone in the top turret: I knew I wouldn't make it this time, we were doomed. We would be killed in a fiery explosion. I cried out as I ducked my head, 'God, if I am killed, take me with you.' Suddenly a flood of peaceful energy flooded through my body and I was no longer afraid. I smiled, sat up and looked around . . . I no longer feared death.

Above: *An Operational Route Forecast sheet, which was an essential item for navigators and pilots on combat and training missions. It gave a good deal of detailed meteorological information—on weather, cloud conditions, icing (the point at which the wings start icing up—in this instance, 6,000ft), and visibility. It included weather conditions from base to target and the return route from target to base.*

"On March 2, our crew was alerted and awakened at 4am. After breakfast we found that 25 B-24s from the 448th at Seething were to be dispatched to bomb an oil refinery at Magdeburg [Germany]. After forming over East Anglia we crossed the North Sea and approached the coast of Holland. At that moment we were suddenly shocked to see two V-2 rockets the size of boxcars race past our formation in a vertical line, trailing white vapor. At first we thought they were a new German fighter but within seconds they were out of sight on their way to London—they were very close, and if by chance they had hit a B-24 they would have destroyed the whole group.

"The trip to the target was uneventful; we were protected by an escort of P-51s, while over the target we received a heavy barrage of flak, and the sky was black with explosions. We received heavy damage with holes under the left waist window and in the left elevator. We dropped ten 500lb [227kg] bombs and observed hits on the target . . . [and then] after six hours and 40 minutes, we returned safely to our base. This was the third long-range mission in three days and everyone was exhausted."

The Waist Gunners

"He smiled at the sight of the well-developed blonde reclining on the nose. The bombsight window was broken, the nose turret cocked out of line. A water truck was drawn up in front of the nose and a hose led up through the broken window and disappeared inside. The ground crew chief turned his white and confused face toward him and said, 'They're washing the bombardier's brains out of the Norden. Flak hit him on the bomb run. In the waist the walls of the fuselage were hanging with three- to four-inch chunks of grey meat. They looked like hacked up chunks of a large fish, bloodless and grey.'"—Staff Sergeant Robert H. Sherwood, *Certified Brave*

All enlisted men in an aircrew were aerial gunners. At the end of the basic training period, men chosen to train as career gunners were eligible to enter the six-week gunnery school. Aeroplane armorer-gunner trainees took a 20-week course in the operation and maintenance of aircraft armaments. Aircraft mechanic-gunner trainees spent 27 weeks training in aircraft inspection and maintenance. At the conclusion of their technical training, specialist gunner trainees were eligible to go to gunnery school. This six-week course covered weapons, ballistics, turret operation and maintenance; gun repairs; air, sea, and land recognition; shooting from a turret; and firing from the air at ground objects, at towed targets, and other aircraft with a gun camera. By 1943, 91,595 gunners had graduated from AAF schools. During 1941–45, 297,000 officers and enlisted men graduated from gunnery schools.

The waist gun positions on early production B-24 models were cramped and higher than on later models, and the

Left: Belt-fed .50 caliber Browning flexible machine gun in the left waist of a B-24H. The K-5 gun mount allowed the gunner to swivel his weapon inside and outside of the window opening.

Lib's huge fins and rudders limited field of fire to the rear. Later improvements included staggered guns, and the replacement of the drum-fed machine guns by ammunition belts. Waist gunners could see what was going on just about anywhere. It was a cold place to be but, when in flak, there was no time to think about being cold. There was no time to think about being scared, either. At altitude the two gunners had to withstand freezing temperatures and other operational problems, such as loss of oxygen supplies, which could soon lead to anoxia—and death. If one waist gunner lost his oxygen supply, in all probability the other waist gunner could come to his aid, unless he was fending off fighter attacks at the time and was unable to help, despite their close proximity to one another. A few minutes of breathing on pure oxygen from an oxygen bottle was usually enough to revive a man, but the after-effects of anoxia could last for the remainder of the mission.

A more general failure of the oxygen supply in one area of the ship, however, could affect several crewmembers all at once. If a regulator froze up and, simultaneously, the oxygen mask froze, it placed an additional burden on the remaining, unaffected crewmembers—who were already overstretched. In the latter case, each ship was furnished with an emergency kit that contained an oxygen mask, so the spare mask would be passed to the gunner and the frozen one taken to the radio room to be thawed out. Given these conditions, it's not surprising that, in the heat of battle, a waist gunner might fire a few rounds into the tail of his own aircraft, especially during sustained attacks.

At the waist gun positions the 170-plus mph [274kmh] winds, coupled with the arctic-like mercury readings, caused much suffering to crewmen. Minor-to-severe cases of frostbite occurred. The advent of electrically heated, snugly fitting "blue bunny" suits minimized the problem. Sometimes, however, the suits shorted out, and in such cases it was essential to don fleece-lined jackets and pants hurriedly. Incidents occurred where a wounded crewman, unattended for just a few minutes while his fellow crewmen fought off enemy attacks, died from exposure; others, still alive and in need of morphine, would endure extreme pain because syringe needles could not be made to penetrate hard, deep-frozen skin, but would break. Conversely, freezing temperatures saved some lives. Reportedly, an artery-severed, blood-spurting limb of a crewman had been freeze-cauterized and his life saved, by baring his injury to icy blasts.

William G. "Bill" Robertie in the 68th Bomb Squadron, 44th Bomb Group, recalls that "there were good and bad things about being a waist gunner. The good things were that you could move around and weren't cramped up like the turret gunners; you had a better view of the outside world than anyone else in the plane; and with those big waist windows and the nearby floor hatch you had a better chance of escape if it ever came to bailing out in a hurry. The bad things were standing over your gun for hours; the cold; and being bucked around by any sudden changes in flight altitude [. . .] There was a slipstream deflector at the forward end of each waist window which could be swung out to keep out the worst of the [wind's] blast but it was still pretty breezy at the gun. The point-fifty gun wasn't difficult to manipulate, but the kick made accurate aim difficult. If I were honest I'd say that you just pointed the gun in the direction of the target and hoped. Any enemy planes shot down by waist gunners were more by luck than skill, and I think most men would go along with that."

Page right, clockwise from top left: The .50 caliber ammunition belt feeds and plywood ammunition boxes containing 600 rounds replaced the bulky ammunition boxes of early B-24s; the staggered waist gun configuration was somewhat less cramped than the directly opposite arrangement of waist gun positions on earlier B-24 models, and allowed for greater freedom of movement in combat; the open hatches, seen here, were later glazed over and the guns fired through mountings in the glass.

Get That Fighter!

The Browning M2 was the standard machine-gun. It was produced in greater numbers than any other US machine-gun and weighed 65lb (29kg), with a muzzle velocity of 2,900ft (884m) per second. However, it was generally accepted that a flexible .50 caliber was inaccurate beyond 1,000 yards (914m).

HOW THE GUN WORKS

GM — TRAINING SERVICE — GENERAL MOTORS WAR PRODUCTS

CALIBER .50, M2 BROWNING MACHINE GUN

THIS PAMPHLET IS IDENTIFIED AS FGC

Prepared by—
AC SPARK PLUG DIVISION, General Motors Corporation
FLINT, MICHIGAN, U.S.A.
FRIGIDAIRE DIVISION, General Motors Corporation
DAYTON, OHIO, U.S.A.

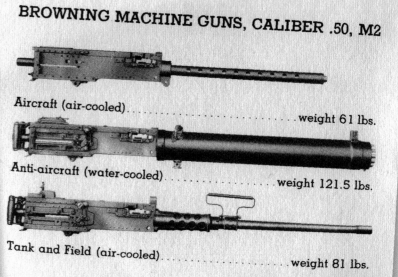

BROWNING MACHINE GUNS, CALIBER .50, M2

Aircraft (air-cooled).................................weight 61 lbs.

Anti-aircraft (water-cooled).................................weight 121.5 lbs.

Tank and Field (air-cooled).................................weight 81 lbs.

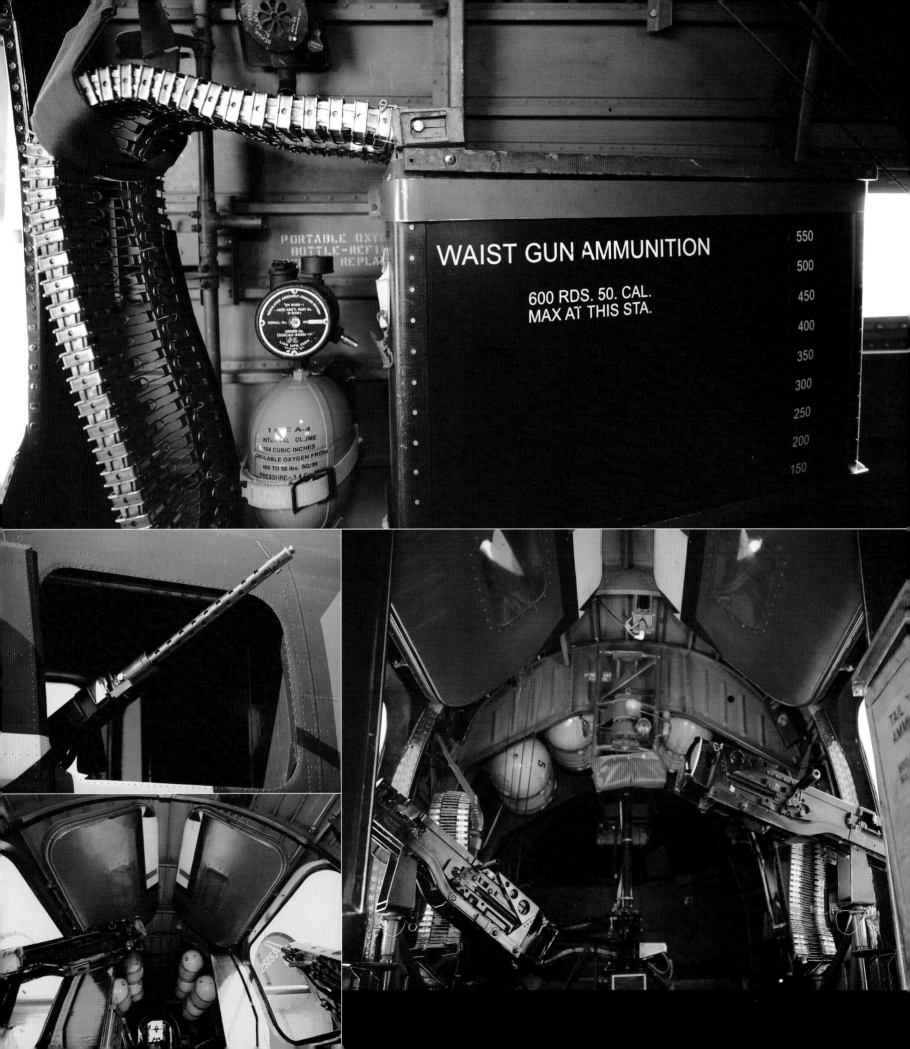

The Traveling Circus

In November–December 1943, Staff Sergeant John W. Butler in the 328th Bomb Squadron in the 93rd Bomb Group (based at Hardwick, Norfolk) flew some missions as left waist gunner in *Tennessee Rambler*:

"Sometimes it was minus 40°F [–40°C] and pretty damn cold. Combat, especially the money [combat aircrew received extra pay], was pretty good if you made it back, but raids were very tiresome as the oxygen and the cold temperature really tired you out. A lot of my good friends went down. At first it bothered you, but later I didn't mind it so much. When you don't make it back the fellows divided up anything they wouldn't send home to your next of kin.

"On [one] raid on Münster [Germany] three Me 109s came up and Haggerty, the right waist gunner, fired a short burst at them. They threw their bellies up and dove downward. An Me 110 came in at 9 o'clock. I gave him a short burst and he lobbed a rocket into the formation ahead of us. I then gave him another burst of about twenty rounds and he started to smoke. He peeled off and came in [again] at 7 o'clock, where I got in another short burst. A P-38 then jumped his tail and he started down. On another mission Red Carey, our right waist gunner, shot a Ju 88 down. Four yellow-nosed Bf 109s came diving down so close I could see the 'chute harness on the Jerry. Carey fired at them, but no luck. I fired over 90 rounds at an Me 110, a Bf 109 and a Ju 88 but I really didn't get a good shot at them. One bandit attacked *Southwind*

and three 'chutes came out. Then five more bandits came down and they shot off the left wing. It went into a spin and burst into flames. The weather was –37°F [–38°C] and I really froze."

Butler's mission to Frankfurt on February 4, 1944 in *Naughty Nan*, was one he would never forget:

"At 21,000ft [6,400m] the temperature was –54°F [–47°C], which is very cold. Before we passed the enemy coast my heated boots went out. I went up on the flight deck to borrow the radioman's, as on the flight deck they had heat. We ran into heavy flak twice on the way to the target. Over the target it was pretty damn good. Carey and I threw the tin foil [chaff] out. It was supposed to spoil the German radar. We dropped our bombs and started for home. My heated suit went out for good. I had the ball turret gunner come back in the waist to take my place as I then went up on the flight deck to try and keep warm. Our bombardier lost his oxygen supply so he came up on the flight deck also. My feet were frozen. The radioman fired a red flare as we came into land and the meat wagon followed us down the runway and took us all to hospital. There were around 20 fellows in the hospital with frostbite. This was the worst mission I was on to have so many things go wrong."

[The next day Butler flew his 22nd mission, when he flew left waist gunner again:] ". . . The CQ called me at 06:30 to fly as a spare gunner. So by the time I made it to the briefing room and out to the plane it was near takeoff time. They didn't pass any candy. I didn't have any breakfast either because everything was in a hurry. They had an oxygen leak in the tail turret so they had to replace the regulator. We then had to take off 20 minutes late and headed for the rally point where

Left: *A gunner is taken from the waist position of B-24H* Liberty Lib *in the 752nd BS, 458th BG, at Horsham St. Faith after returning from the raid on the Dornier factory at Lübeck on August 25, 1944.*

Any Gum, Chum?

Heath, Hershey, and Clark bars were all popular with crewmen, and with the locals, for whom sugar was rationed. Kids would ask, "Any gum, chum?" to which a GI's response was, "Got a sister, mister?" M&M's candy was included in C-ration kits, as its shell resisted high temperatures, and in 1942 the Army (noting its long shelf life) put in an order for $175,000-worth of Heath bars, leading to the bar's commercial manufacture.

Above: *Some special rations available to airmen for in-flight meals and survival packs contained 4oz bars of chocolate and chewing gum. The "air crew lunch," adopted in 1944, held two fudge bars, two sticks of chewing gum, and 2oz hard candy in a pocketsize, two-compartment carton with a sliding cover.*

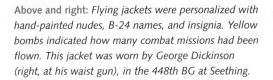

Above and right: *Flying jackets were personalized with hand-painted nudes, B-24 names, and insignia. Yellow bombs indicated how many combat missions had been flown. This jacket was worn by George Dickinson (right, at his waist gun), in the 448th BG at Seething.*

we were finally able to pick our own group. The weather was nice and clear as we were only at 16,000ft [4,876m] so you could see the ground pretty good. Temperature was only –13 [–25°C]. My heated suit worked real good. We had good fighter protection. I saw one P-38 go down in flames but the pilot hit the silk. The plane broke in two and I watched it hit the ground. We got to the primary target and some ships dropped their bombs. We then went on to the secondary where we dropped our twelve 500 pounders. I could see quite a few fires burning.

Fighters shot down *Thunderbird* in the 409th Squadron. Four 'chutes got out. It was a good mission as a whole. We received a large hole from flak in the de-icer boot."

Life-Saving Body Armor

Twenty-four-year-old Staff Sergeant Henry A. Dekeyser, a photographer-left waist gunner in the 576th Bomb Squadron, 392nd Bomb Group (based at Wendling, Norfolk), flew 35 missions—as well as two missions that he did not receive credit for, plus six aborts—between June 7, 1944 and December 23, 1944. He recalls some of the dangers:

"Whenever any German fighters attacked us they made head-on or dead astern attacks. As a waist gunner most of the times I had just a split second to fire my .50 caliber gun, getting off at best two or three rounds, and they were gone. But from the nose or the tail turrets we could get off two or three bursts. You never took the time to see if you had done them any damage as you were too busy searching the sky for the next attack. We never had time to think much under fighter attack, but flak was another story. When you could fire your .50 it gave you a feeling of being able to do something, but with flak you felt completely helpless and unable to protect yourself, so you just prayed, trusted in God, and sweated bullets, as the saying goes. In other words you were scared silly. We had flak suits to wear, which were hung over your shoulders front and back, and if you were in a turret you sat on a thick piece of armor plate. The

Above: *Waist gunners wearing M-3 flak helmets made from GI M-1 infantry steel helmets with hinged ear protectors to permit the use of earphones. The sporran was not normally worn by a gunner.*

Above and right: *At first the Germans relied on flak batteries to protect key sites, and flak towers proliferated. Gun crews numbered some ten men, including a loader, azimuth layer, Kanonier (gunner) and fuze setter; the other men passed the ammo.*

weight of the suit wasn't too bad, but when you had to stand up in the waist position, the weight of the suit pressed the bottoms of your feet flat and you soon had a real aching back and feet. You also had to have the help of one of your crewmembers to get the flak suit on, and we never got into them until the formation was almost ready to cross the mainland coast.

"On a mission with the second crew I was assigned to we were returning from Hanover [Germany]. The sky was clear, the clouds were solid below us, there were bursts of spent flak in the area, and then I saw eight bursts at our altitude and some distance behind us. I called 'Flak!' over the intercom and the crew started to throw out chaff. We were 'Tail End Charlie'—the very last and lowest plane in the formation—and nothing could be seen following behind. The next eight bursts were half the distance from the last bursts and us. I'm sure all of us were saying a prayer for help. I knew that the next eight bursts would be in among us and that some of us were not going to make it. But the bursts did not come. I looked down and could see the sun sparkling off the chaff more than a thousand feet below and there, right in the middle of it, were eight black puffs and then eight more. The hand of the Almighty had made the gunners on the ground change the settings on their fuzes—and not a moment too soon.

"Air battles were fast and you had no time to think about it until it was over. Then you were scared, but flak was nothing but pure terror. I once wasted a couple of dozen rounds firing on a flak battery I could see on the ground. Well, I could see the flashes from the guns and a few seconds later the shells burst amongst us. That is how frustrating

Left: A flak vest consisted of overlapping plates of 20-gauge manganese steel, covered by canvas, to help protect the torso.

Above: A waist gunner wearing an A-11 winter flying helmet, F-2 electric gloves, B-4 life preserver, and A-14 oxygen mask.

The flak vest helped to deflect shrapnel and ricocheting missiles.

it was. The pilot asked me what I was firing at as no one else was firing in the formation. When I told him he said he didn't think I could reach them with a .50 caliber gun, but [to] try [anyway] . . . On another mission we had just been attacked by three Me 109s that had made a head-on attack [but] had kept on going and did not turn to make a second attack. In another minute we found out why. They must have radioed our altitude to the ground because the nose gunner said on intercom, 'Oh my God!'—I was in the left waist position and saw large pieces of B-24 going by and a body curled up in a ball [that] was [soon] gone. We watched for parachutes and saw none. The pilot had thrown the plane into a dive. All the other planes were turning to one side or the other and diving and four more black busts of flak burst directly above us, just about in the place we had been in. Then the nose gunner told us that the three ships in the lead had all gone down. He had seen the command ship explode from a direct hit and the number 2 and 3 ships had also blown apart."

Under Fighter Attack

On November 26, 1944 Al Oliveira was armorer-right waist gunner in a 491st Bomb Group B-24 on the disastrous raid on the oil refineries at Misburg, Germany; he had a remarkable view of the destruction that occurred to his group on that day:

"I was required to remove the bomb fuze pins prior to approaching the target. On each of my 16 missions I kept the pins and jotted information on each tag. On the Misburg raid I noted we carried twelve 500lb [227kg] bombs. Also noted on the tag is the fact that we encountered heavy flak to the point of being 'intense.' After leaving the target area enemy fighters came from high and to the rear of our formation. The 853rd flying high right was hit first and I clearly remember B-24s exploding, with engines falling in flames as well as bombers angling downward trailing smoke and flames. During this action I saw only three parachutes before the fighters turned their attention to the 855th. I clearly recall an FW 190 with cannon bursts exploding by the right wing of our B-24. The German pilot appeared to look straight at me as I returned fire. On the left side of the 190 there was painted on the fuselage below the canopy, five American flag symbols reflecting his record of "kills." I continued firing and saw smoke coming from his engine cowl. Being excited, I fired through our own vertical stabilizer. Between the stabilizer and the tail section, I saw the 190 spiral downward trailing smoke. There was no parachute. Just about this time, a cannon shell exploded by the left waist window and Staff Sergeant Bill Meerdo, left waist gunner, fell against my machine gun and disengaged the .50 caliber from its mount. I applied first aid and morphine to no avail. Bill had taken shrapnel in the neck and was killed instantly. The tail gunner could do nothing but watch as cannon fire hit his turret armor plate. His guns had frozen. Bomb bay doors were buckled and torn from

flak. Control cables were severed and hanging in the waist section. The pilot did an outstanding job of flying the plane back to England with the use of trim tabs."

Below, all photos: A waist gunner had a better view of the outside world than anyone else in the B-24, and, with big waist window openings and the floor hatch nearby, a better chance of escape if it ever came to bailing out. Downsides were having to stand for hours; the cold and the wind; and being bucked around at high altitude.

Above: A waist gunner smiles for the camera; but at altitude things were very different. The kick from the 0.50 made it hard to aim, and, if they were honest, most just pointed the gun at the target and hoped for the best.

A waist gunner on *Boy's Howdy* in the 445th Bomb Group in 1944 recalls:

"On a mission to the Berlin area, we avoided the heavy flak areas but soon encountered German fighters. [At first, there were] about a dozen, which followed us out of range for several minutes, when they were joined by what seemed like hundreds more. They attacked immediately and it seemed the sky was full of burning bombers and fighters plunging to the ground. Our group losses were slight but I'll never forget the sight of all those planes falling and parachutes—both German and American—floating down. On one head-on pass by German fighters a bullet entered the plane above the command deck and took a piece out of a waist window just above my head and went out through the tail turret, taking a piece out of the shoulder of the coat of the tail gunner. After things calmed down he came out of the tail and said, 'Which one of you ******s shot back through the tail?' before he realized that it was impossible for us to swivel our guns around that far. We all had a big laugh about it when we got back home. Sometime during the flight we had a gas line cut and lost a lot of fuel, which left us with just enough to reach home base. Our fuel was almost gone. We had received the word, 'Prepare to bail out' and were gathered around the escape hatch when the pilot spotted an emergency field on the coast. He wheeled in and landed downwind. Just

Left: All .50-inch caliber ammo had copper-colored metal jackets. Distinguishable by the nose were armor-piercing rounds (painted black), incendiary rounds (painted light-blue), and tracer rounds (painted red).

in time too, since we lost all our engines (out of fuel) before reaching the end of the runway and could not taxi in. Since we did not reach home station back at base some crews reported us going down in the North Sea. Needless to say, when we called in they were awfully glad to hear from us.

"During the time of my combat tour I was grounded medically for a few days. I got two to three missions behind my crew so naturally I wanted to make up what I could and finish with them. On a mission to Munich I replaced a sick gunner. Everything was as usual, such as heavy flak over Munich—until we were on our way back. We were a little close to Abbeville, France, and suddenly we were joined by Me 109s. They all had bright yellow spinners and were Goering's 'Abbeville Kids,' as we called them. They were all crack pilots and we knew we were in for a lot of trouble. They made two or three passes at us and got three of our bombers, one of which was our right wing man. We saw him start burning and saw the crew jump. Then the plane seemed to fly straight and level for what seemed an awful long time when it reared straight up, flopped over on its back and went down in a spin. It fascinated me and I watched it all the way down. By that time our fighters had driven off the 109s."

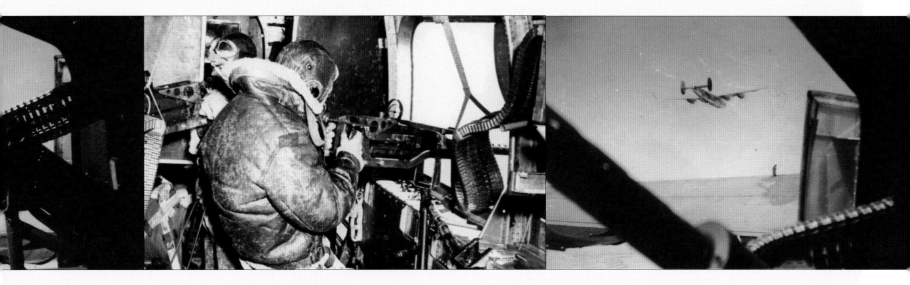

On a Wing and a Prayer

"At 6pm the double doors burst open and a tall angry man dressed in a field jacket, spotted fatigues, and no hat or insignia burst in. Every pure white hair in his head stood straight up in the air. He began to shout. 'All right you fish eaters, you better come to mass! I want to see all you fish eaters at confession and Sunday services! God is going to take care of you and I'm going to help him!' The room was still silent. 'No Catholics at all? Okay. None of you are going to heaven unless you see me first.' With that he exited, slamming doors hard enough to shake the whole hut. A voice in the next cot said, 'Don't pay any attention to "White Flak." He does that performance for all new crews. He's crazy but he's a good guy.'" Staff Sergeant Robert H. Sherwood, *Certified Brave.*

looked up and caught a full splash of water in his face. It was the Group Chaplain asking God to look after them. McClane got to know why there are no atheists in combat. On many missions, he had good reason to pray for God to spare them "just this one more time." He would never understand why God answered this prayer for some and so many others were required to give their all. On one particularly bad mission he prayed out loud for God to let him live through the battle and promised he'd do anything he asked of him if only he would spare him. Like all men, the flesh is weak when the danger is past. Yet, somehow, he felt he was a better person for having experienced these strong emotions. "I did survive the 31 missions and GOD WAS WITH ME!" he said.

Group chaplains, or "Sky Pilots" and "Holy Joes," were well respected and offered benediction and solace to the combat crews. They would close the briefing with a prayer and were always available for those who wished to have Holy Communion before the mission. Robert H. Tays recalled: "Each of us in our own way worshipped by participating in Holy Communion. This was optional, but most of us never neglected it. No matter what the mission, the time, or the weather, Father McDonough and Reverend Clark, the chaplains at Wendling, were always at the takeoff end of the runway for takeoffs or returning missions. They seemed to be everywhere for both officers and enlisted alike. Both [chaplains] were easy to talk to and both liked to party, Clark playing the piano and McDonough leading the singing. Both would take the time and patience to listen to men's problems privately and offer solutions."

Once, before takeoff, John McClane spread out his navigation equipment on the ground. While going over the maps he

This page: *The Chapel on the airfield at Hethel was a sanctuary for men in the 389th BG. In February–March 1944 Charles "Bud" Doyle painted a crucifix on the wall behind the altar. When completed, he asked Father Beck's opinion; the priest's only criticism was that Christ's feet were not properly portrayed. During restoration of the chapel (now a museum), a Madonna was revealed beneath the white paint.*

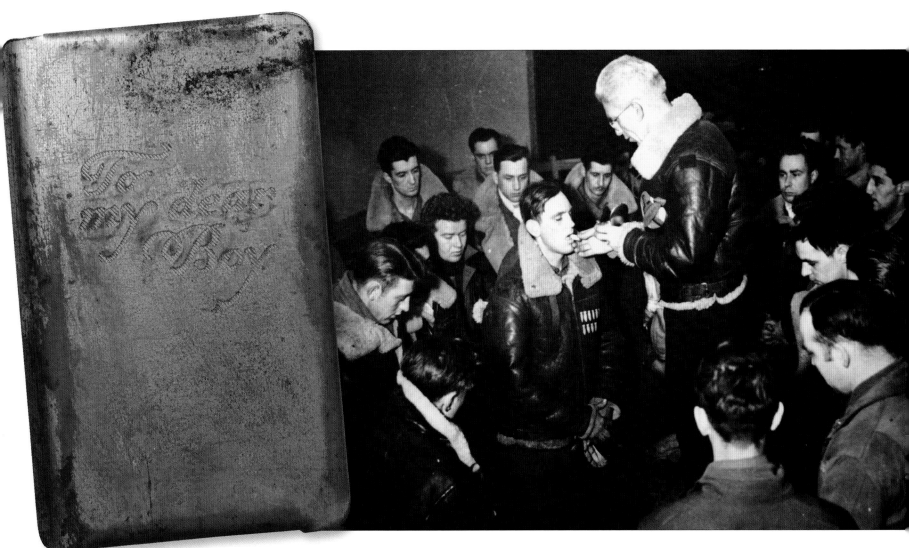

Above left and below: *Metal-covered ("shield") Prayer Book presented to 2nd Lt. Ernest J. Delia, a bombardier in the 712th BS, 448th BG, by his mother. Delia carried it on all combat missions.*

Above right: *"Pappy" Beck, a.k.a. "White Flak," gives Communion to men in the 389th BG. A gunner who had seen heavy flak over Berlin and light flak over St. Lô said that "White Flak" was the toughest if you stepped out of line!*

The Shield *and* Prayer Book

PRESENTED TO

LIEUT. ERNEST J. DELIA

FROM:

By   MOTHER

Open thou mine eyes, that I may behold wondrous things out of thy law.   Psalms 119:18
KNOW YOUR BIBLE SALES CO., Cincinnati, O.

At Hethel, Father Gerald Beck ("White Flak"), the Catholic Group chaplain, distributed Communion to the combat crews in the base chapel. It was not uncommon to see a Protestant lad also receive Catholic Communion, as added spiritual insurance. Father Beck quite often drove his jeep at top speed from plane to plane, making sure that no one was denied Communion before takeoff. One time he was inside a Liberator administering the sacrament at takeoff time and was an observer for that mission. Father Beck often played poker with his boys; officers and EM alike. Shooting craps was his meat. He played baseball with GIs 20 years his junior and drank beer with them in town, after first removing his Chaplain's cross and replacing it with a Field Artillery insignia. "Come to confession and get rid of that load of sin I know you're carrying around. I know you boys; you've got lots of sin. If you'll come to confession you'll shoot straighter and kill more Krauts. That's what the Lord wants. Me too!"

At takeoff time "White Flak" was in his usual place near the end of the runway. Standing erect in his jeep, with both arms outstretched, he was blessing the departing Liberators. Robert Sherwood liked that. It made him kin to the ships and sailors of the past, who left port for high adventure with the benediction of the priests.

Limping Homeward

On July 7, 1944 Staff Sergeant Wally Robinson, tail gunner in William "Jug" Wright's crew in the 767th Squadron, 461st Bomb Group, 15th AF, went on a mission to Blechhammer, Germany. The crew had a lucky escape, as he recalls:

"We developed a rough engine on the way, but we were deep into enemy territory by this time and didn't want to turn back by ourselves. The *Luftwaffe* jumped us over Hungary, and they stayed with us all the way to the target. We were doing a lot of shooting and there were tracers all over the sky. Most of the time the Germans came in two or more abreast from the front, but one loner came in and knocked out the plane on our left. Joe [Jonas Palmer] was letting off a long burst as the fighter went by and he put six holes in our left rudder. He and Smitty [William Smith] were throwing [chaff] out the window to confuse the flak guns, between fighter attacks. This probably saved Joe's life: he was bent over getting an armful of foil when a shell (or flak) entered the bomb bay, and went through the bulkhead to the waist and out the top, making a large hole where Joe's head would have been if he had been standing up. We had to shut down the bad engine over the target, right after releasing the bombs. We were able to stay in formation—again, due to the fact that it was letting down. The fighters hit us again, but didn't stay with us long. About an hour later 'Jug' called us on the inter-phone to tell us we probably wouldn't make it to base because we were too low on gas, and for us to start tossing out the excess weight. Pretty soon 'Jug' called us again and said we had better maintain ditching procedures. B-24s don't ditch well. Every one I saw had broken, though I only ever saw two actually try it. We made it to the Italian coast, however, and put down at Amendola, about ten miles inland. The 2nd and 97th Bomb Groups were located there, both B-17 outfits. We took a terrible ribbing about our 'banana boats' and 'flying coffins'. Some of their people fixed our engine and put some gas in and we took off for home. So that was quite a tour: Italy, Yugoslavia, Hungary, Czechoslovakia, Poland and Germany—and return, and all in nine hours."

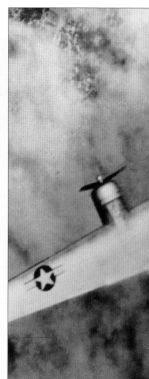

Right: A 376th BG B-24, having lost part of its wing to flak over Toulon, France; the 15th AF bombarded the port in 1944 as part of the softening-up process for the "Anvil" invasion.
Left: Chaff, which consisted of metallic foil strips of varying lengths, was thrown out of planes to confuse the range-finding equipment of the enemy's antiaircraft guns.

Back in England, B. Dale Bottoms, right waist gunner in crew 55, 714th Squadron, 448th Bomb Group, recorded an extraordinary incident on only his fourth mission, on February 4, 1944:

"Well, I have just got in from my fourth raid in the ETO and, boy, I want to tell you I thank God for going with us. I never will forget this one—we started out, and got to the enemy coast about 11:30. We encountered light flak, and then about 30 minutes after that we got the heck knocked out of us. I have never seen such flak. It knocked

No.3 engine out and we had to feather it and [the flak also] put a couple of holes in our wing—one in the fuselage, beside the left waist window. With one engine gone we stayed with the formation until we arrived at the target. When we opened the bomb bay doors, one [door] did not open and one side of the bombs—26 of them, and incendiaries at that—fell into the bomb bay. The bombardier threw 13 of them out the side that was open, and the other 13 'Pop' Blanton, the left waist gunner, and I threw out the escape hatch in the rear. We went without oxygen for a

Above left: B-24L Stevonovitch in the 790th BS, 464th BG, takes a direct hit near Lugo, Italy, on April 10, 1945. Only the "Mickey" operator, who was thrown clear, survived from the 11-man crew.
Above right: Against all odds, this Lib made it back despite a large hole in the roof of the rear fuselage. The feat drew quite a crowd.

while and, at 47 degrees below [–44°C], got frostbite on our faces. We came all the way back on three engines and made the landing fine and dandy."

The Purple Heart Decoration

General George Washington established the award of the Purple Heart in 1782. At that time it was called the "Badge of Military Merit." Following the American War of Independence the award fell out of use until its reestablishment in 1932, on the 200th anniversary of George Washington's birth. Today, it is awarded to those wounded in action while serving in the US armed forces. A posthumous award of the Purple Heart is also made to the next of kin of officers or enlisted men killed in action, or of those who died of wounds received in action.

From August 17, 1942 to May 15, 1945 the 8th Air Force alone awarded 6,845 Purple Hearts and 188 Oak Leaf Clusters. No decoration is ever awarded more than once to any

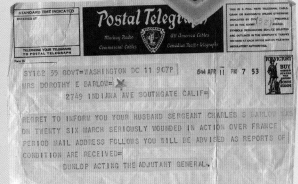

Purple Heart for South Gate Man

Staff Sgt. Charles S. Barlow, U. S. army air corps, and husband of Dorothy Barlow, 2749

CHARLES BARLOW

Indiana ave., South Gate, was

individual—*except* a posthumous award of the Purple Heart—but for each succeeding achievement sufficient to justify an award, a bronze Oak Leaf Cluster may also be added. Decorations were awarded by the War Department acting for the President, the exception being in the field, when the commanding general of a separate army of a higher unit could award all decorations, other than the Medal of Honor.

Left: Staff Sergeant Charles S. Barlow in the 714th BS, 448th BG received the Purple Heart after being wounded on his 13th mission, on March 26, 1944.
Above: The Postal Telegraph bearing the news, sent on April 11th at 7:53pm to Charles' wife, Mrs Dorothy E. Barlow. Charles did make it home.
Top: The medal is a purple enameled heart within a bronze border; its purple ribbon has white edges.

The Ball Turret Gunner

"Of particular interest was the ball gunner cramped into a tiny compartment: he could not scratch his nose or go to the 'bathroom' and when an attack was under way, the empty shell cases and cartridge links filled what empty space was left. Because of the cramped quarters and the inevitable cold from flying at high altitude in an unpressurized aircraft, gunners often suffered from frostbite."—Bud Markel, engineer, 827th Bomb Squadron, 484th Bomb Group

Although the ball turret was no place for a person **of a nervous disposition, official postwar analysis declared that it was the safest crew position on a B-24 Liberator.** The Briggs/Sperry retractable ball turret was hydraulically suspended from inside the aft fuselage, and could be raised and lowered externally while in flight using an electric/hydraulic retraction mechanism. The *Air Forces Manual No.20* on flexible gunnery had this to say about getting into the turret: "To start getting acquainted with the Sperry Ball, get in. You will have to be careful—men have been injured and even killed because they did not know the right way to get in, or they were careless about it. The turret ball is heavy and yet delicately balanced; unless it is locked in place, it may swivel and break a man's leg or snap him almost in two as he attempts to enter."

The ball turret could only be entered from inside the B-24 after the Liberator had become airborne, and then by rotating the guns straight down, which brought the entry door inside the aircraft. Each gun had an ammunition box with a chute for feeding the guns and leading away the links and fired shells. The top box (maximum capacity 505 rounds) fed the left gun; the

Left: The ball turret gunner could only climb into his ball turret once the Liberator was actually in the air. The guns had to be rotated and the entry door brought inside the fuselage.

lower box (maximum capacity 425 rounds) fed the right gun. Controlled power drives gave tracing rates from 0° to 45° per second in azimuth and 0° to 30° per second in elevation. The gunner's hand controls and elevation limit stop were in a unit, which regulated the amount of turret movement in azimuth or elevation. When the handgrips were released they returned to their center position. The gunner sighted his twin .50s through a Sperry gun sight located between his knees. Gun-firing switches in parallel were located at the end of each handgrip. Either switch fired the guns. The gunner operated the range control with his foot. Foot pressure in the support increased the range up to 1,000yds (914m).

Often a ball turret would be removed, and sometimes the opening would be used to house an H2X radome instead. Actually, the ball turret was not even a true ball. The Perspex side panels, which completed the spherical appearance of the ball turret on the E and F models, were removed from the G model.

Being a ball turret gunner was a lonely job, as was the tail gunner's—but a tail gunner could at least swing round to catch a view of the two waist gunners. Though some ball turrets had a very small 3-in (7.6cm) window above the head, which made it possible for the gunner to see inside the ship, many did not. Which made it doubly lonely.

Furthermore, as ball turret gunner Ed Smith remembers, "The guns and feed only allowed good vision straight ahead so, to search, the turret had to be continually revolved. In fact, to pick up an enemy coming in you needed a warning of his approach if you were to stand a chance of hitting it. The only time I was able to get fighters in my sight was in tail attacks as they dived away under our ship."

Stuck under the belly of the Liberator, it was too easy to worry about what would happen if things went wrong. One of the ball turret gunner's greatest fears was that if something happened to his plane, he would not have time to get back up and get his parachute on—there were stories about the turret mechanism jamming, the retraction gear failing, being isolated by a fire in the fuselage, and the turret dropping off. Grisly imaginings about the likely consequences if the ball turret failed to

retract into the aircraft, trapping its occupant—especially if there were landing gear problems—could never have been very far from the back of a Liberator crewman's mind. John Rickey, tail gunner in *G.I. Jane Pallas Athene* (578th Squadron, 392nd Bomb Group) recalls his "most harrowing experience . . . [It was] landing a Liberator with the ball turret down and the ball gunner still in it. My pilot called the tower for instructions on what to do. They told him to get the rest of the crew ready to bail out. Better to lose one man instead of ten. He called back and told them he thought he could land the plane only if he had the rest of the crew in the front of the plane and bring it in on the nose. Luckily that's what he did. It took the ground crew two hours after we landed to get the ball gunner out."

Page right, clockwise from top left: *The Briggs/Sperry ball turret seen in relation to the right and left waist gun positions; view from the bomb bay catwalk looking aft, with the ball turret in the raised position at the rear of the Lib; close-up of the Briggs/Sperry ball turret (through the tiny pane, the gunner could signal in alarm); the B-24J seen from the Sperry ball turret of a B-17 Flying Fort, which, unlike the Liberator's Briggs/Sperry turret, could not be retracted.*

Mechanical Brains

The January 24, 1944 issue of *Life* magazine ran an illustrated feature (left) showcasing the new "mechanical brains" on the Liberator: "For a great many years, the Sperry Gyroscope Company of Brooklyn, New York, have been in the business of building mechanical brains and putting them up in metal containers . . . One of the newer Sperry gadgets is the automatic gunsight, which is used in US bomber gun turrets."

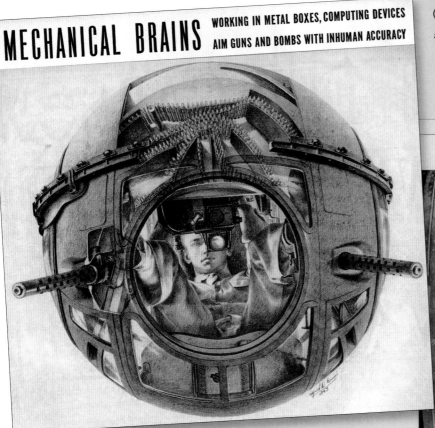

MECHANICAL BRAINS — WORKING IN METAL BOXES, COMPUTING DEVICES AIM GUNS AND BOMBS WITH INHUMAN ACCURACY

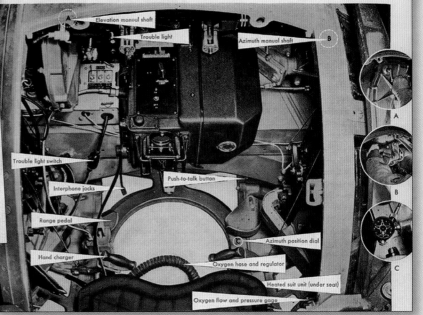

Using the Auxiliary Units

Elevation manual shaft
Trouble light
Azimuth manual shaft
Trouble light switch
Push-to-talk button
Interphone jacks
Range pedal
Azimuth position dial
Hand charger
Oxygen hose and regulator
Heated suit unit (under seat)
Oxygen flow and pressure gage

The illustration (above) was by Alfred D. Crimi, who would become a renowned artist. "Using The Auxiliary Units," from the Sperry manual (right), pinpoints the different ball turret controls.

Reluctant Witness

Colonel James J. Mahoney in the 492nd Bomb Group (stationed at North Pickenham, Norfolk) would never forget his attempt to rescue the ball turret gunner after a crash landing:

"The ball turret gunner on Lieutenant Dave McMurray's crew was Sergeant Pat Tracey, a good-natured, hard-working Irish-American from Bayonne, New Jersey. By his own choice, Tracey was a ball turret gunner, which to me was the least desirable position in the plane. Also, he was a little on the chubby side to be squeezing into the extremely limited confines of the turret. Returning from one mission, McMurray broke out of formation, firing red flares [to warn the control tower, and the medical and fire crews, that there were wounded aboard the plane, and that it should be given priority in landing]. Smoke was coming out of one engine and he had feathered another on the opposite side. He was given number one priority in landing, dropped his wheels and made a close-in approach. We saw that his ball turret was in the 'down' position instead of being retracted, as it should have been for landing. When the tower called Dave on this, he quickly explained that it was jammed, nor could he

Left: This B-24J in the 389th BG ran out of fuel on its return from Magdeburg on February 15, 1945, crash-landing in a field near Hethel. It narrowly missed a cottage and left its left wingtip in the garden.

communicate with Tracey, [who was] still inside it. Tracey was going to be in a very dangerous position during landing as the bottom of the turret was sure to scrape along the runway—how badly would depend upon how well McMurray could execute the landing . . . Should he land tail-heavy, it could be rough on Tracey.

"The fire trucks and meat wagons were readied for whatever McMurray and crew had concocted for them this time. Under difficult conditions, he made a beautiful landing with weight well forward and the turret barely touching and sparking along the runway. At the end of his roll, he pulled off onto the grass to clear the runway for our planes coming in behind him. He cut his engines and the crew scrambled out of every opening. The smoking engine was quickly brought under control, so our next concern turned to Tracey. As the firefighters were working on the engine, we saw that the circular, heavy armor-glass window between the ball turret's two .50 caliber machine guns was shattered and had a cannon shell hole in its center. There was little doubt that the projectile that made that hole had put an end to Pat Tracey. Hoping against the obvious, we climbed into the plane and tried without success to manually open the doors atop the turret. A couple of ground crewmen with some tools pried it open. Tracey was slumped forward with only the back of his neck showing, and blood everywhere. The firefighters, crash crews, and medics were trained and fully capable of handling this situation . . . but because of my concern for a long-time GI friend, I found myself taking over where I had no business doing so. The smallness of the hatch opening was such that it wasn't possible for two people to get into position to lift Tracey out. By getting on my knees I could put my arms down into the turret with my hands under his armpits. It was an awkward position for lifting and it was not going to be easy to extract about 165lb [75kg] of Tracey plus all that equipment. Having set myself for that weight, I gave a mighty heave and to the astonishment of all— especially me—Tracey, or rather, the top half of poor Tracey, came out of the hole easily and wound up on top of me as I tumbled over backward. That shell had literally cut him in half just above the belt. At that point I quietly turned over the rest of that job to those who should have had it in the first place, and climbed out of the plane . . ."

Below: B-24 Stinger in the 791st BS, 467th BG, crash-landed by Lt. Thomas Murphy at Watton-Griston in Norfolk on May 8, 1944, following the mission to Brunswick.

Above: *Five B-24s crashed at Seething on April 22, 1944 after the mission to Hamm; 13 from the Second Bomb Division crashed or crash-landed in Norfolk that night.*

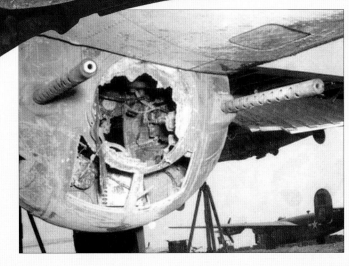

Above and right: All that remains of a ball turret from a 489th BG Lib that was ripped apart by a direct hit. In combat, armor-glass could deflect flak and bullets only to a degree. This turret's armor-glass (right) has been shattered by a projectile; the gunner would have been killed instantly—a fate that befell Sgt. Pat Tracey (see opposite).

Ball turret gunner Ed Smith in the 514th Bomb Squadron, 376th Bomb Group in Italy recalls:

"The ball turret was no place for a nervous guy. Stuck down there under the belly of the B-24 it was too easy to worry about what would happen if things went wrong . . . My greatest fear was if something happened on the ship, I wouldn't have time to get back up and get my 'chute on. The ball had an electric/hydraulic retraction mechanism, which brought it way up into the fuselage until only the ends of the gun barrels stuck out below the fuselage. It had to be that way when lowered so that the hatches could be opened to allow entry. The general rule was for the ball to be lowered when we started over enemy territory. It was reckoned to take 10–15mph [16–24kmh] off our speed so the pilot didn't have it down any longer than necessary.

"While they didn't pick big fellows to ride the ball, I'm no small man and I could fit with fair comfort. It was no place to be for a long time as there wasn't a mite of room to stretch. You prayed the electric heating in your suit didn't go out because it could quickly become an icebox.

"And curled up there looking between your legs you soon wanted to move. The worst problem was urinating; I had my own set-up for getting around the problem. The view from the ball was certainly sensational; there's nothing more humbling than to realize that all there is between you and a five-mile [8km] drop to earth is a canvas safety strap and a glass panel . . . When you fired you'd think the ball was going to rip right outta the ship. The thing I hated most was going into a flak cloud. I'd bring the guns up to the horizontal so the armored door at the back was facing to the ground. I'd swing the ball so I faced the tail going into flak and swing round to the front as we went out of it. It may not have made things safer, but this way I didn't get to see how close it was coming!"

"Balls are Out"

Changes on the production lines and the addition of a nose turret increased the gross weight of the B-24 to between 50–70,000lb (23–32,000kg) and, as a result, fuel consumption and overall performance suffered. With little reserve power available, takeoff in particular became quite critical. Thus in East Anglia late in July 1944 ball turrets were removed from many Liberators to improve stability and altitude performance. The 467th Bomb Group was one of the first groups to dispense with the ball turret, as Colonel James J. Mahoney recalls:

Left: A 15th Air Force B-24J in the 449th Bomb Group—pictured with its ball turret in the straight-down position—dropping a string of bombs over an enemy target.

"We were continually trying to analyze the patterns of attack by German fighters in order to arrange our formations [to give the] best defense against them. We set up a program to track the number of rounds fired, by gun location, against attacking Jerries. An analysis of the data, together with consideration of our gunners' claims of 'destroyed' and 'probable' against the attackers, made evident what we'd long suspected: that the ball turret on a B-24 was of little or no defensive value against enemy air attacks. It was a rare occasion when this position had an opportunity to fire its weapons, and even more rare when a ball gunner claimed even a 'probable.' Looking at the ball turret, then, in realistic terms, we were risking a life, using up a lot of system oxygen, carrying his weight and that of a 2,100lb [952kg] turret, for nothing. He wasn't getting any effective shots because the most damaging attacks being made on us were from frontal and high positions. Adding the attacker's speed to our own, the rate of closure was at least 800mph [1,287kmh]. With a maximum effective range of about 500yds [457m], our top and nose turret gunners who could see the attacker coming in all the way had only a couple of seconds for possible effective fire. The ball turret gunner, who couldn't see the attacker until after he had fired on us, had virtually no opportunity to position his guns for effective fire as the 'bandit' zipped by.

"After building up our case against the ball, we went to the Old Man [the CO, Colonel Albert J. Shower] with the recommendation that we should eliminate ball turrets from at least some of our planes and see what effect, if any, it might have on our vulnerability. We already knew

Above: B-24H Poop Deck Pappy in the 577th BS, 392nd BG in the 8th Air Force with its ball turret facing rearward and the ball gunner keeping a look out.

Right: B-24J Libs in the 706th BS, 446th BG en route to the Messerschmitt Bf 110 plant at Gotha on February 22, 1944. All ball turrets are retracted.

center of gravity, increased speed, reduced fuel consumption minutely, and made the plane less tail-heavy for landing. Our test worked so well that within a couple of months you couldn't find a ball turret in any of our planes. Not long thereafter other groups started eliminating their ball turrets also."

John McClane also talked about the removal of the ball turrets:

"The removal of the ball turret from our Liberators did two things, one being the reduction in weight so we could gain higher altitude as a defense against the stiffer flak barrages being built around every major target in Europe. Secondly, it improved the stability of the B-24s in tight formation flying. We hated to lose our ball turret gunner, 'Swoose' Alexander. He was the 'character' of our crew and a fun person to know. Swoose was assigned to another crew and soon completed the required 30 missions. What happened to Alexander, I do not know as he volunteered for a second tour. All I know is that he had a job with our crew that I could not have made myself do. His job was to curl up inside the ball turret, then the doors were shut and the waist gunners cranked him down below the belly of our plane. He could not get out unless someone cranked him back up. A threat of being court-martialed and a stick of dynamite could not have forced me into what my mind's eye perceived as a 'Death Trap.' As strange as it may seem, records after the war showed that ball turret gunners suffered fewer losses than at any other position of the plane. Maybe it was because he was best protected from flak but even if I had known it then, no one could have made me get into that contraption."

Above top: Smoke markers from a 565th Pathfinder Squadron, 389th BG PFF Lib (with its H2X radome extended) mark a target for the "Sky Scorpions" formation.

Above: A Ford-built B-24H with its ball turret retracted. (Note its Willow Run "wavy demarcation line" between the OD upper and gray lower surfaces.)

Right: Ball turret gunner Staff Sgt. Charles J. Alexander, known as "Swoose," with (left) Lt. John W. McClane Jnr. at Shipdham in 1944.

it would increase the performance of the plane. Although he was a confirmed 'do-it-by-the-book' West Pointer and sometimes strenuously resisted our frequent attempts to do things otherwise, he readily recognized the significance of our case and gave a reluctant okay. We then removed the turrets from one squadron's planes and reassigned the gunners to a crew pool. We had checked pretty carefully what the effect of weight loss would be on the center of gravity along the MAC [Mean Aerodynamic Chord], and on the elevator controls. It moved forward the

Desperate Measures

For Benedict Yedlin, a Sperry ball turret gunner in the 449th in Italy, the June 6, 1944 mission to Ploesti was noteworthy not because of the intense flak encountered—but for an altogether more personal reason: "We were returning to our base, Giottaglie on the instep of the Italian boot from a bombing mission. Our plane *The Buzzer* . . . was one of 39 B-24 bombers from the 449th Bomb Group that took part in the raid. We did not know that this was to be an historic day . . . This was our crew's second mission to the Ploesti oil fields. We were doing our part some 1,500 miles [2,414km] from the Normandy landings to render Hitler incapable of continuing the war by cutting off his source of petroleum . . .

"As far as I could tell from my ball turret position on the underside of the plane the mission had been reasonably successful as evidenced by huge pillars of black smoke which penetrated the defensive white smoke screen. Even from my vantage point I had yet to see the city of Ploesti or to track our bombs down as they left the bomb bay and see them explode on the ground. Ploesti was the third most heavily defended target in Europe next to Berlin and Vienna. As usual the flak there was 'IAH'—'Intense, Accurate, Heavy.' Some B-24s were seen to explode, others dive crazily to earth with some 'chutes seen. Luckily, holding our collective breaths, we got through the flak barrage sustaining very little damage. Some holes in the fuselage, left tail, and right wing. No mechanical damage that we could tell.

"Our pilot, 'Buck' Rogers, now that the tension was gone [as the bomb run had been completed successfully], got a little chatty on the intercom. He told the crew that we were letting down from our 24,000ft [7,315m] bombing altitude to around 9,000ft [2,743m] and [said] we could then remove our oxygen masks which were by now wet with saliva. I was reasonably comfortable in my ball turret. Since we were still over enemy territory, Yugoslavia, some caution was necessary. Returning to base from a mission to the Balkans, when we reached the

Adriatic I would position the turret for exit, open the hatch, get out and retract the turret by hand pumping [it] into the well in the fuselage. The B-24, unlike the B-17, could not land with the ball turret in position. The turret, which rotates in azimuth 360° was now positioned with my twin .50 caliber machine guns and round glass window pointed aft.

"Early in combat our crew learned from experience that if the ball turret was pointed to the front of the plane, in the direction of flight and a crewmember used the fore relief tube, urine would spray on my circular safety glass window and my vision would be completely obscured. There

Right: Losses on the early low-level Ploesti missions resulted in the 15th air Force flying high-altitude bombing raids on the Romanian refineries. In this photo, B-24s in the 449th Bomb Group are seen triggering widespread fires in the Astro Romano oil refinery complex.

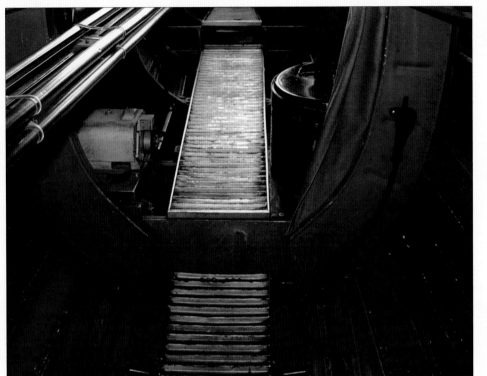

Above: *The .50 caliber ammunition belt feed to the left of the bomb bay catwalk supplied the rear turret, while the "can" to the right and the relief tube were used by all crewmembers—as Benedict Yedlin discovered to his cost. Sometimes gunners who failed to use the relief tube, however, and urinated where they sat or stood, died when their heated suits shorted out and they literally froze to death.*

was no way to clean the window in flight and this would create a serious problem—the turret would be useless and the use of two of the ten .50 caliber machine-guns would be lost. My arrangement with the crew in the forward compartment—[the] pilot, copilot, navigator, bombardier, nose gunner, and flight engineer—was that if they had to use the relief tube to let me know via intercom and I'll turn my turret aft 180°. Just a flick of the control handle.

"We were now flying west over the mountains in Yugoslavia with the blue Adriatic in sight. I was facing west listening to popular music on Armed Forces Radio. I was musing about our just-completed mission, wondering about the fate of the men in the planes that went down. Did some safely parachute to ground? Did the ball turret gunner get out? Were they picked up by Germans or Romanians? What was the fate of Jewish crewmembers taken as prisoners of war? At the time we had no news or information on how many in the plane were KIA, wounded or PoW, or evaded capture. Group headquarters didn't share this information with the crews. On the other hand I had no concern about

what our bombs did to people on the ground. As far as I was concerned they were all Nazis and enemies.

"While thinking, listening to music, speculating in a very comfortable, almost supine, position, I noted drops of yellowish liquid leaking through my hatch door. My very first thought was that it was hydraulic fluid. Many of the systems on the B-24 were operated by hydraulic systems, brakes, flaps . . . and a loss of fluid could cause serious landing problems. Through my head went the thought that the hydraulic lines in the bomb bay had been damaged by flak. I was in a panic but not yet ready to notify the pilot on the intercom of the 'hydraulic line leak.' Removing my glove I applied my finger to the liquid [that was] still leaking in, and then put my wet finger to my lips. It tasted salty! It then dawned on me that what I tasted was not hydraulic fluid, but pee. I screamed on the intercom: 'Who in the hell is taking a piss? It's leaking into my turret!' I was greeted

Above: *This Sergeant Flakbaite cartoon from* Short Bursts *points out, in inimically comical fashion, the hazards of using the relief tube in flight.*

by return calls of both denial and amusement. It had to be someone in the forward part of the plane. Finally 'Baldy' Hinds, the bombardier, owned up to using the relief tube . . . This is one of my few vivid recollections of 'combat.' I'm glad it was pee not hydraulic fluid!

"Randall Jarrell, one of the most respected writers of the Second World War, wrote *The Death of the Ball Turret Gunner.*

'From my mother's sleep I feel into the State,
And I hunched in its belly till my wet fur froze.
Six miles from earth, loosed from its dream of life,
I woke to black flak and the nightmare fighters.
When I died they washed me out of the turret with a hose.'

I prefer my story."

Turrets in the Big League

"'12,000ft. Oxygen check,' brings satisfactory replies from all positions from tail turret to nose turret. 'Boy, these guys are the original squirrel hunters' offers one of the gunners, as black puffs appear just off our wing. 'Tail gunner to navigator. There's a plane going down at 5 o'clock. B-24. Left wing on fire.' 'OK, Keep an eye on it and watch for 'chutes.' Silence follows. The gunners scan the skyline for fighters. '18,000ft. Oxygen check.' Everyone answers but the top turret. After a pause, 'Top turret OK.' 'How about trying to stay awake up there?' 'MMmmm.'"—Charles E. Clague Jnr., bombardier, 93rd BG.

At first the Liberator was armed only with a Martin dorsal turret and Consolidated-built tail turret. The B-24C, and the first 82 B-24Ds were armed with seven .50-caliber guns: one in the nose, two in a Martin A-3 turret forward of the wing, two in the waist, and two in a tail turret. Some 2,900 rounds of ammunition fed the guns. Finally, three machine-guns were installed in the nose of the B-24D and a Bendix power turret with periscopic sights provided belly protection before the Bendix turret was replaced by a single handheld tunnel gun. In the Pacific in 1942 where the B-24D was the first significant version to see service with the USAAF, many Ds were modified at the Hawaiian depot so that a tail turret could be installed in place of the Plexiglas nose. The final 93 B-24D-CO models and all subsequent B-24 production models (except the first five B-24Gs) carried the Briggs/Sperry A-13/A-13A retractable ball turret. Experience in the Pacific and European theaters revealed that the Plexiglas-nosed B-24D was vulnerable to head-on attacks by fighters. In the Southwest Pacific the 90th Bomb Group pioneered the installation of a Consolidated tail turret in the nose, while in Europe, two nose guns were lashed together but these proved difficult to operate. The B-24G/H/J series were the first Liberators to have a nose turret containing two .50-inch machine-guns fitted on the production lines but their installation affected overall aircraft performance.

The B-24G was very similar to the B-24D, some having a nose turret containing two .50-inch machine-guns built by Emerson and Consolidated. The B-24G served only with the 15th AF in Italy. The

Both pages: Ambitious victory claims by aerial gunners helped gloss over the fact that, though better than the fixed-gun arrangement, turret guns were little more than a deterrent in the face of fighter attacks. Pictured here are pages from instruction manuals for various types of ball turret. Innovations were largely restricted to improvements like the Martin High Hat, which gave better all-round visibility.

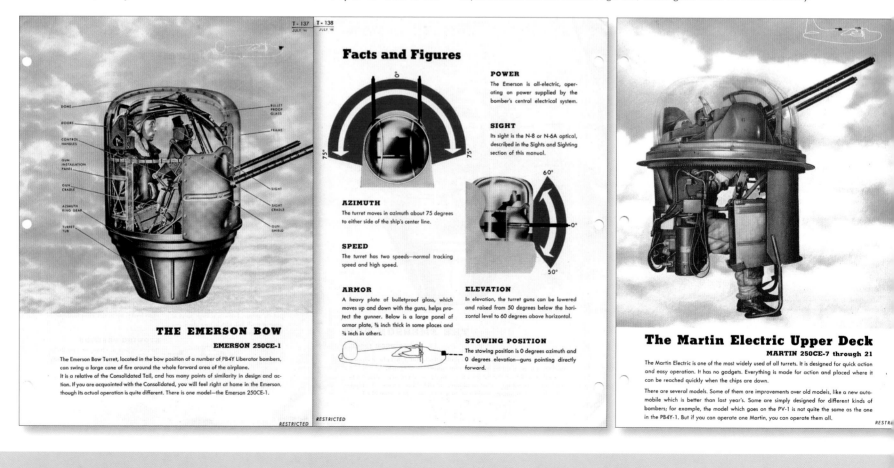

THE EMERSON BOW
EMERSON 250CE-1

The Emerson Bow Turret, located in the bow position of a number of PB4Y Liberator bombers, can swing a large cone of fire around the whole forward area of the airplane.
It is a relative of the Consolidated Tail, and has many points of similarity in design and action. If you are acquainted with the Consolidated, you will feel right at home in the Emerson, though its actual operation is quite different. There is one model—the Emerson 250CE-1.

Facts and Figures

POWER
The Emerson is all-electric, operating on power supplied by the bomber's central electrical system.

SIGHT
Its sight is the N-8 or N-6A optical, described in the Sights and Sighting section of this manual.

AZIMUTH
The turret moves in azimuth about 75 degrees to either side of the ship's center line.

SPEED
The turret has two speeds—normal tracking speed and high speed.

ARMOR
A heavy plate of bulletproof glass, which moves up and down with the guns, helps protect the gunner. Below is a large panel of armor plate, ⅝ inch thick in some places and ⅜ inch in others.

ELEVATION
In elevation, the turret guns can be lowered and raised from 50 degrees below the horizontal level to 60 degrees above horizontal.

STOWING POSITION
The stowing position is 0 degrees azimuth and 0 degrees elevation—guns pointing directly forward.

The Martin Electric Upper Deck
MARTIN 250CE-7 through 21

The Martin Electric is one of the most widely used of all turrets. It is designed for quick action and easy operation. It has no gadgets. Everything is made for action and placed where it can be reached quickly when the chips are down.

There are several models. Some of them are improvements over old models, like a new automobile which is better than last year's. Some are simply designed for different kinds of bombers; for example, the model which goes on the PV-1 is not quite the same as the one in the PB4Y-1. But if you can operate one Martin, you can operate them all.

RESTRICTED

B-24G and H carried ten .50 caliber guns with 4,700 rounds of ammunition, paired in the nose, top, belly, and tail turrets, and at hand-operated mounts in the waist. Waist windows were provided on later blocks. The all-electric Emerson nose turret was introduced on the Consolidated B-24H in June 1943. A total of 6,678 B-24Js were built by all five Liberator plants, the greatest number of all Liberator variants. Convair used hydraulically operated Consolidated nose turrets, but from spring 1944 both San Diego and Fort Worth changed to Emerson nose turrets only, while Douglas built all 582 with the electrically operated Emerson turrets. Two other types of nose turret—the Consolidated with staggered guns and the hydraulically operated Motor Products turret (an improved version of the Consolidated turret)—were also used in the tail.

The B-24L differed from previous models primarily in having a lighter tail turret designed by Consolidated's Tucson Modification Center, which gave a greater field of fire, was easier to manipulate, and saved 200lb (91kg) in weight. It contained two handheld .50-inch machine guns. Consolidated built 417 B-24Ls at San Diego, but only 186 of these received the handheld guns in hydraulically assisted M-6A "stinger" tail mounts (which were also used on some B-24Js). The rest were fitted with standard turrets and it was not uncommon for the M-6A installation to be replaced in the field by an A-6 turret or an open twin-gun mount. Tests carried out using a Bell power boost twin .50 caliber mounts in a modified B-24D nose proved quite successful, but was not proceeded with. Consolidated and Ford were the only plants to build the B-24M, which was fitted with a light power tail turret.

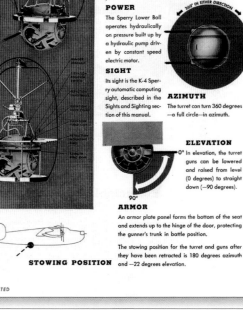

The Sperry Retractable Ball Turret

SPERRY 250SH-1

The Sperry Lower Retractable Ball mounted in the belly of the PB4Y-1, is the deadly and efficient defender of the bomber's once soft underside. It was built especially for the PB4Y-1 whose ground clearance calls for a ball turret that can be kept out of the way on takeoffs and landings. Its guns sweep in a full circle and offer protection from any fighter who dips below the bomber's level. Its sight, the Sperry K-4, computes deflections automatically even when the gunner, swinging around below the plane, is unable to tell exactly which way he is facing.

FACTS AND FIGURES

The retractable mechanism to pull the turret up into the belly of the bomber is simple. The big hydraulic cylinder is secured to a supporting beam in the top of the plane and the turret is suspended from a piston riding within the cylinder. A hand pump mounted on a fuselage wall supplies hydraulic pressure to force the piston up and raise the turret, which can be locked in place with safety hooks on the upper trunnion housing. A valve on the fuselage releases the hydraulic pressure and permits the piston and turret to slide down.

POWER
The Sperry Lower Ball operates hydraulically on pressure built up by a hydraulic pump driven by constant speed electric motor.

SIGHT
Its sight is the K-4 Sperry automatic computing sight, described in the Sights and Sighting section of this manual.

AZIMUTH
The turret can turn 360 degrees —a full circle—in azimuth.

ELEVATION
0° In elevation, the turret guns can be lowered and raised from level (0 degrees) to straight down (—90 degrees).

ARMOR
An armor plate panel forms the bottom of the seat and extends up to the hinge of the door, protecting the gunner's trunk in battle position.

The stowing position for the turret and guns after they have been retracted is 180 degrees azimuth and —22 degrees elevation.

STOWING POSITION

RESTRICTED | RESTRICTED

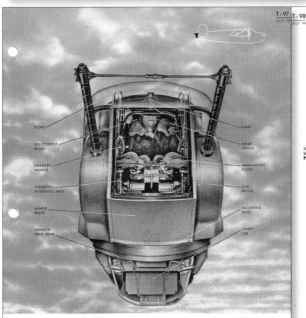

THE CONSOLIDATED TAIL

CONSAIR 250CH-3 OR M.P.C. 250CH-6

The Consolidated tail turret is a double stinger in the tail of the PB2Y-3 Coronado and the PB4Y Liberator. In some Liberators it is also used as a bow turret. It is a versatile gun mount providing a large cone of fire.

There are two models—the original Consair 250CH-3 and the new MPC 250CH-6, which is now in general use and has some marked mechanical improvements.

In operation the two models are basically the same.

RESTRICTED

Facts and Figures

POWER
The Consolidated Tail operates hydraulically, on pressure built up by a hydraulic pump driven by a constant speed electric motor.

AZIMUTH
The turret moves in azimuth about 75 degrees to either side of the ship's centerline — from almost straight out to the left to almost straight out to the right.

SIGHT
Its sights is the MK 9 reflector described fully in the Sights and Sighting section of this manual.

ARMOR
A bulletproof glass panel, 2⅛ inches thick, protects the gunner in front. Directly below it is a ⅞-inch armor plate panel, and to the right and left of the gunner's knees are two more small panels, ⅜ inch thick.

ELEVATION
In elevation, the turret guns can be lowered and raised from 45 degrees below the horizontal level to 71 degrees above horizontal.

STOWING POSITION
The stowing position for turret and guns is 180 degrees in azimuth and 60 degrees in elevation—guns pointed back from the tail and two-thirds of the way between level and straight up.

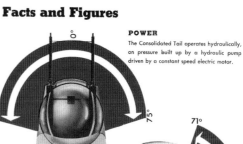

The Kid Rides Again

Sergeant William "Billy The Kid" McCullah, a ball and nose turret gunner in the 712th Bomb Squadron, in the 448th BG at Seething, Norfolk, from 1943 to 1944, remembers a duel at 20,000ft [6,096m], when he was manning one of the waist guns—and how the new ball turret gunner panicked at his first taste of action:

"Once when we were not flying lead I took the right waist [gun position]. That left the ball turret for the new gunner. We dropped our bombs and were on our way home when we lost an engine. Unable to keep up, we fell behind our formation. We flew alone, 2,000yds [1,829m] behind the first section and a mile in front of the second section. With an engine out we were a cripple—a dangerous situation. Sure enough, fighters commenced to attack. One of the fighters broke away, flying a parallel course to our line of flight. He was far in the distance, a speck. The new gunner had not yet entered the ball turret and it was high time that he did. With a possible fighter attack pending, I indicated for him to get into the turret. He violently shook his head, 'No.' That was mildly disturbing. I watched as the German fighter gained a position athwart us, 90 degrees off our right wing.

"'Fighter coming in, 3 o'clock level two thousand yards,' I said over the intercom. Exactly what I wanted him to do! 'Come on. Come on, you Bastard!' I said to myself, squeezing off 20 rounds to warm my gun. Excited chatter began over [the] intercom. My crew, aiding, abetting, urged me on. Still out of my range, the Focke Wulf fired his 20mm cannons at us. I positioned my waist gun behind and above him (allowing for bullet drop). The right outer circle of my three-ring rear sight was centered on the iron bead of my front post. It was a maximum deflection shot. At 1,100yds [1,006m], I commenced firing. The deafening sound of my gun got the full attention of the new ball gunner . . . He jumped onto my back, wrestling me, spoiling my aim and pulling me from my gun! He panicked! (What in hell was he trying to do?) One of the other gunners grappled him, pulling him off [and] holding him in a headlock! I went back to work.

Right: Amazing photos of Focke Wulf 190 pilots attacking B-24 formations show the skill deployed in head-on attacks. High closing speeds meant shooting enemy fighters down was nearly impossible, and FW 190s picked out stragglers in their droves.

"The FW 190 was eating the distance. On the last 500yds [457m], I braced my right elbow hard against my waist to prevent gun climb. I locked the trigger, firing full blower, 850 rounds per minute. His apparent motion increasing, the closer he got, the faster he seemed to fly . . . " [McCullah trailed off when recounting this story, so it is unknown whether or not he hit the attacking fighter—but he lived to tell the tale!]

While most B-24s in England had their ball turrets removed in 1944—many were faired over or used to house radar equipment—on the "Carpetbagger" Liberators (used on night air drops over occupied Europe: see pages 66–67), they became cargo hatches nicknamed "Joe Holes," through which secret agents, or "Joes," dropped. A static line was installed for them and, to facilitate bailouts, the hole had a metal shroud inside the opening. If the Liberator did not have a ball turret, a hole was made there instead. Charles D. Fairbanks, the ball turret gunner in Lieutenant W. G. McKee's crew which arrived in England in November 1943, recalls one of the seven night missions that the crew flew in May 1944:

"Plywood was used to cover the floors and blackout curtains graced the waist windows and navigator's compartment, while blister side windows were installed to give the pilots greater visibility. Later models had their nose turrets removed and a 'greenhouse' was fashioned instead to allow the bombardier a good view of the drop zone and to enable him to assist the navigator by spotting landmarks. Suppressors or flame dampers were fitted to the engine exhausts to stifle the telltale blue exhaust flames. Machine-guns located on both sides of the waist were removed, leaving only the top and rear turrets for protection. In flight the entire aircraft would be blacked out except for a small light in the navigator's compartment. Oxygen equipment was not needed at the low levels flown, and was removed. At the same time a variety of special navigational equipment and radar aids had to be installed. The aircrews learned that during the non-moon period, flights at night would be made with the use of 'Rebecca' [an air-to-ground device that enabled the navigator to home in on the drop zone] and an absolute radio altimeter. By means of all this equipment, a greater degree of accuracy could be achieved on a drop than was possible even with ordinary visual pilotage.

"Since the Carpetbaggers had no ball turret I was moved to the tail. At Alconbury [in Cambridgeshire] we were assigned 'C' for Charlie, a B-24D Liberator painted dull matt black. The 'C' and the serial number were about the only markings on it. There were no large emblems on the wings. Later, about halfway through our tour we were given B-24Js with the nose and ball turrets out [too] . . .

"I recall one clear night with a full moon. We were just on top of a haze layer and the moon was reflecting off the layer. It gave a very definite horizon. All at once I saw an airplane coming from my right. A Me-110 was so close I could see both people in the 'greenhouse' on top of the aircraft. He was maybe 100ft [30m] above us. It seemed to me he was a sitting duck but we had orders not to shoot unless we were shot at so I didn't open fire. He floated right on by. Another night we were just cruising along nice and quiet. The noise of the aircraft kind of blows itself out after a while and you can't hear it any more. Suddenly, it sounded as if someone was shaking a couple of buckets full of rocks. All of a sudden the Ju-88 had banked toward us and started shooting. It was machine-gun fire I'd heard. The ball turret hatch was clear and I watched him go underneath. We didn't get hit. The Ju-88 made one pass and never came back. We didn't get one hole in the aircraft."

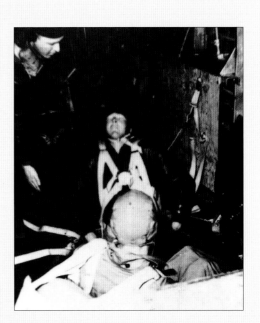

Above: A parachutist tries out the "Joe Hole"—named for the "Joes" dropped through it—in a Carpetbagger Lib.

Below: Crew of Lt. W. G. McKee (far left, standing) in the Carpetbaggers at Harrington in 1944.

The Tail Gunner

"[When] we arrived at the 44th 'Flying Eightballs' Bomb Group base at Shipdham, an officer's driver came over to us and asked, 'Who's the tail gunner on this crew?' I told him I was. He said 'See that B-24 over there?' pointing to a bullet-ridden plane on the runway. 'It got a direct hit in the tail today and they're sucking out what's left of the tail gunner.' Some welcome, I thought, but they're not going to do it to me!"

—Eddie S. Picardo, tail gunner, 44th Bomb Group

Positions on the B-24 crew were interchangeable, none more so than the gunnery positions. It was quite commonplace for a trained aerial gunner to fly alternate missions in the tail, waist, or nose turret position while, on occasion, the radio operator would man one of the waist guns and the other waist gun might be manned by the armorer. The man who rode the tail turret was the man "who looked steadily at the past." Apart from being an excellent gun position, the tail gunner's station provided a convenient location for a copilot to check on formation. The tail turret, like the ball, nose, and top turret, sported twin .50s and all were equipped with fire interrupters to keep the gunners from shooting themselves down. Being flexible .50 calibers, the waist guns could shoot down their own airplane, usually by firing into the wing, rupturing a fuel cell, or shooting off their own tail and causing the tail gunner much consternation. Nothing, however, protected their friends in formation around them from any overexcited gunner. The tail gunner did not enter the turret until the B-24 was airborne and he was not supposed to land in it. If he did, the whip and acceleration

Left: Consolidated rear gun turret on the B-24H Liberator, which was armed with twin .50 caliber machine guns. The hydraulically operated Motor Products turret was also used in the tail.

could pitch his head on to the gunsight when the main wheels impacted. Some tail gunners considered the Consolidated turret a sturdy mount for the guns, and could shoot more accurately with it than with the power-boost Stinger turret fitted to a few of the later B-24s. The Stinger turret was less cluttered and gave better visibility, but the Consolidated gave more protection.

Although he was the assistant radio operator, Forrest S. Clark flew his first mission on November 5, 1943 as tail gunner. "We had just passed over the Dutch coast. I had never seen the sky so steely blue and such good visibility. I could see for many miles to the rear. We were in one of the lead groups and I could see spread out behind us most of the entire formations of the US 8th Air Force. 'What a sight. What am I getting into? Wow. I never saw so many aircraft,' I said to myself as I swiveled the turret about to check the operating mechanism. I looked down at the line of the coast as we passed over, a thin line edging a blue sea, the North Sea. We were bound for Germany and the target was the industrial city of Münster. We were on oxygen having exceeded the 10,000–12,000ft [3,048–3,657m] altitude. I could smell the rubber of the oxygen facemask and the faintly sweet odor of pure oxygen. It gave me a little high, a kind of euphoria of the heights.

I asked myself if I had remembered to check everything and if the guns would work when called on to do so if there was an attack. Many times I checked the .50 caliber cartridge belts. The air was smooth and there was little or no turbulence. We were making our way inland over Nazi occupied Europe now and yet no enemy fighters were in sight. I thought this might be a 'milk run' and began to think of life back at the base.

"Just then a violent vibration shook the plane and it seemed to rear up in the front dipping the tail section downward, 'We've been hit,' was the call over the intercom. 'Check for damages. Any reports? All report in.' Again and again the plane rocked from side to side. From then on all hell broke loose. I saw planes going down, flaming wreckage as planes exploded and others spiraling down leaving a trail of smoke. Suddenly, I had more respect for the small blackish clouds. I realized that the war had begun for me and that the enemy was actually after us, after me, and I began to sweat through my heated suit and nervously pressed the facemask to my face. This was my baptism under fire, in a tiny cramped turret 25,000ft [7,620m] over Germany on the way to Münster with a load of 500 pounders [227kg bombs]. We were lucky and got back to the base. I thought, 'If I see anything with a wing and a propeller and it points its nose at us, I'll shoot.'"

Page right: *Convair rear turret (top two photos) with gunner's yoke or Clark Control Valve (DO5C), which hydraulically operated the turret's side-to-side movement and the gun's vertical moves (note the two triggers); above it is the N-6A optical gunsight, protected by armor plate and bulletproof glass; the ammunition belt feed track (below right); and the escape exit area (below left).*

46 MORE BLASTS AT THE AXIS...thanks to PLASTIC

McDONNELL Aircraft Corp.

Manufacturers of PLANES · PARTS · PLASTICS · SAINT LOUIS

Armored Glass and Plexiglas

Lightweight armored glass helped to offset the weight of the ammunition load and of boilerplate added to the cockpit sides. In reality, though, the lighter weight of the Plexiglas—for safety first and foremost—was quickly counterbalanced by the fact that crewmembers would carry as much ammo as possible for use against fighters, especially on long missions, and also often stowed more than one heavy flak suit for protection from shrapnel.

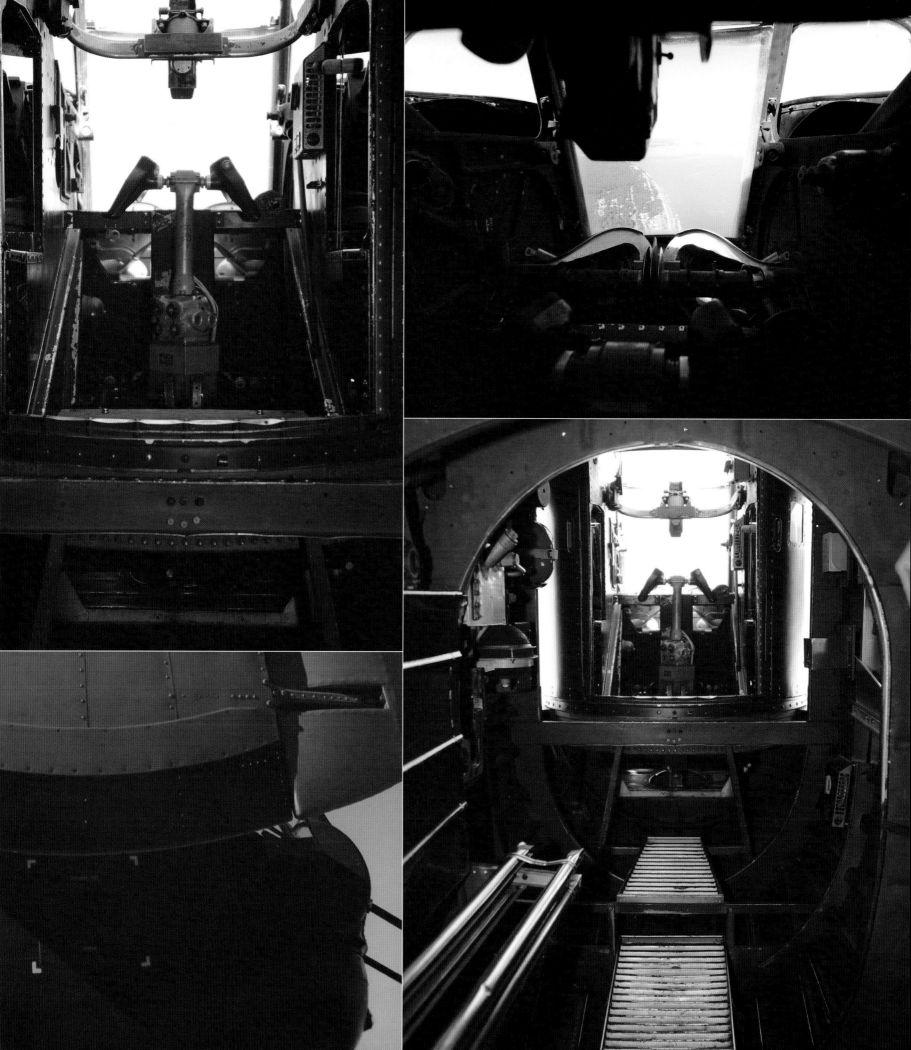

Innocence and Death

Most crews were fatalistic and Forrest S. Clark was no exception.

"The night before the Oslo raid, [on] November 18, 1943, Sergeant 'Alabama' Gilbert got into a heated and lengthy blackjack game. Finally, he lost all his pay and threw down his wallet. 'I won't be needing that any more,' he said. Next day as we came up the Skaggerak and the Oslo Fjörd I could see everything plainly etched in newly fallen snow. Sitting in the tail position, I could look back and see a line of seven to ten fighters lining up to attack our rear. 'They're waiting in line to get at us,' I called over the intercom, pressing the mike to my throat. Suddenly they attacked from all sides. Two shells went through the turret directly over my head, missing me by inches. I followed one after the other as the *Luftwaffe* pilots zoomed in at our tail and then dove beneath us to come up in front, swing, and line up for another pass. One after another they came.

Closer and closer. I tracked them with my twin .50 caliber guns, but could not get a good lead on any until they passed under us and then shot up again for the waist gunners to get shots at them. Finally, I fixed one in my sights as he leveled out and came in faster and faster. 'So close,' I said to myself. 'He's going to hit us: he's going to ram us.' I gripped the triggers of both guns, leveled them out and pressed down. I kept holding the triggers down, hoping they would not jam the belts. I could see my tracers going out in long lines right into his wing roots. Bright flashes of fire and traces kept boring into his wings until he came so close I could see the outline of the German pilot's head in the cockpit. Just as he slipped under us I saw a thin trail of smoke coming from the engine.

"Some 62 2nd Division men were lost and 'Alabama' Gilbert was one of those who never returned. We cleaned out his clothes and found a

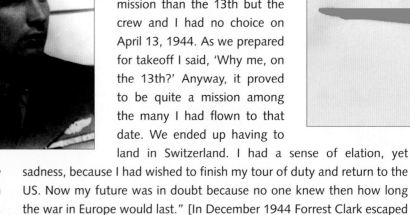

dollar bill. It seemed that the more we faced death, the more superstitious we became about everything. I would have preferred another date for a mission than the 13th but the crew and I had no choice on April 13, 1944. As we prepared for takeoff I said, 'Why me, on the 13th?' Anyway, it proved to be quite a mission among the many I had flown to that date. We ended up having to land in Switzerland. I had a sense of elation, yet sadness, because I had wished to finish my tour of duty and return to the US. Now my future was in doubt because no one knew then how long the war in Europe would last." [In December 1944 Forrest Clark escaped from Switzerland with the aid of US agents in Berne and the French Resistance, making his way to Lyons, France, just before Christmas 1944, during the Battle of the Ardennes.]

Above left: *Technical Sergeant Forrest S. Clark, pictured here, was a tail gunner in the 44th "Flying Eightballs" Bomb Group at Shipdham for much of 1943 to December 1944.*
Below and left: *Booklets like* You Can't Miss It *(the stock answer when GIs asked for directions in England) and friendly cartoons helped to keep aircrews up to date. "Sad Sack" was a famously sloppy cartoon character.*

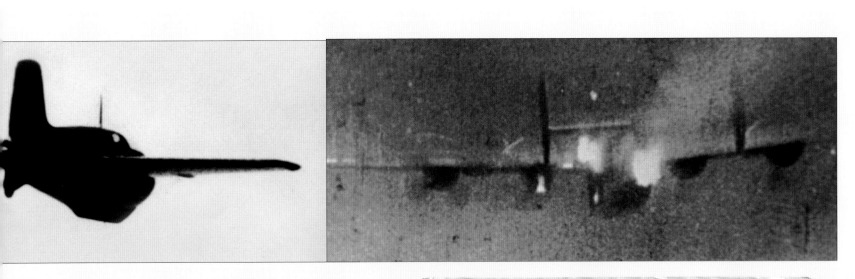

Above left: The tailless Messerschmitt Me 163 Komet rocket-powered interceptor was one of Germany's Wunderwaffen (wonder weapons) but it arrived too late, and in few numbers, to pose a serious threat.
Above right: A solitary Lib—especially one already damaged by flak and with engines out—was easy prey for enemy fighter pilots, who favored fast passes against the nose or tail, with deadly results.

Tail gunners had to keep a cool head—and steady hands—at all times. The tail turret was often vulnerable to fighter attack, and there was always the risk that the occupant could become trapped. This is what happened to John Rickey, tail gunner, *G.I. Jane Pallas Athene,* **578th Squadron, 392nd Bomb Group, piloted by Captain Neele Young. Rickey could not remember any one specific mission that was the worst but he remembers one where an airplane flying on their right wing received a direct flak hit—either that, or one of their bombs exploded prematurely:**

"It caused him to go down and did a lot of damage to our *G.I. Jane* plane. It severed a control cable to the tail turret hydraulic pump and twisted the tail turret around so that I couldn't get out. But they cranked it around by hand and I went forward to the flight deck for the rest of the mission. Another time my flying suit shorted out and my socks caught on fire. That was some sight, seeing me come out of my turret tearing off my boots and socks and beating out my smoldering socks."

Right: Aircraft recognition was a difficult part of an American aerial gunner's existence in combat. Enemy fighters were fast and nimble, and left little time for positive recognition. It was commonplace for bomber gunners to mistake their "Little Friends" for the enemy.

Stone-Cold Fear

Staff Sergeant John W. Butler flew a few missions as tail gunner, including one to Emden, Germany, in *Exterminator*.

"It was 39° below zero. My heated suit worked very good back in the tail. Being a tail gunner was nice as you had armor around you and all the bad stuff has gone by. We ran into a lot of flak at the target and it was pretty accurate. I heard a loud noise in the tail and I got out of the turret to see where we were hit. The flak [had] put a large hole in the vertical stabilizer. Then some fighters came in at 6 o'clock and in my hurry to get back in the turret I pulled my heated connection off on my right boot so my gloves and boots were not working. I checked all my circuits and even checked my fuzes. I was beginning

Both below: Flak and fighters knocked out tail assemblies and devastated gun turrets, which, once out of action, allowed Fw 190s and Bf 109s to home in to administer the coup de grâce. Against the odds Margaret Ann *(left) in the "Flying Eightballs" made it back.*

Above: Olive drab and natural metal B-24s of the 44th "Flying Eightballs" Bomb Group in formation. Late in the war, aircraft were no longer painted; this saved weight, sped up production, and enabled a modest increase in speed. (Tail code markings were retained.)

to become real cold. Then I happened to check my right boot. I put the plug back in and the heat came back to my feet and hands again. A Ju 88 came in on the tail but he was gone before I could get a shot in. I fired around 30 rounds at some Me 109s but no results. Flak also hit us in the waist. The tunnel gunner passed out from lack of oxygen. [An additional crewmember, the tunnel gunner was located in the underbelly of the B-24D, to give that model some added firepower; this was before the introduction of the ball turret gun.] He fell forward on top of the camera hatch. Flak came through the side of the plane and passed the spot he was in, the lucky stiff . . . [On their return] the Red Cross had hot cocoa waiting for us. It sure tasted good. Harry Fargo, flying tail gunner on *N-for-Nan* froze his hands and feet and they had to land at another field so they could get him to a hospital. *Q-for-Queenie* made a crash landing on our home base but no one was hurt. My guns worked OK.

"I flew another mission in the tail in *O Carole N Chick* when we took off at 07:50 to bomb Cognac airfield in France. It was quite a long way to the target area, which we reached with no mishaps. We were escorted by P-47s and P-38s. Temperature was minus 30°. The weather over the target was 10/10 cloud cover [completely covered by cloud] so we couldn't drop our bombs. We were not allowed to drop our bombs just any place over occupied territory except a direct military target. I had just called the navigator over the interphone that it would be nice if we could run into some flak so we could get credit for a mission, when all of a sudden I had all the flak I wanted. A ship in the 389th received a direct hit. He blew into a million pieces. Two 'chutes came out. The whole wing came off in one piece and it dropped by itself turning lazy circles. It was all on fire and it reminded me of a cartwheel from the Fourth of July."

Butler's 10th mission, in *Birmingham Express* on December 16, 1943, was also eventful:

Above: *The shattered tail turret of a 448th BG Liberator, which limped back to Seething from Buchen, Germany, on March 25, 1945.*

"We took off at 08:40 to bomb Bremen. The flak over the target was very good and Jerry wasted a lot of money trying to shoot us down. My right glove burnt out so I had to get out of the turret to get a new pair. Just when I was getting back in I heard our right gunner firing so I started firing at some yellow-nosed Me 109s. I counted seven. I fired about 100 rounds but couldn't see any hits. Jerry would attack in pairs on a diving approach from 5 to 7 o'clock. I received my first oak leaf cluster to my Air Medal that day. [An oak leaf cluster was awarded on completion of five missions *after* the first five missions. Butler

Rewards for gallantry, determination, and ésprit de corps: *The Distinguished Flying Cross (far left), the Air Medal, and the Silver Star.*

Above: *Back at base, this relieved rear turret gunner ponders what might have been after a flak shell ripped out the lower part of his turret. Although uninjured, the gunner would have lost power and been trapped in the turret until landing.*

received his second oak leaf cluster on February 7, 1944, his 15th mission, flying tail gunner in *Texas Rambler*:] I noticed four Me 109s at about 1,200yds [1,097m], at 7 o'clock. I had my guns set on them to see what they would do. They were just milling around. Then one peeled off and came into attack. I held my fire until he was about 500yds [457m] away. Then I opened up. I fired about 70 rounds. He was then in to about 200yds [183m]. He started to burn and he peeled off toward 8 o'clock. He threw his belly up. I let loose about 30 rounds. He bailed out and the plane started down and then exploded. My right waist gunner shot down an FW 190 and the pilot bailed out as the plane exploded. Also, I was credited with one plane destroyed, so I also received another oak leaf cluster. On my 25th and final mission of my tour when I left the French coast behind I was very happy. I never wanted to see the French coast again except on a postcard or on a newsreel. It was a good mission to finish up on. I was a pretty happy guy when I landed."

Flak and Fighters

Staff Sergeant James H. McMahon in the 409th Bomb Squadron in the "Traveling Circus" was tail turret gunner on *Baggy Maggy* on the March 6, 1944 raid on Berlin:

"We were in the high element and 'coffin corner.' [McMahon does not say precisely where his plane was positioned, but presumably it was the last plane in the last formation.] The sky was perfect, no clouds, which meant that the German fighters were going to come up and that the flak would be accurate. I should have been as nervous as hell but I thought of my brother Thom in a Nazi prison camp and all the other fellows I had seen go down. I figured if I came back, okay, but if I went down it would be for Thom. Thinking this I felt glad. I believed that I was going to die and was fully prepared to die right over the target. I felt that what I was doing was the most important thing I had done on all my nine previous raids. All of the men felt the same way. We felt that if we could hit Berlin and survive we would probably survive to go home. Of course this was rationalizing but it worked for a lot of us.

"All the way into the target the flak was bad and the Jerry fighters sure played hell. Our fighters sure gave them hell, too. I didn't get any

Left: Fred Meisel fought for Germany in World War I, and won the Iron Cross. Inducted into the US Army on December 29, 1941, he helped drive the Japanese out of Dutch Harbor.

shots at fighters till the target. I saw one FW 190 shoot down one of our B-24s, which went into a dive and went straight down. Then all hell broke loose. The flak was terrible at different places going to the target and coming out. It was very heavy over Berlin itself. It looked like we had flown through a black thundercloud as we were going away from the target area. The plane shook and was buffeted and shrapnel hit the ship like a tree branch whipping a metal roof. German fighters were everywhere and lots of the time I didn't get a chance to squirt them. Fighters going away were the hardest to hit. I had a feeling of hate for the Germans and I wished that I could have gotten a clear kill. The group behind us was catching hell. We kept flying through the flak and made two runs on the target. We went directly over the center of the city. It took 20 minutes. Man; there were B-24s and B-17s all over the place. Our bombs hit smack on the target and my heart bled for those damned Krauts down there. The whole lousy place was on fire. Everything was blowing up. Well, after that for a 100 miles [160km] I could see the fires and smoke. Boy did I feel good. I was laughing like hell for some reason. I guess it was because I was still there. We lost six planes on this raid."

In April 1944 the 15th Air Force began bombing oil and transportation targets in the vicinity of the Ploesti oilfields in Romania. One of the airmen who eventually wound up at Cerignola near Foggia, Italy, in the 456th Bomb Group was Sergeant Fred Meisel who had last served in the Aleutians. One of his first missions was on April 21, 1944 when he flew as tail gunner. John L. "Jack" Dupont, his copilot, recalls:

"We set out for Bucharest to bomb the railroad marshalling yards. We were carrying 500lb [227kg] demolition bombs. The weather was bad and we could not see to bomb Bucharest. We tried secondary targets of Tumu Severins and Belgrade with no success. With no fighter escort, we encountered a heavy fighter attack and our plane was badly damaged. We salvoed our bombs and with two engines out, we started across the Adriatic. About halfway across and still losing altitude, we called to the

Left: 15th Air Force B-24s pick their way through flak over the burning oil refinery at Blechhammer, Germany. The oil campaign in Europe cost many lives. A posthumous Medal of Honor was awarded to Lt. Donald Puckett, a pilot in the 98th BG, who tried in vain to get his crippled Lib home after bombing Ploesti on July 9, 1944.

who had climbed down in the turret to retrieve the ball turret gunner's gloves! We immediately jerked him up out of the ball. Kenny assured us he was all right and it wasn't any big deal but we observed that he had totaled his wristwatch in trying to free himself. We managed to maintain our altitude at a little over 200ft [61m] and after making an emergency landing at a field near the Adriatic coast for repair and refueling, we finally reached our base at Cerignola. Our pilot, Rex Wilkinson, was awarded the DFC for this mission. Our plane never flew again due to extensive structural damage and the ball turret gunner had a very frightening ride across the Adriatic, one that he will never forget. Nor will I."

Below: The rear turret position with the doors half closed. Tail gunners liked to keep the doors open but, if the B-24 did not have enclosed waist windows, they would get very cold indeed, as they received an air blast in the back of the turret whenever the bomb bay doors were opened.

Top: Rear of the waist section leading to the Consolidated tail turret. With the doors left open, its occupant could see his waist gunner buddies, giving a greater sense of comfort and well being. (Note the yellow oxygen cylinder, top left.)

Right: The fireman's ax was placed in the crash position behind the bomb bay. It was used to chop through tangled wreckage, and could help get a trapped gunner out.

crew to prepare to ditch. The response was a frantic call from the radio operator, telling us that our ball turret gunner [Sergeant Kenneth Mayberry, or 'Kenny'] could not align his turret to get out. Our total concentration was now on his predicament as we continued to lose altitude. We were now below 500ft [152m] elevation above the water and gradually losing more. Our flight engineer called: they had tried everything and could not get the ball door to align with the ship to release the gunner. In desperation, I headed back into the waist section carrying my .45 automatic and the fire ax. I was determined to somehow get the turret to rotate. To my amazement when I reached the waist, there stood the ball gunner, looking more composed than anyone else. I could see the top of someone's head in the ball turret and was told that it was Fred Meisel, our tail gunner,

Lib' Livery

"Most bombers have fantastic names scrawled across their elongated noses. Many are illustrated by out-of-this-world characters, in brilliant colors . . . A pilot from Maine is apt to come out any rainy morning and find that his plane has been named 'Texas' . . . [top] brass suggested that the names should be ones that could be used in conversations—at tea in Claridge's [the swish London hotel] . . . there were to be no more *Vulgar Virgins*, or *T. Ss.*"— Andrew A. Rooney, *Stars and Stripes*.

The B-24 was lampooned by artists and aircrews alike. Much of the derision originated from the shape—a long, graceful, high-aspect ratio wing, offset by a vast billboard-styled body. But it served as a perfect canvas for Air Force artists and cartoonists the world over. Inspiration came from memories of sweethearts at home, in the form of shapely figures on the noses of the Libs. Like figureheads on ships, they flew through the extremes of the Atlantic to England, the dusty deserts of North Africa to Italy. Some carried their sweethearts' names beneath the artwork, while others made their intentions clear to the enemy with taunts of *Flak Dodger* and *Hitler's Hearse*. They epitomized the spirit of these young aircrews,

Left: Lucky, *in the 409th BS, 93rd BG "Traveling Circus,"* *returned from Ploesti on August 1, 1943, flak hole 'n' all.* Below: 854th BS, 491st BG badge. The colors are those of the 95th Combat Wing, which was deactivated in August 1944—the group joined the 14th Wing.

though their exuberance sometimes landed them in trouble with those in authority. Almost all Liberator nose-art centered on the female nude. Headquarters initiated, without much success, a short-lived campaign to "clean up" the artwork of some of the more revealing models. Their creators responded with skimpy briefs and negligées, which made their designs appear even more alluring. Double entendres like *Virgin On The Verge*, *S.O.L.*, and *Arise My Love and Come With Me* escaped the censor.

One of the greatest influences upon the abundance of work to be found on the noses of aircraft were the superb pin-up calendar girls created by the likes of Alberto Vargas, George Petty, and Gil Elvgren. Vargas' scantily clad females appeared in the magazine *Esquire* well before the catastrophe of Pearl Harbor. Later, the "Varga" girl became the symbol of a serviceman's dreams, and he adorned his

Row below: 8th AF leather patches worn on the A-2 jackets of the crew. The first four are from the 713th, 712th, 714th, and 715th Bomb Squadrons in the 448th BG at Seething. Next is the 784th BS in the 466th BG, then the 392nd BG "Crusaders," and the 329th and 409th Bomb Squadrons in the 93rd "Traveling Circus" BG.

barracks with calendars, and played cards with decks emblazoned with these figures. Then, he set about painting his aircraft. The "Varga" girls appeared throughout the war and became a symbol of the American fighting man.

Another influence was the Li'l Abner comic strip characters created by the legendary Al Capp, who had begun his salty satirical strip in the Depression year of 1934. The hillbilly village of Dogpatch, which satirized Washington and its Presidents from Franklin D. Roosevelt onward, introduced Abner Yokum, the innocent country boy and his community of rural loafers and greedy politicians. At its peak the cartoon strip featured in 900 newspapers, and many Britons' first introduction came from the comic sections of American newspapers which were wrapped round postwar food parcels.

Walt Disney's Mickey Mouse (which also lent its name to the "Mickey" radar bombing aid) and Donald Duck, and Warner Brothers' Bugs Bunny also appeared on B-24s. Others were unique creations of single Liberator groups and squadrons. In 1942 the 44th Bomb Group, soon to join the 8th Air Force in England, called themselves the "Eightballs" after the black ball in the game of pool. The 44th was broken up to form other groups and those personnel that remained kept the moniker the "Eightballs." A distinctive emblem was designed, and was painted on the nose of each of the group's B-24Ds. When the 44th began flying to England in late 1942 the group became known as "The Flying Eightballs" and each aircraft sported a

Left: 707th BS and 706th BS, 446th Bomb Group leather patches worn by crewmembers at Bungay (Flixton), in Suffolk.

Both below: The 44th BG "Flying Eightballs" was among the most famous B-24 groups in the ETO. The unofficial insignia adorned not only all of its early B-24Ds, but also featured on a Christmas card (left) and a wall, still visible today, in the 14th CBW HQ site at Shipdham, Norfolk. The nose shows the four squadron colors.

FROM "SOMEWHERE IN ENGLAND" THE "FLYING-EIGHT BALL" BRINGS BEST WISHES FOR

A MERRY CHRISTMAS AND GOOD CHEER FOR THE COMING YEAR

black "Eightball" with a nose, wings, and a bomb for a body. The list of artwork is endless, and their origins manifold. Some named their Liberators for their favorite drink, movie, or girls, while others painted *Consolidated Mess* on their B-24, which sums up the humorous and often masochistic "respect" Liberator crews had for their aircraft.

Tail-End Charlies

On May 10, 1944 Staff Sergeant Wally Robinson, tail gunner in William "Jug" Wright's crew in the 767th Squadron, 461st Bomb Group, 15th AF, flew his 10th mission, to the Messerschmitt factory at Wiener-Neustadt in Austria. Robinson wrote:

"About 30 enemy fighters were concentrating on our group as we approached, attacking from the front . . . By the time I saw them from the tail turret they were practically out of range, the combined speed of the fighter and the bomber going well over 500mph [804kmh]. When we got to the target the fighters left and the flak took over. The sky . . . was full of it, and it didn't seem possible that we could fly through it. We started taking hits all over the plane. Shrapnel came through the bottom of my turret and rattled around me, but I wasn't hit. However, the track carrying the ammo to the turret was cut off, though I didn't realize this until we got out of the flak area and the fighters came at us again. I started shooting, and after firing a few bursts, the guns quit—but I kept the guns and turret moving anyway to make the fighters think I was still in business. The B-24 on our right dropped back and started down. I counted ten 'chutes. Another was spinning and burning but there were no 'chutes from this one. Our P-51s were coming in now and there were dogfights all around us, and a lot of the fighters were going down too. A few P-38s were out there as well and I saw one turn into a ball of fire . . . A Liberator from another group slid in behind us with an engine out. We were having engine trouble, too, and were dropping behind the formation, so we 'escorted' the other B-24 back to Italy and luckily weren't spotted by any of the *Luftwaffe*. Jug made a remark back at the base that I'll never forget: he said that when the 109s were coming in, their guns looked as big as GI cans. We got 33 new holes on this mission."

Right: *A rear view of a B-24 tail gunner, crammed inside his turret and concentrating furiously. He is wearing a B-8 back parachute pack, and a yellow-painted walk-around bottle is stowed on the right.*

Left: *Ed Chu with George Walker, a young English friend, pictured at Seething in 1944.*

Back in England, in his 1945 mission diary Ed Chu vividly described fending off enemy attacks:

"I was the tail gunner with pilot Gordon Brock's crew, 714th Squadron, 448th Bomb Group. Much of what happened in the front of the plane was not known to us in the back—in flight, myself and waist gunners Deane and Anthony, who were in the rear half of the plane, were in our own little world, separated by the chasm called the bomb bay, and [we] only knew what was going on up front through the intercom. Fortunately, we never completely lost communication with the front end.

"Mission 16: Target, underground oil storage depot, Buchen, Germany. March 25, 1945. Duration 7 hours 30 minutes. Before the IP,

Max, our copilot, called 'bandits in the area.' I saw three planes approaching out of the sun at 6 o'clock level. When they got within range, I recognized them as Me-262s. I opened fire at approximately 1000 yards [.9km] at the closest one; I continued firing until he broke away through the squadron toward 2 o'clock high. I observed no hits or damage to confirm hits, although my tracers appeared to go right into the jet. P-51s [then] boxed one up in front of the squadron, and he exploded. Out of the corner of my eye, I could see the plane on our left wing flying the left element—'Purple Heart Corner'—peel off, and in flames. No 'chutes were observed, and the plane was later seen hitting the ground and exploding. Another Me-262 appeared at 6 o'clock and this time I opened fire at extreme range. My left gun jammed, the ammo locking up in the booster motor sprockets. P-51s kept this jet from the formation.

"P-51s and P-47s dove by our formation after [more] jets, one P-47 cutting real close to our tail. I saw a B-24 explode and another one spin down in flames, as jets hit a trailing squadron . . . Another plane flying off our left wing feathered an engine and dropped behind.

"Mission 18: Target, jet airfield, Parchim, Germany. April 4, 1945. Duration: 7 hours 50 minutes . . . At the IP there were broken clouds beneath, with the ground visible in glimpses. Mendus, our top turret gunner, called two unidentified fighters at 5 o'clock low which came out of the clouds; they were going in a direction opposite to us and then turned toward our squadron. At extreme range, possibly 2000 yards [1.8km] at 5 o'clock low, I recognized them as Me-262s, and opened fire at the nearest one. I continued firing to point blank range, and could see my tracers going into him. He then dipped below the tail and broke away at 10 o'clock low. As he was coming in, I could see the flashes of his cannon firing from the nose. He was so close that I could see the white of the pilot's face and his helmet when he looked up at us under our tail.

"A moment later, I saw a piece of B-24 fuselage with the tail section intact and attached, falling and twisting slowly down below my turret. I watched it fall until it was quite a ways down beneath our formation; at first, my mind wouldn't register what it was, and then it hit home. Just after this happened, the plane flying right element off our right . . . peeled off out of formation, [with] the number two engine on fire. I could see men bailing out; it looked unreal, like chunks of debris falling

Left: US Army Signal Corps Instruction Sheet for the T-30-C throat mike, which pilots and flight crew wore around the neck, over the larynx, to enable inter-crew radiotelephone communication. Type A-10A and A-14 demand oxygen masks had built-in mikes for inter-crew or radio communication.

off the plane. Again, I didn't realize what I was seeing until I saw the parachute opening out. We counted nine 'chutes and the plane was now a ball of fire.

"On the bomb run . . . I saw a jet approaching the squadron at 5 o'clock low. He climbed and made his attack from 6 o'clock high. I noticed puffs of black smoke as he fired his cannon, and he broke off toward 12 o'clock high . . . I had opened fire on him, probably [at] about 1,000 yards [.9km], and continued firing until he was past the limit of my turret. The tracers from the squadron filled the air.

Above: B-24H-25-FO 42-95083 My Buddie in the 714th Bomb Squadron, 448th Bomb Group, pictured on its hardstand at Seething, Norfolk, in 1945. It was flown by Lieutenant Gordon Brock. This particular Liberator, which was built by the Ford Motor Co., survived to the end of the war.

'We didn't drop our bombs on the second run, and eventually brought them back to the base. Our plane suffered no flak or fighter damage, but it was a waste of life. On this mission, I fired half my ammunition, or 700 of my 1,400 rounds. Mendus used up all his ammunition in the upper turret, around 800 rounds, and Anthony and Deane fired quite a bit of their ammunition from the waist."

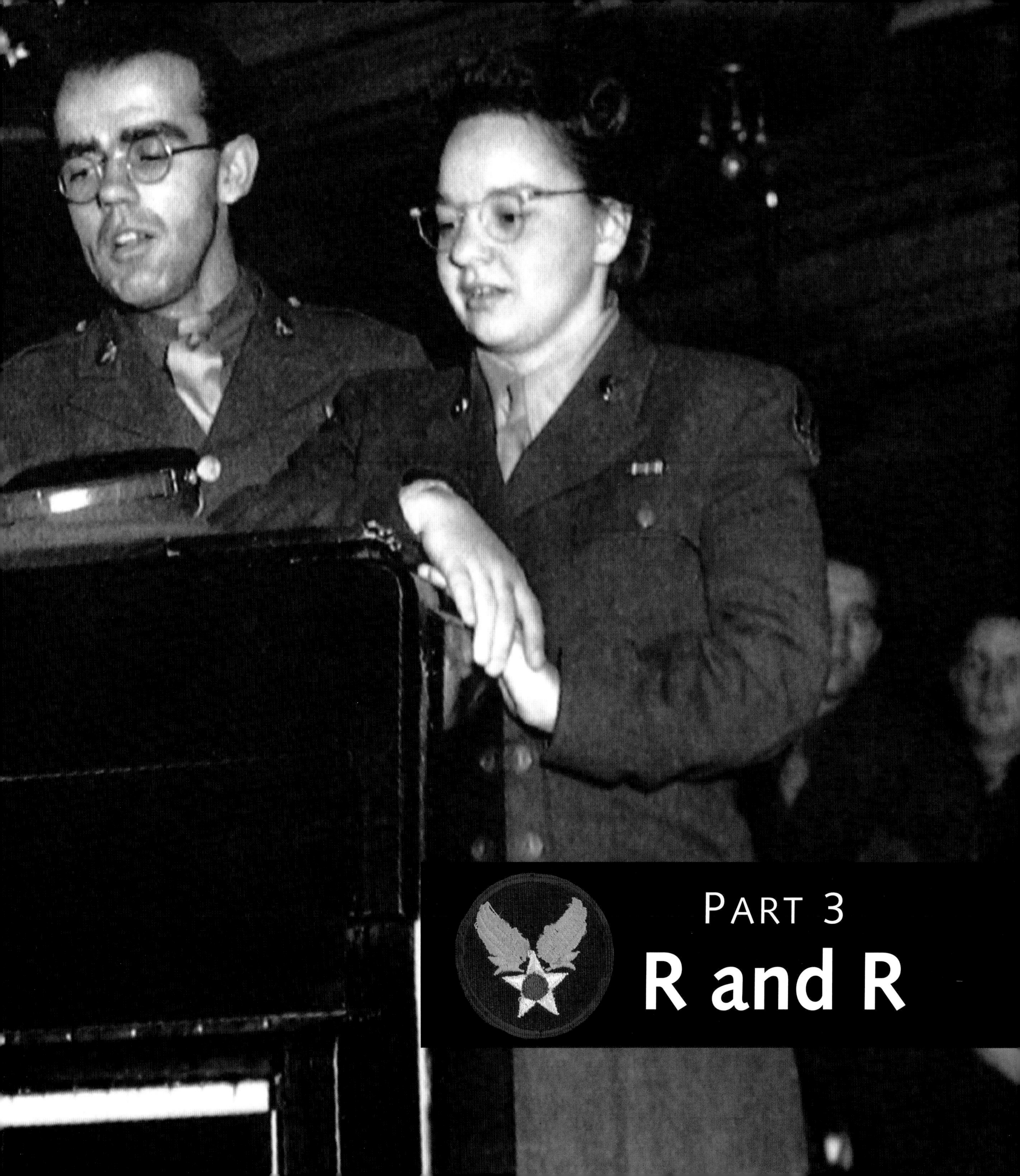

Part 3
R and R

Rest and Recreation

Her mother never told her
The things a young girl should know.
About the ways of Air Force men.
And how they come and go.
Now age has taken her beauty.
And sin has left its sad scar,
So remember your mothers and sisters, Boys,
And let her sleep under the bar.

—Popular wartime ditty (Anon.)

"At Shipdham in the early days of powered eggs and Brussels sprouts," recalls Lieutenant (later Colonel) William Cameron, "we carried our mess gear to the club. Beer was served from a barrel on a rickety table, using our Mess kit cups." At the end we had a fine club, linens, silver, and all the rest, which we paid for, but it was never so welcome. We even built our own movie theater, using materials bought from a bombed-out movie house.

We fixed up a small open bay at the end of our barracks, which was building 200, so we called it the '200 Club.' It was a place for parties and sitting around 'shooting the bull' when we didn't have anything else to do. A favorite stunt was to drop .45 caliber ammo in the little potbellied stove, secretly of course. That used to stir things up. I once let go a smoke bomb . . . almost ruined our clothes and bedding with the stench. On one occasion I was definitely the 'square' of the group . . . It was decided to strip me of my clothes. The girls thought it was very funny but I got as mad as hell (this was about 3am) and almost had a fistfight with Bob Brown, one of my best friends. He would have killed me. I was the type who got into trouble trying to do the right thing . . . like getting transportation for the girls at 4am, when all my buddies went to bed and left them there. On one occasion I woke old 'George' and 'Gentleman' Jim DeVinney at

Below, left to right: Gunners in the crew of Shoot Luke in the 328th BS, 93rd BG at Hardwick get Service Dress or Class A uniforms ready for a three-day pass in London (S/Sgt Floyd Mabee, on the bed, sews a button); crewmen in the 44th BG at Shipdham wait for a bus to take them into Norwich (the nearest liberty town for most B-24 groups in this area) in 1943; inside the 448th BG Officers Mess at Seething.

Below: *Base Consolidated Mess card belonging to Sgt. Charles S. Barlow in the 448th BG at Seething; the back of a meal ticket pass, part of which reads, "This meal ticket must be presented at each meal;" center roundel of a V-Disc, My Pin-Up Girl, from the Fort Hamilton show, Stars & Gripes. V-Discs were supplied by the War Department Music Section.*

5am for the practice mission—not realizing they had a couple of girls in the sack with them—and was met by a barrage of .45 gunshots over my head in the dark. I hit the floor of the hallway and crawled out! They were quite a bunch and when they were gone there was no one who ever quite took their places."

"One of the more hilarious aspects of military life," recalls Ronald D. Spencer, was attendance at GI movies—standard Hollywood movies shown at theaters on military bases: "The worse the movie was, the better we liked it. The typical Grade B movie was what we liked best. The 'show' associated with these movies was the comments by the audience. While always good for a lot of laughs, those at Rackheath were truly hysterical. The theater was a large Nissen hut, perhaps 100ft [30m] long. About 20ft [6m] or so at the back was raised a couple of feet and was reserved for the officers. Hanging from the ceiling just in front of the officers' section was a small platform for the projector and the hapless projectionist. He had a ladder, which he used to climb up to the platform, which he then pulled up and stowed on the platform during the showing of the film. With the more common B pictures, the place was a total zoo. When a rare good picture was available, the audience was a model of decorum. On one memorable night, an actor in the film accidentally killed a young lady, whereupon he more or less looked at the camera and spoke the world's greatest straight line 'what'll I do?' As might be expected, the audience had a number of rather carnal suggestions—one of the better being that he might consider doing something before she got cold. There being a number of Red Cross girls and nurses present, a senior officer arose and said the film wouldn't continue until the culprit identified himself. After a rather lengthy and deafening silence the officer gave up and said to get on with the film. It was all good fun and no one really cared one way or the other since the primary purpose was really to keep us out of bed, or out of trouble.

Above and below: *Enlisted men playing darts, drinking beer, and carousing during a spell of relaxation at Seething. Although racial tensions in the services could at times run high, African Americans received a generally warm welcome from their English hosts, as the pub scene below shows well—the engineer battalion personnel who were building runways at Debach airfield are seen enjoy an evening with the locals.*

"One obvious advantage we had in serving in England during the war was the fact that you lived in a highly civilized country with, relatively speaking, all of the amenities. Off the base, that is. Outside the gate we had pubs, buses, taxis, and within 5 miles [8km] or so a city of some 200,000 people. Thus, we had access to just about

Above: A "tuppenny" (two-pence) program and admission ticket to the Hippodrome Theater in Norwich. Shows were popular with GIs who also liked to dance with, romance, and sometimes marry, the local girls they met at the "Samson & Hercules" ballroom in town.

everything that wasn't rationed or in short supply. Norwich was the obvious destination of choice if you wished to make more of a night of it. The so-called liberty run (Army trucks) left for Norwich around seven and returned somewhere around eleven. The liberty run was a pretty cold, uncomfortable ride which was also a deterrent. Most used the trucks since they were free . . . The typical British

double-deck buses . . . [also] passed by the base so you could take those if the schedule was appropriate. If you really wanted to splurge, you could take a taxi, but I don't ever recall taking the taxi either way. I did walk back to the base once but I don't recall the circumstances. Norwich, being a good-size city, had a lot to offer, subject to shortages of course. It had a legitimate theater, a movie theater, a big dance hall called the 'Samson and Hercules' (better known as the 'Muscle Palace'), a large outdoor market, a castle (mentioned in Robin Hood), the huge cathedral, some restaurants, but best of all a Red Cross club where you could stay overnight and, most important, get a hot bath—a true luxury to us. Most of the troops sampled all of the various spots when they first arrived, with the novelty wearing off after they'd been there awhile. By the spring of 1945, most people hung out in the club on the base as opposed to pubbing or going into Norwich. Also, by that time, the officer's club had so much money in the treasury that they began handing out free beer and sandwiches later in the evening. That was enough of an incentive to stay on the base.

"Another was the occasional party where girls were brought in from town in a bus or buses. The big problem was getting them off the base after the party. Our base was pretty straight in that regard. But some bases were notoriously lax. On one, I was told, they put up a sign on the following Monday saying that all women will positively be off the base by Thursday—I guess to get ready for the following Saturday night's influx. A not unreasonable request, we thought.

"One thing that I always found intriguing was the dichotomy of our lives. During the day you could be deep in Germany exposing life and limb and that night be all dressed up and sitting in a theater in town watching a very good stage show. Sitting all around you were people who

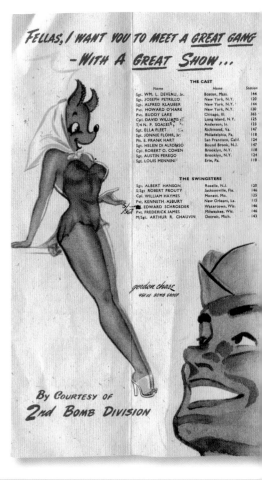

Above: Boating was another favorite pastime; these GIs from Seething have made an ingenious boat from a fighter drop tank!

Below: 2nd Bomb Division, 8th AF souvenir program for "It's All Yours Buddy." Another of the shows, "Skirts," was put on at Norwich's Theater Royal in 1944.

had spent their day in the office or some other mundane place. I'd look at someone next to me and think that while they'd been shopping that morning, I'd been 4 miles [6.5km] over Brunswick at 50 below zero with the flak banging around—wild!"

On one occasion, Ralph H. Elliott decided to go take a look around Great Yarmouth, a coastal resort 20 miles (32km) east of Norwich. He took a noon train and returned to Rackheath about 8:55pm after having had quite a good time. First thing he did at Great Yarmouth was walk along the waterfront, then he went to see a show called *Rose Marie* with Jeanette McDonald and Nelson Eddy. He then had "a real good supper: chicken and ice cream" in a restaurant. By then it was time to catch the train back. John McClane Jr. also visited the resort: "One of the many nice customs I enjoyed in England was that a person could not travel far in any city without coming to a 'fish and chips' stand. For a nominal charge, the vendor dispensed a very tasty, as well as nutritious, 'quick food.' The chips were potatoes . . . cooked in the fish grease. On an outing to Great Yarmouth, we ate our fill of fish and chips out of newspaper, as well as other foods."

Allan Healy recalls that "There were many places we went to. Cambridge was not too far away and for some there was great attraction in its University atmosphere, the Cam, and the 'Backs,' King's College Chapel, the Bull Hotel taken over for GIs, bookstores, and antique shops. We saw the cathedrals, Ely, Peterborough, even York or Durham. The ruined Abbey at Walsingham was not far off. Some few got to Devon and

Above: The American Red Cross Club at the Bull Hotel in Trumpington Street, Cambridge. The town boasted six clubs: five for EM, one for officers. Historian G. M. Trevelyan would meet GIs at the Bull Hotel every Saturday at 4 o'clock.

Below: An Old Buckenham and Seething American Football game in progress in 1944. It gave a welcome bout of fresh air and exercise for these GIs, clearly not sufficiently taken by the English game of soccer to want to take it up instead.

Cornwall, some to Liverpool, or the Lake District. Best of all, perhaps, was Scotland. The girls seemed prettier there, the people less reserved, life a bit more like that in America and yet more foreign, too. You had a fine time, found hospitable people who seemed to like you, and had gotten a long way from the war and the life of the base."

IT'S ALL YOURS BUDDY

8th Air Force, England Souvenir Program

Above: A GI dancing with his date at a London dance hall. Local girls learned new dances, such as the "Jitterbug" and "Jive." The capital was the most popular destination for GIs on a 48- or 72-hour pass.

"By and large the people of England had very good reason to feel that we were 'Over paid, over fed, over sexed—and over here,' recalled Arthur L. Prichard, a copilot in the 467th Bomb Group. "We were well-fed, well-paid— and the well-paid part probably accounted for the 'over-sexed' portion of the saying because the men didn't know how long they would be there or, if [they were] flying personnel, how long they would live. So they flaunted their money and got any favor they could."

William "Bill" Head, a navigator/staff officer in the 445th Bomb Group, believed that the "Four Overs" were justified in many cases: "Many of us Americans had come into the service just out of school or college. We [had] never had a paying job before. Suddenly we became better fed and better paid than we had ever been. Moral restraints from the American family, church, and friends disappeared and 'everything' seemed to be available for the buying, asking or taking. Boasting

seemed to be a popular pastime. We believed that America really was what was depicted in movies and the magazines, although down deep we knew that this wasn't so, I guess. It was a bit of bravado that we had to put on to cover some of our insecurities. I can understand the British Tommy's 'Four Overs' attitude. I can understand how an occupying military force, loaded with money, eating the best food, dating their women would draw resentment from an army that had been at war for years, received low pay and only adequate rations."

Al Zimmerman recalls that "the place to go in London to dance was the converted opera house near Covent Garden. It was here that I first took the floor with a British gal. All was going fine until another girl tried to cut in, grabbed me by the arm and tried to pull me away. I'd been told the English girls were shy and reserved—and here's one trying to pull me away from another! Embarrassed, I just held on to the girl I had, said 'How do you do,' and kept dancing. My partner's immediate reaction was to be offended. What was I doing not taking the other girl? I was bewildered until it was explained that this was a ladies' 'Excuse Me' dance. When a girl tapped your shoulder you changed partners." A lieutenant in the 93rd Bomb Group said that dancing with English girls was "like learning a new language. She is shy, very patient, and tells you she is 'thrilled to death.'"

Lieutenant John W. McClane Jr. had his first experience of a British dance hall in Belfast. "The dance floor was very large with several hundreds of couples dancing. Whereas Americans dance in a small area of the floor, maybe getting around the whole floor once to a

Above: A bicycle permit issued to Charles I. Graves in the 93rd BG at Hardwick on August 28, 1944.
Right: So many bikes ended up being "borrowed" that checks were introduced at Rackheath.

Left: *Contemporary, wartime map of North Suffolk and South Norfolk. The map has marks on it made by Bill Schwinn, showing the places he cycled to on his trips from the base. Cycle trips to pubs, which were near each and every one of the bases, were known as "Pubbing Missions."* Inset: *Bill Schwinn (second from right) and friends on their bicycles outside the control tower at Seething.*

In today's coin, it would be like giving over $1,000. I did have at least two of the three attributes the English credited to all Americans: I was overpaid and I was over there. Money meant nothing to me."

"Bicycling was a major pastime," recalls Allan Healy. "English cycles were issued to many of the ground men. The aircrews felt free to borrow. 'Borrowing' became so bad that on one occasion all cycles were called in by the MPs [military police] and their numbers [were] checked. Many were then returned to their original owners." Myron Keilman, a pilot in the 392nd Bomb Group said, "Can you imagine a gaggle of 18 bike riders charging down those narrow Norfolk roads, in daylight or dark? I can assure you it was not like a Hell's Angels act—it was more like a Wild West scenario where the cowboys came to town after months on the trail and stormed the Longhorn saloon. Nevertheless, these Yanks were totally accepted and—I dare say—appreciated."

dance number, the British move fast, almost run, with the whole floor of couples moving like a wheel. Also, they did not like to talk much or carry out a conversation like American couples do. However, they will all burst out in song if a catchy tune gets their attention. This was our first experience of a mixed group singing *'Roll Me Over in The Clover'*—that to us seemed a little off color for mixed company."

It seemed to McClane that the enlisted men could not hold onto money from one payday to the next. "I gathered from what I heard that within a few days of being paid, all their money was lost in crap games or gambling of some sort. I often would loan them just enough money to get the necessities they needed from the PX; anything more would soon be gone . . ."

Many an afternoon McClane and the Colman family he had befriended would cycle out to Shipdham airbase from Norwich. "Mr. and Mrs. Colman had a tandem bicycle. Mr. Colman, wearing his billed cap, occupied the front seat while Mrs. Colman, pedaling with all her might, sat on the rear seat. Between them they made a picturesque sight. The older daughter and husband often came along. Margaret's bicycle had a wicker basket attached to the handlebars. In it she invariably carried her dog, a small shorthaired terrier. I rode the bike that I kept at the Red Cross in Norwich. Mr. Colman almost had a fit when I told him I bought it for £50 ($25.00) from an airman who had completed his tour of duty.

Above: *Wearing their Class A uniforms and "best pinks," these officers in the 44th BG at Shipdham cycle along a Norfolk country lane near the base during a break from combat in 1943. Cycling was a hazard for some GIs; one has an arm in a sling.*

"Flak Shacks"—the 8th Air Force Rest Homes

"Coombe House and the others like it represent the best work of preventative medicine in the ETO. Very definitely I can say now that rest homes are saving lives—and badly needed airmen—by returning men to combat as more efficient flyers. The natural impersonal friendliness of Red Cross girls who set the atmosphere is a huge factor in making these houses home. Lack of Army demands and freedom from regulations help create the free and easy tempo of the place. The whole feeling is one of such warmth and such sincerity that men come away knowing they have shared an experience of real and genuine living the first and frequently only time while they are over here."—Captain David Wright, Psychiatric Consultant for the 8th Air Force, who once spent six weeks in careful observation to decide upon the value of rest homes.

Air crews known to be "flak happy" were sent to Rest and Recuperation Centers which were better known as "Flak Shacks" or the "Flak House"—"that delightful, full-fed, pleasant English country estate, which helped to cure both operational and flying fatigue." Statistics showed that a remarkable percentage of men who finished their missions had a chance to be in rest homes sometime during their combat tour. At first, the Air Force ran these rest homes alone. After two had been established, a large part of the responsibility was then transferred to the American Red Cross, in an effort to make them as unmilitary as possible. Army Quartermaster outdid itself on food, and "Cooky" in the kitchen cooked it to perfection. Fried chicken, steaks, ice cream, and eggs were regular items on the menu, and they were served by attractive waitresses.

Rest Home For U.S.A. Flyers

This page: *England had at least 17 rest homes, or "Flak Shacks," as they were known, including Coombe House in Shaftsbury, Dorset (above) and Pangbourne House (top and left). They were opened between 1943 and 1944 for use by 8th Air Force Combat personnel suffering from "combat fatigue." These delightful English country mansions were taken over by the military. All were run by the American Red Cross, who ensured that the "flak happy" officers and men received the finest food and were able to relax and enjoy recreational activities in tranquil surroundings.*

Above, left to right: A US officer boating on the Thames at Pangbourne House in Berkshire; 44th BG combat personnel at Walhampton House, Lymington, Hampshire, with an American Red Cross girl; Frederick G. Kieferndorf (left), bombardier, with a Red Cross girl and a fellow flyer at Eynsham Hall, Whitney, Oxfordshire, in 1945.

When Charlie Peretti's crew took official combat leave the enlisted men went to a rest home near Pangbourne, Berkshire (west of London), while the four officers proceeded to the opulent Roke Manor at Ramsey, Hampshire. John McClane recalls: "A reception committee of young ladies attired in attractive civilian dresses greeted the four of us. It was apparent from the first encounter that their duty was to make us feel at home, as if the war were nonexistent. We were escorted to our rooms and given the admonition to chuck our military uniforms in favor of civilian clothing, which had been selected on the way. After being acclimated to uniform dress for so long, the sight of seeing each other in multicolored, checked, and striped shirts and [pants] was almost too much. Our stay was only seven days so we had to make a quick adjustment to our new environment. One of the rules was that we were not to talk about the war or combat. I can't recall a more pleasant week in my life as the stay at Roke Manor."

Captain Alvin D. Skaggs' crew joined the other "flak happy troops" at Moulsford Manor, also in Berkshire, following a mission when a shell burst just 20ft (6m) from their right vertical stabilizer and killed the tail gunner. Again, they were not allowed to wear uniforms but were each issued with an old pair of blue jeans, a shirt, and a pair of tennis shoes. Recreation facilities included tennis, golf, horseback riding, punting on the Thames, croquet and club games such as checkers, dominoes, and cards. There was even breakfast in bed most any time they wanted it from about 6am to 9am, served by a waitress, who would knock on the door at the time requested the night before when the young lady at the desk had asked, *"What time would you like to be knocked up in the morning?"*

Robert Tays' crew, meanwhile, was sent to Knight Hays Court near Tiverton in the Land's End area of Cornwall. "The manor house had 99 rooms, well kept by its owner, vaulted ceilings, fireplaces, dining room, library, game room, and special rooms like one might expect a Knight to have," recalled Tays. "Several thousand acres belonged to Knight Hays, which were worked by his tenants and supervised by gardeners, game wardens, and others. Wearing civilian clothes given to us by the Red Cross, who operated the place, we romped in non-military fashion for 10 days. A herd of cattle grazed nearby so the crew challenged me to ride rodeo style. They were very docile and soon all were riding. The Texas image faded. Playing much bridge, eating well, drinking well, playing golf in civvies, the war was forgotten for a few days."

Right: Between August, 1 1944 and December 31, 1944, the Air Force Rest Homes together accommodated 6,581 officers and 6,809 enlisted men.

Robert Tays recalls that "Once a month, we had a party at the officers club. Eight or ten trucks were sent to the neighboring villages to pick up the young ladies that were eager to entertain or be entertained by those daring combatants. Americans seemed to fascinate these gals. Many of them would love to have married an American and come stateside or, as they would put it, 'move to the colonies.' A good meal was served, followed by dancing and a floorshow. USO (United Service Organization) shows came to us in the hanger, about once a month. Bob Hope, Glenn Miller and many more, a host of comely young gals with each entertainer. The shows were clean and much fun, with

Left and above left: American Red Cross "Donut Cluster" brooch, worn by Red Cross girls; Rainbow Corner was the most famous Red Cross Club and was open 24 hours a day throughout the war.
Right: The London ARC Light (American Red Cross) map, showing events, was published weekly.

down on those special days. The day was filled with parades, athletic events, good food, drink, dance, and endless flying stories. Just another way to make us feel proud of our accomplishments and motivate us to continue to do better. About every two weeks we were given a three-day pass to do as we pleased and relieve the tension of combat. London town was our destination on almost every occasion. Good old London."

During his first trip to the capital in June–July 1943, their first time off base, Jim Johnson and his buddy Hoffman arrived at Liverpool Street Station when a man came up to them and said, "Say, have you gentlemen been to Petticoat Lane?" "Why, no we haven't," they said. "Today is your lucky day, because I just happen to

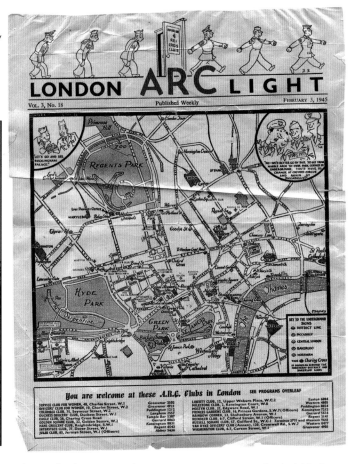

Above: American servicemen enjoy a boat cruise on the river Thames and a view of London's famous landmark, Tower Bridge, on leave on a gloriously sunny day in 1944.

GI participation. For an hour or two, we forgot that we were scheduled to fly tomorrow. A touch of home or something familiar always seemed to lighten the stress load. Glenn Miller played our base just a few days before he was lost. Special parties that lasted all day were the 100th mission and 200th mission party. We were stood

have the last two tickets to Petticoat Lane," he babbled. "Tell you what, I'll let you have them for half a crown each. Taking their money he said, "Now then, walk up those stairs, turn left and you'll soon see Petticoat Lane." They did and soon saw what they took to be a marvelous display of merchandise and wares of many shades and

Art Swanson got to know the Underground subway system very well. "Sometimes I'd see Britishers standing around on a platform looking lost. I'd go up and offer to give directions. Got a kick out of the look on their faces when a Yank told them which train to catch."

One of the things Sergeant Robert "Bob" S. Cox, a mechanic in the 466th Bomb Group liked was "railroad trains." He liked the English railroads. "They were just real neat. The cars ran smooth; they were fast; everything worked good. Seemed like better than ours. But the only chance that I got to ride a train was when we went to London. I only went twice while I was there. London wasn't a bad town but it was tore up."

Major Frederick D. "Dusty" Worthen found out about several American Red Cross clubs that were hotels for the US military. "They were clean and completely adequate, plus they served free coffee and donuts all day and night. The Red Cross is an organization that has to

Both above, and right: Any bomb group that reached the magic number of 100 and 200 missions was stood down for one and two days, respectively, and a party (above, for the 466th BG at Attlebridge) was held on base. On Christmas Eve 1944 a party for 1,250 local children and Blitz orphans was held at Old Buckenham, and toys for 300 French children were flown in B-24 Liberty Run to the ARC Center in Paris.

varieties. Walking up to a woman stallholder Johnson said, "Who collects these tickets?" "What tickets?" Johnson gave them to her and she read, "Admit one to Petticoat Lane." "You've been had. No one has to pay to walk down this street."

Returning from London one very foggy night a few months later Johnson and his buddies caught the train back to East Anglia. The word "Bovril" appeared at one of the stations. Nothing else was on the sign. Later in the journey, said Johnson, "Another GI said to me, 'It's a bad fog, really bad, he's going round in a circle. We've been through Bovril twice before!' We did not know, being foreigners, that Bovril was a drink!"

When Colonel James J. Mahoney and his buddy Spivvy checked in at the Savoy (a swish hotel in London), the clerk said that he had passed their room several times and had heard the water running continuously. He asked if they were aware of the restrictions on the use of water for bathing because of its need for fighting Blitz fires. He also wanted to check to see if they had exceeded the 3in [7cm] allowed for a tub. "He turned off the faucet, pulled a ruler from his pocket and plumbed the depth. Sure enough, we had substantially more than doubled the allowable [quantity], then, despite our vigorous protests, he did the unthinkable—he let that precious hot water go down the drain until it reached the three-inch level on his ruler! *Rules, you know*."

be well respected. How well we would realize this in the future! There were 17 Red Cross clubs scattered around London and their main headquarters, Rainbow Corner, was just off Piccadilly Circus. We chose the Jules Officers' Club on Jermyn Street near Piccadilly where most of the action was. Only once did we venture to another city besides Norwich and London. We spent a 72-hour pass in Cambridge, the university town. I don't know what inspired us to go there. It was unlikely that we were thinking of our higher education there after the war was over. Again, more sightseeing, visiting the university, some good eating, and pretty girls."

Bill Campbell had quite a time "awful drunk out." "We stayed in a place called King's Palace. Some joint, except that half of it had been blown off by buzz bombs. A lot of loose women live here [and] are running in and out of your room constantly. Moved out the next day to the Howard Hotel, uptown; extra nice place—beds a foot thick and a great big bathroom, which we fought over all day and all night. Paid £18 for a quart of Scotch, but it was worth it. Walked around Piccadilly half the night, fooling around with the 'Commandos' [ladies of the night]—swell time. Ate dinner in ritziest places we could find and paid a small fortune for taxi fares." Rufus Webb, a 19-year-old air gunner, remembered meeting a lady of the night around Piccadilly Circus—"a sweet young thing; she came from Scotland. The night we met we had just got back to her room when the alarm sounded. She was terrified and shaking with fear. I remember we got under her bed and I put my arms around her and held her tight all night. For some strange reason I felt really good in the morning—sweet thing, I will always remember her."

W. J. "Red'" Komarek best sums up London: ". . . A city of pomp and splendor, a panorama of history, theaters, restaurants, some of the best pubs in England . . . and plenty of girls. You could go to a dance in Covent Garden and find a ten-to-one ratio of women to men and fifteen-to-one of women to Yanks . . . For the less adventurous, there was the Red Cross Rainbow Corner Club. The neighborhood had a questionable reputation, being in Piccadilly Circus and frequented by . . . 'Commandos.'" Ronald D. Spencer adds that "London was really the major attraction when you got a three-day pass. The train ride took three or four hours. I would stay at a Red Cross Club near Piccadilly Circus. Like the one in Norwich, it had rooms and baths at very reasonable prices. Being close to Piccadilly, it was in the heart of a lot of activities, particularly theaters. A wartime favorite was the Windmill Theater, which took great pride in the

fact that it never closed during the Blitz. It was sort of like a US burlesque but with better comedians. It was at that time that I found that English comedy could be very funny. I occasionally went to a stage show in one of the other theaters. One of the better haunts in London was the Grosvenor House on Park Lane, around the corner from Oxford Street, which had been turned into a very large and sumptuous officers' club. It was a great place to go with food, drinks, and music in a very nice setting. It was a very popular hangout at the time.

Sightseeing was a common pastime in London with many famous places to see. Buckingham Palace was a must, as was Westminster Abbey. I used to stroll through Selfridges [department store] on Oxford Street, which I considered their Macy's. At night, the hookers came out in force. Bed and Breakfast was what they were usually selling. The term obviously has a different connotation today. Prices reached their peak on payday and declined to bargain rates just before the next one. The payday asking price was usually around £10 on payday. This was a truly princely sum, about $43 dollars [about $600 today]. I expect that the negotiated price was a lot lower. With a legitimate office job paying about $20 a week, you could see why a lot of the girls were drawn to the trade. In Piccadilly you'd get propositioned about every ten feet. The standard question for anyone returning from London was 'what are

the latest quotations?' It was somewhat of an academic question since few of those I knew ever partook—a lot of talk, but not much else . . . Unfortunately, after a time even London ceased to interest most people. I think most of the troops tended to be more interested in finishing their tours and going home. In short, the novelty had worn off."

Lieutenant Robert H. Tays in the 392nd Bomb Group concludes, "Yes, we visited Harrods, the Bank of England, Madam Tussaud's Wax Museum, Hyde

Left: *RAF personnel on bicycles at RAF St Mawgan in Wales wave "cheerio" to a B-24 Liberator taxiing prior to making the long flight home to the US in late 1945.*

Opposite page, bottom: *Happy American personnel at Watton, Norfolk, in May 1945 hold up copies of newspapers with the long-dreamed-of headline, "GERMANY QUITS."*

Below: *Victory in Europe (VE) Day celebrations get into full swing with a joyously extravagant firework display at the base at Seething, Norfolk, on May 8, 1945.*

Park, Governor's House, City Hall of London, 10, Downing Street [the British Prime Minister's house], Trafalgar Square, St. James's Park, and all the government buildings. Flyboy on pass gets around by taxi, yes, to see it all. Next day back in the air to who knows where until after briefing . . . VE (Victory in Europe) took place on May 8, 1945. Having finished my combat tour I was part way through my two-week leave in London when VE Day occurred. London went wild and we partied for several days and nights. Lights came on and thankful prayers were said. After ten days of the good life in London, I phoned the base and orders had been cut returning us to the ZOI (Zone of the Interior). Back to Wendling, we went to prepare to go home."

Pat Everson, a 12-year-old Norfolk schoolgirl at Seething and Mundham County Primary School when the 448th Bomb Group were based at Seething airfield, cried as they fired flares and rockets to celebrate VE Day. "My mother explained they were so happy to be going home. After the war, the base was used to store bombs and in my teens, I went on the runway to pick cowslips. The runways stretched out into the distance, so empty yet so full . . . I swore out loud that I would never forget them."

Glossary

ETO Eurpoean Theater of Operations

CBI China–Burma–India Theater

FTR Failed to Return

GI General Issue; a US serviceman

H2S British experimental airborne radar navigational and target location aid

Happy Valley Ruhr Valley, Germany

HE High Explosive (bomb)

Heavies Bombers

HEI High Explosive Incendiary (bomb)

Holy Joe Chaplain

Hot Crock Garbage, nonsense, untruth

IAS Indicated Air Speed

IFF Identification Friend or Foe

IO Intelligence Officer

IP Initial point at the start of the bomb run

Iron Ass A hard, demanding, tough officer

Jug Short for Juggernaut, P-47 Thunderbolt

Junior Birdman An inexperienced pilot

KP Corporal Punishment, fatigues

Kriegie From the German word *Kriegsgafanganen* (PoW)

Latrine Rumor Unfounded rumor

Liberty run Night off in town

Light colonel Lieutenant Colonel

Little friend Allied fighter aircraft

Looie Lieutenant

LORAN Long-Range Navigation

Lucky Bastard Someone who has completed his tour of missions (and who has been awarded a certificate for The Lucky Bastards' Club)

Lufbery A fighter maneuver

Milk Run An easy mission

NCO Non-Commissioned Officer

Noball Flying bomb (V-1) or rocket (V-2) site

Non-com NCO (see entry above)

Over the Hill To be absent without leave

P-38 Lightning fighter

P-47 Thunderbolt fighter

P-51 Mustang fighter

PFC Poor [expletive] civilian, or private first class

Piccadilly Commando A London prostitute

Pill roller Medic

POM Preparation for Overseas Movement

Poop Information (slang)

PoW Prisoner of War

PR Photographic Reconnaissance

Prop Wash Air disturbed by preceding planes

Pubbing mission A pub crawl

Purple Heart Medal awarded for wounds received in combat

Purple Heart Corner Reputed to be the most vulnerable spot in a bomber formation

PX Post Exchange: the military store

R&R Rest and Recuperation

R/T Radio Telephony

RCM Radio Countermeasures

Red-lined To be canceled

Re-Tread An older officer who has been recalled to active service

RP Rocket Projectile

Sack Bed

Sack Time Bedtime, sleep

Sad Sack, Sack Artist GI who was always asleep

Second John Second lieutenant

Section Eight Discharge given for mental breakdown, insanity, etc

Shack Job An easy woman

Shack Up To sleep with a woman

Shortarm A VD inspection

Shuttle Long bombing mission with a stop en-route

Sky pilot Chaplain

Snowdrop Military policeman, so-called because of his white helmet

Tour A series of missions

TS Tough Shit

UEA Unidentified Enemy Aircraft

UHF Ultra-High Frequency

USAAF United States Army Air Forces

VHF Very High Frequency

V-Mail A letter greeting card written on a special form; they were photographed on microfilm, flown to the US, and delivered in hard copy format

WAAF (British) Women's Auxiliary Air Force

WREN (British) Women's Royal Navy

Wolfpack A fighter outfit

ZOI Zone of the Interior (i.e., the US)

Zoot Suit Flying suit

Further Reading

Baynes, Richard C. *Replacement Crew* (Irvine, CA: R.C. Baynes publisher)

Birdsall, Steve. *The B-24 Liberator* (New York: Arco Publishing Co., 1979)

———. *Log of the Liberators* (Garden City, NY: Doubleday & Co., 1973)

Blue, Allan G. *The Fortunes of War* (California: Aero Publishers, Inc., 1967)

Bowman, Martin W. *The B-24 Liberator 1939–1945* (New York: Rand McNally, 1980)

———. *The Bedford Triangle* (Stroud: Sutton Publishing, 1996; PSL, 1988)

———. *Consolidated B-24 Liberator* (Crowood Aviation Series, 1998)

———. *Fields of Little America* (Cambridge, England: PSL, 1977)

Blue, Allen G. *The B-24 Liberator* (New York: Charles Scribner's Sons, 1976)

Carigan, William. *Ad Lib: Flying the B-24 Liberator in WWII* (Kansas: Sunflower University Press, Manhattan, 1988)

Campbell, John M and Donna. *Consolidated B-24 Liberator* (Pennsylvania: Schiffer Publishing Ltd., 1993)

Chapman, Willie. *Booster McKeester & other Experiences, 98th Bomb Group Middle East Theater 1942–43* (Long Beach, CA)

Chase, Donald V. *Combat Record of Technical Sergeant* (1982)

Clark, Forrest S. *Innocence And Death In Enemy Skies: A True Story of WWII Adventure and Romance* (Jawbone Publishing Corp., 2004)

Collar, George M. *Reflections of a Bombardier*

Cundiff, Michael J. *Ten Knights in a Bar Room: Missing in Action in the South Pacific, 1943* (Iowa State Press, 1990)

Dorr, Robert F. *B-24 Liberator Units of the 8th Air Force* (Osprey, 2000)

———. *B-24 Liberator Units of the Fifteenth Air Force* (Osprey, 2001)

Dugan, James & Stewart, Carroll. *Ploesti: The Great Ground Air Battle of 1 August 1943* (Fletcher & Son, 1963)

Fagan, Vincent F. *Liberator Pilot: The Cottontails' Battle for Oil* (California: California Aero Press, 1991)

Freeman, Roger, *B-24 Liberator at War* (Osceola, WI: Motorbooks, 1983)

———. *The B-24J Liberator* (Leatherhead, England: Profile Publications, 1965)

Hughes, Walter F. *A Bomber Pilot in WWII— From Farm Boy to Pilot, 35 Missions in the B-24* (Fremont, CA: privately printed, 1994)

Healy, Alan. *The 467TH Bombardment Group September 1943–June 1945* (privately printed, 1947)

Johnson, Frederick A. *B-24 Liberator* (Osceola, WI: Motorbooks, 1993)

———. *B-24 Liberator, Rugged But Right* (Walter J. Boyne Military Aircraft Series, McGraw-Hill, 1999)

———. *Liberator Lore Vols. 1–4* (Tacoma, WA: Frederick A. Johnson Publisher, 1989)

———. *The Bomber Barons* (Tacoma, WA: Bomber Books, 1982)

Mahoney, James J. & Brian H. *Reluctant Witness: Memoirs from the Last Year of the European Air War 1944–1945* (Trafford, 2001)

McDowell, Ernest R. *Consolidated B-24D-M Liberator* (NY: Arco Publishing Co., 1969)

Moyes, Philip J.R. *Consolidated B-24 Liberator Early Models* (Oxford, England: Visual Art Press, 1979)

Moxley, Gene F., (compiler). *The 465th Remembered Book I and II* (Warrenton, MO)

Newby, Leroy W. *Target Ploesti* (Novato, CA: Presidio Press, 1983)

Parnell, Ben. *Carpetbaggers* (Austin, TX: Eakin Press, 1987)

Picardo, Eddie. *Tales of a Tail Gunner* (Seattle, WA: Hara Publishing, 1997)

Reynolds, George A. *ETO Carpetbaggers* (privately printed, 1987)

Sentry Books Inc. *Wings, Sentry Magazine* (Granada Hills, CA, 1991)

"Second Thoughts." *2nd Air Division Journals*

Sherwood Robert H. *Certified Brave* (Trafford Publishing, 2004)

Skaggs, Gene. *Crew Sixty Four*

Smith, Ed. *Ball Turret Gunner, B-24 Liberator At War* (1983)

Spencer, Ronald D. *There We Were . . . or The Saga of Crew No.8* (1993)

Squadron Signal Publications. *B-24 Liberator in Action* (Carrollton, TX, 1987)

Tays, Robert H. *Country Boy–Combat Bomber Pilot*

Westheimer, David. *Rider On The Wind* (England: Sphere, 1979; NY: Walker, 1984)

Wilson, Paul and Mackay, Ron. *The Sky Scorpions—The Story of the 389th Bomb Group in WWII* (Schiffer, 2006)

Wolf, Leon. *Low Level Mission* (New York: Berkley Publishing Corp., 1957)

Worthen, Major Frederick D. (ret.) *Against All Odds: Surviving World War II* (Fithian Press, 1996)

Yedlin, Benedict. "In My Sperry Ball I Sit." *Briefing, Journal of the International B-24 Liberator Club* (Spring 1999)

Picture Credits and Acknowledgments

Page number and position are indicated as follows: L = Left, TL = top left, TR = top right; C = center; CL = Center left; B = Bottom, BL = Bottom left, etc:

Author's collection: 15: TL, BL, BR; 16: TL, TR, BL; 17: T, B; 18: T, B; 19: L, TR, BR; 20; 21: BC; 22: BL, BR; 23: TR, BR; 24: TR, B; 25: TL, TC, B; 26–27; 33: TL; 34: L; 35: BL; 37: BR; 38: T, BR; 39: CL, TR, CR. BR; 40: L; 41: TC, BL; 44: BR; 46: L, R; 49: T; 50: L, R, C; 51: BL, BR; 52: BL, BR; 53: TL, TR, BL, BR; 54: L, R; 55: BL; 60: L, TC; 61: T, BL, BR; 62: T, BR; 63: L; 64: T; 65: T; 66–67: all photos; 68: BL, BR; 69: BL, BR; 72: BR; 74: T, B; 75: BR; 76: L; 78: C; 79: B; 80–81: all photos; 82: T, B; 83: TR; 88: T; 89: TR; 91: T; 92: T, B; 93: T, B; 94: BL; 95: CR; 96: L, TR; 102: B; 104: T, BC; 105: TR; 106: T; BC; 107: BL; 108: T, BL, BR; 109: TR; 110: BR; 111: TC, BL; 116: T, B; 117: TR; 118: T, BL, BR; 119: BR; 121: CR; 124: T, B; 125: T, B; 128: TL; 130: T, C; 131: TR; 132: T, BL, BR; 134: T, B; 135: BR; 136–137: all images; 138: B; 142: BL, BC; 143: BR; 144: TR; 145: TR; 146: TL, BR; 147: BR; 148-149: all photos; 150: TL, BL; 151: TC, BR; 152: B; 153: T, B.

Patrick Bunce: 70, 77 (T), 112, 114 (B). (*All the other B-24 interior and exterior photos are by Patrick Bunce and are © Elephant Book Company Ltd*.)

448th Bomb Group Collection (archive photographs only listed; see credit, right, for artifacts and other memorabilia. *Photos of such artifacts and memorabilia are the copyright of Elephant Book Company Ltd*): 21: TL; 33: BR; 37: T; 38: T; 49: BR; 63, CR; 91, CR; 94: BR; 96: CR, BR; 103: B; 104: BL; 106: BL, BC; 107: BR; 119: T; 133: TL; 138: T; 139: BR; 142: BR; 143: TR; 145: BR; 147: T (inset).

93rd Bomb Group Collection (archive photographs only listed; see credit, right, for artifacts and other memorabilia. *Photos of such artifacts and memorabilia are the copyright of Elephant Book Company Ltd*): 69: T (illustration by T/Sgt. Harry L. Tower Jr., 93rd Bomb Group, 409th Bomb Squadron; used by kind permission of the Tower family); 95: TR.

Liberatorcrew.com: 114: BL (artwork by Alfred D. Crimi; published in *Life* magazine, January 24, 1944; copyright Sperry Gyroscope), BR; 117: B; 122–123: all images.

Library of Congress: 12–13; 48; 51: BC; 89: BR; 119: BL; 120: R

National Archives: 133: TR

National Museum of the US Air Force/USAF photo: 14; 15 (TR).

All the B-24 interior and exterior photos featured in the book, with the exception of those listed above, were made by Patrick Bunce and are the copyright of Elephant Book Company Ltd.

All the memorabilia and artifact photos featured in the book, with the exception of any listed above, were made by Mark Winwood and are the copyright of Elephant Book Company Ltd.

Jacket and front cover illustration: *Under Attack: Tall, Torrid & Texas* by Roy Grinnell, Artist of the Aces
Historical Aviation Art & More
Website: www.roygrinnell.com

Editors' acknowledgments

The editors particularly wish to thank the following for their help in preparing this book: Pat Everson of the 448th Bomb Group Collection and the veterans of the 448th Bomb Group, and also the people involved at Station 146 USAAF WWII Control Tower, Seething, Norfolk; Paul Thrower, Curator, 93rd Bomb Group Museum, Hardwick, Norfolk, England; Pat Bunce for all his advice and help. Thanks also to Jonathon Moran at Liberatorcrew.com and to the Tower family, for allowing us to use the illustration by T/Sgt. Harry L. Tower Jr.

Museums

The great majority of the items of memorabilia featured in this book were photographed at the 448th Bomb Group Collection, Seething, Norfolk, England, and at the 93rd Bomb Group Collection at Hardwick, Norfolk, England. The great majority of the B-24 interior and exterior photographs were made at the Collings Foundation, Stowe, Massachusetts, USA, home of the only B-24J Liberator flying in the world today. For more information on flights in the Liberator, visit the Collings Foundation website: www.collingsfoundation.org